This book is due on the last date stamped below.
Failure to return books on the date due may result
in assessment of overdue fees.

FINES .50	per day	

SCARECROW PRESS, INC.

Published in the United States of America
by Scarecrow Press, Inc.
A wholly owned subsidiary of
The Rowman & Littlefield Publishing Group, Inc.
4501 Forbes Boulevard, Suite 200, Lanham, Maryland 20706
www.scarecrowpress.com

PO Box 317
Oxford
OX2 9RU, UK

British Library Cataloguing in Publication Information Available

Library of Congress Cataloging-in-Publication Data

Multiracial America : a resource guide on the history and literature of interracial
issues / [compiled by] Karen Downing, Darlene Nichols, Kelly Webster.
    p. cm.
  Includes bibliographical references and index.
  ISBN 0-8108-5199-7 (pbk. : alk. paper)
  1. United States–Race relations–Bibliography. 2. Racially mixed people–
United States–Bibliography. I. Downing, Karen E. II. Nichols, Darlene P.
III. Webster, Kelly, 1971–
Z1361.E4M86 2005
[E184.A1]
016.3058'00973–dc22   2004027757

Contents

Acknowledgments vii
Introduction 1

1 Accessing the Literature
  Karen Downing 5

2 Teaching an Interracial Issues Course
  David Schoem 13

3 Hot Button Issues
  Karen Downing and Kelly Webster 23

4 Core Historical Literature
  Chuck Ransom 37

5 The Politics of Being Interracial
  Karen Downing 55

6 Interracial Dating and Marriage
  Alysse Jordan 79

7 Interracial Families
  Renoir Gaither 105

8 Transracial Adoption
  Darlene Nichols 119

9 Books for Children and Young Adults
  Darlene Nichols 137

10 Multiracial Identity Development
  Kelly Webster 149

11 The Intersection of Race and Queer Sexuality
  Joseph Diaz 167

12 Representations of Interracial Relationships and
  Multiracial Identity on the American Screen
  Helen Look and Martin Knott 179

Appendix I   Subject Heading / Descriptor Vocabulary to
              Assist in Searching
              Karen Downing   203

Appendix II   Definitions of Terms Used in
              Interracial Literature
              Karen Downing   211

Appendix III Sociology 412—Ethnic Identity and
              Intergroup Relations Syllabus
              David Schoem   219

Appendix IV   OMB Directive 15   231

Appendix V   Resources by Race   235

Index   237
About the Contributors   251

Acknowledgments

The authors would like to thank:

Tom Hubbard for his wonderful assistance in editing and preparing the manuscript;

Barbara MacAdam for her support and encouragement;

The good folks in Interlibrary Loan at the University of Michigan Library for their fast and friendly service;

Emma Smith for her hard work at the beginning of the project;

Leslie Doty Hollingsworth for her guidance on transracial adoption issues;

Judy Avery for her support and keen eye in reviewing the manuscript.

Introduction

Forty years ago, it was socially taboo. It was an embarrassment if it happened in your family. Some thought it unnatural. In many states it was even illegal. If anyone found out, you risked losing your job or your home. Offspring were pitied, or despised, or outcast and expected to repudiate part of their own heritage. Marriage across interracial lines—it had no place in American society.

But interracial marriage is no longer illegal—even if still taboo within many social groups—and the children that result from these unions are no longer peculiar to society. The number of interracial marriages has doubled in the past twenty years and with these marriages has come a baby boom of interracial children joining the previous generations of interracial Americans. The parents of this new generation as well as those now grown who have a mixed-race heritage are increasingly balking at having to choose one racial category with which to define themselves or their children. Sparked in part by changes in the U.S. Census of 2000, new political and social movements have developed to challenge the predominance of "Black or White" thinking—the concept that the races are mutually exclusive and that a person cannot possibly be more than one race.

Research and writing on mixed-race people and interracial intimacy has exploded in the past fifteen years. Literature, film, and other popular resources are increasingly reflecting the changing American demographics by including positive images of interracial people and relationships. There is no question that both personal and professional interest in this topic is growing and will continue to grow.

Why a Resource Guide on the History and Literature of Interracial Issues?

This book is designed to address that growing interest in interracial people and relationships in America. Barely a day goes by when the authors are not contacted by individuals of all ages looking, and often failing, to find articles, film/videos, and books to satisfy their curiosity on one interracial topic or another.

Over the past decade there have been an increasing number of books and articles published on the subject of being interracial. Despite the growth in publishing, it remains challenging to locate these materials. For example, there are no commonly accepted terms to provide consistency in searching electronic databases or print indexes. This guide not only provides researchers with useful lists of articles, books, websites, movies, and more, but also assists them in navigating the mass of publication that is often scattered and almost inaccessible. This book brings together annotated lists of representative works on a wide range of related topics and guidance to help researchers more easily locate further information themselves.

While it may have been an early dream to be totally comprehensive, it quickly became apparent that our goal for the book would be to include the most substantive and balanced resources that are readily available to those wishing to find them. Our criteria for including resources in this book include:

Quality of the argument—whether it is an editorial or a lengthy research-based resource, the author must be able to support his or her premise adequately.

Quality of the content—sensational literature is, for the most part, not found here, since it is rarely supported by facts or evidence.

Supportable evidence—consideration was given for research-based resources that use quantitative or qualitative data.

Substantive—we excluded very short news items often found in newspapers, popular magazines, and websites. The resources found here are for those who are seeking substantive information.

Balance of perspectives and media types—we include the viewpoints and perspectives of authors from within the interracial community as well as those who are not. Many of the historical resources are viewed today as extremely racist and misogynistic, but they are extremely important to contextualize our current understanding of interracial issues. We also attempt to present a variety of types of resources, from popular magazines and newspapers (which may be the only resources available in smaller communities), along with scholarly research-based publications. Because different media speak to the issues in myriad ways, we have attempted to include as many media types as possible.

With these criteria in mind, the book contains information on:

Chapter 1, *Accessing the Literature*, attempts to teach the researcher how to find information on a variety of topics related to interracial issues in order to be self-sufficient. Major roadblocks and the strategies to overcome them are described.

Chapter 2, *Teaching an Interracial Issues Course*, lends context to teaching about race and interrace at the university level. It also discusses the content and pedagogical issues the instructor considered before, during, and after teaching the course.

Chapter 3, *Hot Button Issues*, includes information on issues relating to appearance, passing, and blood quantum. All three issues are potentially highly emotional in nature, with significant current ramifications directly tied to historical injustices.

Chapter 4, *Core Historical Literature*, delves into the earliest American literature on interracial issues, including the fiction, nonfiction, and so-called "scientific" literature of the 1800s through the Civil Rights era.

Chapter 5, *The Politics of Being Interracial*, includes background on how interrace and politics intersect. Federal and state laws are discussed, including anti-miscegenation laws. This chapter includes resources on the politicizing of racial classification and categorization of people, including enumeration of individuals and groups, as well as on the growth of the political strength of the multiracial movement.

Chapter 6, *Interracial Dating and Marriage*, discusses the social science research relating to the reasons and choices individuals make in dating and marriage across race and public opinion on interracial dating and marriage.

Chapter 7, *Interracial Families*, examines the literature on the growing number of mixed-race families in the United States. Issues such as parental influence on child socialization and family identity are central to this chapter.

Chapter 8, *Transracial Adoption*, examines the abundance of literature on adoption across racial lines. A short history of interracial adoption within the United States is provided, along with a discussion of the controversies surrounding the practice.

Chapter 9, *Books for Children and Young Adults*, responds to the needs of families and researchers of children's literature who are searching for materials that include interracial families and children. This literature is often "hidden" because interracial subject headings are not always assigned to these items.

Chapter 10, *Multiracial Identity Development*, provides a selection of literature on the development and expression of interracial identity. This section includes autobiographical works by mixed-race authors, as well as resources from the fields of psychology and sociology.

Chapter 11, *The Intersection of Race and Queer Sexuality*, examines the small but growing body of literature on interracial LGBT issues. The works fall primarily into three categories including: biography/autobiography/testimony; clinical literature authored by therapists; and theoretical/literary analysis, often referred to as cultural studies.

Chapter 12, *Representations of Interracial Relationships and Multiracial Identity on the American Screen*, examines motion picture works relating to interracial issues. The evolution of images of interracial individuals and relationships is discussed.

The appendices include information that will be helpful to researchers trying to find information not contained within these pages, and future works that have yet to be published.

Appendix I, *Subject Heading/Descriptor Vocabulary*, gives the reader an idea of the range of vocabulary that is used to describe interracial topics by those catalogers who compile indexes and catalogs. These subject headings lend entrée into the literature.

Appendix II, *Definitions of Terms*, is a short compendium of terms used in interracial literature. These terms, some of which are outdated and even offensive, are important to know as they may aid the researcher with further searching.

Appendix III, *Sociology 412*, includes a full syllabus and reading list of the course on interracial issues taught by professor of sociology, David Schoem. It will be useful to anyone who is considering teaching a similar course, and it points to additional resources on interracial literature.

Appendix IV, *OMB Directive 15*, is the full text of the Office of Management and Budget's definition of how the Federal Government classifies people by race. It is a useful tool for examining the way in which our U.S. culture delineates races as separate from one another.

Appendix V, *Resources by Race*, allows readers to locate resources in this text that deal with specific combinations of races.

1   Accessing the Literature

Karen Downing

Many Needs, Many Strategies

In the process of assisting hundreds of researchers to access literature on interracial issues over the last several years, it has become apparent that there are a multiplicity of information needs among them, and that they often experience great difficulties in finding what they need. Students at all levels, from elementary school through the doctoral level, need information for papers, art projects, master's theses, and doctoral dissertations. Parents want resources to help their interracial children cope with social isolation and develop a strong sense of pride in their mixed heritage background. They seek picture books or young adult fiction that portray interracial children in a positive light. They look for materials that reflect their children's experiences and realities. University researchers in many disciplines require access to scholarly sources including case study, qualitative, and quantitative data that will inform their research and teaching activities. Counselors, teachers, and school and university administrators need access to resources to help them with the growing numbers of interracial individuals they are charged with assisting.

With these varied needs for information and materials come significant challenges to finding the resources. The authors of this book regularly hear from exasperated students, parents, teaching faculty, and other librarians about their fruitless searches to find substantive information on interracial issues. In order to access these important resources, it is necessary to know a bit about the commonly experienced difficulties in order to deal with them. To aid all researchers, from the general public to experienced librarians, these difficulties are detailed below along with methods to address and overcome them.

Improved Subject Access

There are many barriers to accessing information on any underrepresented minority groups in the United States. When you add in the additional factor of *interracial* issues, it becomes even more difficult, in many instances, to find quality information resources that offer bias-free or at very least, balanced perspectives.

Why the Library of Congress Matters to You: Subject Headings and Classification 101

The Library of Congress constructs standardized terminology, or subject headings, to describe books, magazines, videos, and other items libraries may own. In practice these terms should be consistently applied to describe every item on a given topic so that they can all be retrieved in a single search from an online library catalog or by looking in the right location in a card file. Although these terms do evolve over time—"Negroes" eventually became "Afro-Americans" and later "African Americans," for example—the evolution is slow and often inadequate to reflect that of society. Subject headings are an important tool for retrieving information in library catalogs but they, too, are a product of our social environment and can be limiting and frustrating.

It would seem that better subject access to information sources is an important topic no matter what the subject matter. A recent search of *Library Literature,* an index of the professional literature in the field of librarianship, turned up close to one thousand such articles on topics as far ranging as better subject access for fire emergency materials to feminism to music. There are however, very few articles in *Library Literature* on subject access as it pertains to underrepresented minority groups, and nothing on access to literature on interracial issues. Judging by the difficulties researchers and librarians have tracking down this literature, and because the body of relevant material is growing rapidly, this is an area that will need to be addressed by the Library of Congress (L.C.) soon.

Sanford Berman, perhaps the ultimate authority on outdated and offensive Library of Congress Subject Headings, described how it took L.C. years to change offensive and useless subject headings on minority groups throughout the seventies, eighties, and nineties. He described how it took almost two decades to get rid of the Library of Congress subject heading "Yellow Peril" (Berman, 1992, p. 133). Others have advocated for changes in classification schedules (call numbers) for at least as long. Subject headings have changed over time, but often without links to previous headings. An example of this can be seen when the Library of Congress changed their heading "Children of interracial marriage" to "Racially mixed children," and "Racially mixed people," thereby allowing those of us who are multiracial to finally become adults!

The Library of Congress also constructs the call numbers, or classification schemes, into which all literature is fitted by catalogers, who assign the call numbers to the materials in libraries. Although there are some relatively newer classification areas such as "Racially mixed children" found in HQ777.9, and "Intermarriage" in HQ1031, currently today, "Interracial offspring" remains sandwiched between "Inbreeding" and "Degeneration" in the G Schedule, and the topic "Interracial Marriages" appears between "Inbreeding" and "Marriage of Degenerates and Defectives" in the H Schedule. This is an outrage, but by no means a unique situation in an antiquated and biased schema.

Given the snail's pace of change, information seekers will need to be armed with knowledge of how the system works (or doesn't work), in order to find a full array of information on interracial topics.

Problems and solutions to unearthing information on interracial people and issues are outlined below. Appendix I lists a sample of subject headings from numerous indexes as well as Library of Congress subject headings as they exist today. These lists will give the reader a thesaurus to aid in their information searches.

Language Usage Difficulties

Echoing Kathleen Bethel, in her article on cataloging the Afro-centric way, I feel obliged to warn the reader that I am not a cataloger, nor have I played one on television (two of our co-authors are catalogers). However, as a frequently frustrated user of information resources myself, and as a reference librarian helping other users who have even greater difficulties accessing this literature, I will share some of the pitfalls that befall many library users searching for literature on interracial themes.

Language difficulties are many when looking for information on any racial group. The plethora of synonyms used by authors, publishers, indexers, and catalogers prevent easy and straightforward access to these resources. Terms and their meanings can change over time as well, making historical research very different from accessing current information. Calling one a mulatto in the pre-civil rights era was a fact of life; today, the term is usually taken as insulting and offensive.

Inconsistent Vocabulary and Definitions: Finding Tools

In order to find books and articles on interracial themes, it is often necessary to use both library catalogs as well as multiple indexes to periodical literature in many disciplines. Search engines for the World Wide Web also offer entrée to many resources, and some unique challenges as well. Each of these finding tools connects the user to different types of information resources, and each one utilizes different vocabulary to get at those resources.

For instance, the Library of Congress Subject Headings have used terms such as "Children of Interracial Marriage," "Mulattoes," and "Miscegenation" to describe books about individuals who are interracial. Sometimes subject headings are updated, and the old terms are used as cross-references to the new. Other times headings are added without necessarily replacing related terms. Ultimately, it is up to the individual cataloger to decide how many terms to use to describe any one book or journal, and there are no guarantees that cross-references or multiple headings will be used. Many libraries are not economically able to retrospectively change from the old to the new subject headings. Therefore, if you search using only one heading, you will miss many excellent resources. A savvy user must know a range of subject headings to use (see Appendix I) in order to find a robust array of information available.

The searching becomes even more complicated when using indexes to find scholarly and popular articles. Each index uses different subject terms and there is no consistency between them. Hence, savvy seekers must be able to use a plethora of synonyms to find the information they seek. In the online environment, they must know the difference between subject and keyword searching as well. Subject searching uses the controlled vocabulary of the index (you must use their terminology for topics). Keyword searching, however, allows you to use your own vocabulary, but will inevitably miss many relevant resources, and will probably find many irrelevant resources. For example, doing a keyword search on the term "interracial" in many indexes finds articles on topics such as relationships between racial groups, cross-race labor organizing, and housing patterns.

Terms such as these have been used in indexes, catalogs, books, and articles to describe interracial resources:

American Indian	Hybridism	Mulatto
Anglo-Indians	Integrated Family	Multiethnic
Asian	Intercountry Marriage	Multiracial
Asian-American	Intercultural	Native American
Biracial(s)	Interethnic	Negro(es)
Biracial Adolescents	Interrace	New People
Black Seminoles	Interracial	Octoroons
Children of	Interracial Marriage	Quadroons
Interracial Marriage	Latino/a(s)	Race
Creole	Metis	Race-Crossing
Eurasians	Miscegenation	Racially Mixed People
Hapa	Mixed Bloods	Transracial
Hispanic	Mulata	

These are but a few examples of how inconsistent the vocabulary used to describe interracial people can be. In order to find the best information on your topic, it is best to use the index's subject descriptor list, if one exists, as a guide to doing subject searching. We also recommend using broad terms such as "interracial" as keywords for keyword searching. When you find a relevant article or book during a keyword search, look at the record closely to find the relevant subject terms used by that particular catalog or index.

Outdated or Offensive Language

The meanings of words change over time. Words that were used by oppressors to refer to those who were oppressed are no longer acceptable to many today. Words such as "mulatto" illustrate this point. Mulatto's meaning is derived from the Latin word for "mule," or a sterile hybrid animal. The term was (and still is) routinely used in book and article indexes. Another example is found in the term "miscegenation," which, by its dictionary definition, refers to a sexual act rather than a relationship between two people of different races. The Library of Congress, Readers' Guide to Periodical Literature, and many indexes still use the word "miscegenation" to refer to the latter meaning, although this is viewed as derogatory today. We do not use these words in everyday language, yet they continue to appear in current indexes, and remain as reminders in the historical indexes of the past. For this reason, the savvy searcher will be familiar with these terms, even if they are offensive, in order to find historical materials. See Appendix I for a list of these terms to search for materials published in the pre-civil rights era.

Bias and Perspective in the Literature

Differences in bias and perspective are inevitably found in any body of literature between authors who are within the studied group and those outside of the group. It is interesting and important for users to understand the differences in perspective in order to critically evaluate the content and methodology of the work. In the case of in-group interracial literature, there are many works such as biographies, personal narratives, works of fiction, and poetry. Increasingly, as interracial scholars are conducting research within higher education, there are more scholarly studies and interpretations as well. Authors sometimes identify themselves as being multiracial in the preface, introduction, or biographical sketch of their works.

Early literature (pre-civil rights) was rarely written by in-group authors and tends to be much more critical and negative in nature. It was a different time; interracial marriages and people were seen as "degenerates." Unfortunately, its influences can still be seen today in the Library of Congress classification schemes outlined earlier, and the content of many authors of that era. In psychology, for instance, articles included very clinical and negative studies performed on interracial children and couples. Now that interracial psychologists are entering the field, there are articles on healthy identity development and studies about the longevity of interracial marriages.

Mainstream vs. Nonmainstream Literature

When searching for information on any racial or ethnic group, the seeker will have to become familiar with resources beyond the usual "mainstream" resources (e.g., Readers' Guide to Periodical Literature and Psychological Abstracts). Indexes such as Alternative Press Index, Index to Black Periodicals, Ethnic Newswatch, Chicano Index, and others will be very important finding tools, especially to lend entrée into the literature written by interracial authors. Unfortunately, these resources are usually less accessible for the average user because fewer libraries subscribe to them. Larger public and academic libraries are the best sources for such tools, and increasingly, smaller public libraries are gaining access through state and regional consortia.

Recommended Reading

Berman, Sanford. *Prejudices and Antipathies*. Jefferson, N.C.: McFarland & Company, Inc., 1993.

————. "Things Are Seldom What They Seem: Finding Multicultural Materials in Catalogs." In *Alternative Library Literature, 1990/1991*. Jefferson, N.C.: McFarland & Co., 1992.

Bethel, Kathleen E. "Culture Keepers: Cataloging the Ethnocentric Way." *The Reference Librarian* 45/46 (1994): 221-40.

Clack, Doris Hargrett. "Collection Access through Subject Headings." In *Social Responsibility in Librarianship: Essays on Equality*, edited by Donnarae MacCann. Jefferson, N.C.: McFarland & Company, Inc., 1989.

Hyman, Richard Joseph. "Libraries in the City University of New York: Adaptations in Cataloging and Classification." *Urban Academic Librarian* 6/7 (Fall 1988-Spring 1989): 58-66.

Milstead Harris, Jessica L., and Doris Clack. "Treatment of People and Peoples in Subject Analysis." *Library Resources and Technical Services* 23, no. 4 (Fall 1979): 374-90.

Moorcraft, Heather. "Ethnocentrism in Subject Headings." *Australian Library Journal* 41 (February 1992): 40-45.

Olsrud, Lois, and Jennalyn Chapman Tellman. "Difficulties of Subject Access for Information about Minority Groups." In *Multicultural Acquisitions*. New York: Haworth Press, Inc., 1993.

2   Teaching an Interracial Issues Course

David Schoem

In this chapter I will discuss how I came to teach a course on interracial identity, and, in doing so, will share some of my experience with students about issues of racial identity over the course of a career of teaching. I will consider the intellectual importance of moving beyond some of the common approaches to teaching about race in higher education and why teaching on interracial issues and about interracial people is critical. I will also present information about the course, its development, structure, and pedagogy, and share some of the memorable experiences from the course. Finally, I will provide examples of courses offered elsewhere on interracial issues.

Deciding to Teach an Interracial Issues Course

I have been teaching undergraduate courses on race and ethnicity and on intergroup relations for over twenty years. Over this time I have seen the number of interracial students in my classroom grow significantly, both as a result of the growing numbers nationally and also as a result of these students' greater willingness to publicly self-identify as interracial. In contrast, in the early 1980s a few of my students would typically make known to me in a quiet way midway through the term, in papers or in office hours, that they were mixed-race. To be mixed-race was still not an affirmed public identity and my students felt vulnerable, marginal, and isolated.

I would refer my interracial students to a small, ad hoc, but very important support group for interracial people on the University of Michigan campus organized by this book's co-editor, Karen Downing. This marvelous group provided my students with their first opportunity to share their experiences while offering support with a network of mixed-race faculty, staff, and students. For many, it was their primary anchor at the university and provided the support needed for them to succeed socially and academically at college. Over time, the numbers and percent of students in my courses who are mixed-race has grown, as has their confidence in their social identity.

In discussions in my classes, as the numbers of interracial students have increased over time and public attitudes have shifted, there has often been speculation that the view that a mixed racial identity carries some social stigma might be entirely reversed. Students wonder aloud whether those who are mixed-race might move from the margins to the center, and that a societal view could emerge that a mono-racial identity is somehow less rich and interesting than a mixed identity. However, there is less hope expressed that the societal focus on racial categories as a way of stratifying and organizing society will disappear.

Today, my interracial students still have many questions about their personal, racial, and other social identities, but so do all my students in the eighteen to twenty-five year old age group. What is different for the interracial students is that they have never or only as an exception had a chance to read or study about their social identity throughout their K-12 education or in almost any of their college courses.

As part of my interest in race and ethnicity, and out of my own personal identity, I have long held a strong intellectual interest in issues facing the Jewish community. In addition to courses on race, ethnicity, and intergroup relations, I teach courses on the "Sociology of the American Jewish Community" and have written and published in this area. Since a 1990 Jewish Population Study (Kosmin et al., 1991) showed that over 50 percent of new marriages involving Jews were interfaith marriages, there has been tremendous interest and concern about this topic in the Jewish community.

In a manner that was familiar to me from my experience with mixed-race students, I began to see a growing number of interreligious or mixed faith students in my classroom. These students would initially hide their identity until they felt sufficiently comfortable with me or with the class to announce their mixed identity through papers, office hours, or class discussion.

Although racial identity and categorization have, unquestionably, held a much more precarious and dangerous position in the history of the United States compared to religion, there were some similarities in the issues with which interracial and interreligious students approached me. Then, as now, I remain interested in exploring the comparisons and learning from them.

First, the Jewish interfaith students faced invisibility. They were made to feel invisible for fear of the reaction of their Jewish peers, the larger Jewish community, and the larger society.

Second, they had been told that the affirmation of their identity, as mixed, was a virtual impossibility. For interracial students, there was a long legal history of one-drop rules and strictly enforced categorization of people either with agency status as White persons or of subordinate status as persons of color. For interreligious students, the persecution of people based on religious categorization, whether self-affirmed or conferred by the superordinate group, remains a dominant lesson throughout history. While religious authorities proclaim that theological differences preclude the possibility of a mixed faith identity between, for instance, Jews and Christians, most Jewish and Christian students, in fact, have little idea about the ideological underpinnings of their self-identified religious group.

With all of these intellectual and social questions in mind, and with the strong encouragement and support of my mixed-race colleagues, I decided to substantially revise my existing course on racial/ethnic identity and intergroup relations to put interracial issues at the center of the course. It was an experiment that I took on with some trepidation and much enthusiasm.

How We Teach about Race and Racial Identity

The absence of courses on interracial issues, and the exclusion of any content about interracial people from most courses focusing on race are instructive about how we think about race. Race is still too often taught as a biological construct with fixed, unchanging categories, and certainly this is how it is understood by most students. Even for those teachers who teach about race as a social construct and are reflective about the pedagogy of teaching about race, it is easy to fall into the trap of essentializing racial groups and racial characteristics in order to draw broad comparisons and understandings. When we teach about different racial groups in the United States, we often introduce the categories of African Americans, Asian Americans, European Americans, Latinos, and Native Americans and leave students with the impression that these categories are distinct (in a biological sense) and unchanging.

The issue of race, if anything, is a complex one and one of inestimable importance in the history and structure of this and many other countries. And yet, our understanding of race is exceedingly simplistic and misguided. We need only look at the history of the U.S. census to appreciate the very public changes in racial categorization according to political changes, popular sentiment, and shifts in power. Recent books, such as *How the Irish Became White* (Ignatiev, 1995) and *How the Jews Became White* (Brodkin, 1998) attest to the political and social constructions of race in recent U.S. history.

As a Jew, my own group's recent historic experience with race is telling. In twentieth-century Germany, Jews were identified by the Nazis as a racial group and one of such disdain that they were the subject of an unspeakable campaign of genocide. Determination of who was or was not considered Jewish was a matter that the Nazis took upon themselves to determine, regardless of the self-identification by individual Jews. In the United States, however, Jews are not even considered a race, but rather are identified primarily as a religious group. Further, according to the stratification of races in this country, Jews are considered White, and thus over time, have gained many of the privileges that accompany that powerful racial categorization. Clearly, in the Jewish experience, race has had nothing to do with biology, but has indeed been a most powerful marker of social position in society, targeting the group in its extreme forms for a privileged status, or for death, based on society's shifting constructs.

Within the U.S. racial categories, interracial persons are so recognized only if they cross the essentialized groupings. Thus, the daughter of African American and Asian American parents is considered to be mixed-race. The same would hold true for the son of a European American and a Latina. However, the daughter of a Chinese American and Japanese American would no more be considered mixed-race in mainstream U.S. categories than would the daughter of a Mexican American with a Cuban American, or an Czechoslovakian American with a German American. Because today we are wed to specific categories of race within the United States, even longstanding and historic enmities between peoples of different nations cannot override the rigid constructs that are in place at any given moment.

While the examples above might today be considered inter-ethnic rather than inter-racial marriages in the United States, it begins the blurring of the lines about race, ethnicity, and how we construct our definitions. That is not to say, of course, that families and ethnic groups within racial categories do not still hold strong feelings about inter-ethnic relationships and marriages. Nevertheless, most Whites consider themselves as almost pure racial stock in their Whiteness, but that is only because of the racial power realignment in the United States of what were formerly bitter national/ethnic foes in Europe. Why is it that my heritage as a son of Russian/Latvian/Lithuanian and Austro-Hungarian parents makes me White in the United States, and does not make me mixed-race?

When students come away from these classes with a sense of fixed racial categories, they are unable to conceptualize that there are interracial people. More experienced teachers will do some comparative study of these racial groups and challenge biological theories with the theory of the social construction of race. Yet most teachers still do not go beyond the primary categories and exclude interracial people from their syllabi. When we teach about race without acknowledging interracial people, we reinforce misunderstanding, spread misinformation, and restrict students' abilities to reach beyond limited, but popularly held constructs. Students hold onto not only rigid notions of racial categories, but rigid notions of the biological foundations of race, the immutability of racial stratification, and a vision of intergroup relations based strictly on racial power.

Course Content

We began the course with discussion of our communication styles in the classroom in order to explore how we would talk and examine issues together during the semester. Next we moved on to the topic of group identities and personal identities, reading articles by Chesler (1995) on talking about race, Tatum (1997) about racial identity development, Njeri (1991) and Pinderhughes (1993) about multiracial identity, and Parker (1997) about an individual's personal and group identities. (See Appendix III for a complete list of course readings.)

We then moved on to a discussion of the meaning of race, racism, and racial identity. We read about definitions of race in U.S. history and more broadly about the social construction of race and the changing categorization of race, looking at articles by Cose (1995), Hacker (1992), Hoffman (1994), Omi and Winant (1986), and Spickard (1992). We also continued to consider racial identity development with readings from Tatum's (1997), *Why Are All the Black Kids Sitting Together in the Cafeteria?*

Weeks four and five were devoted to discussion of assimilation, cultural pluralism, and multiculturalism. We read about Jewish assimilation (Waxman, 1990), Asian American panethnicity (Espiritu, 1992), Mexican American multiethnicity (Fernandez, 1992), and mixed-race and interfaith identities (Alba, 1990; Russell, 1992; Shrage, 1995).

The next three weeks we focused on topics and readings on multiracial identity and relationships. In this section of the course, we relied extensively on selections from three of the required books: Maria Root's *Racially Mixed People in America*, Naomi Zack's *American Mixed Race*, and Maria Root's *The Multiracial Experience*. We looked at the experience of multiracial people in the United States and other countries and the experience of people of different racial mixes. We also examined the racial identity development of mixed-race people, different approaches to experiencing multiracial identity, and the experience of people in multiracial relationships.

Next we looked at the experience of interfaith relationships and interfaith identity. We read a number of articles (Bayme, 1992; Wertheimer, 1996) about different ways Jewish individuals and the organized Jewish community were facing these issues. As we discussed these topics, we compared our insights with our earlier discussion and understanding of interracial relationships and identity.

In the final weeks of the semester, in addition to students presenting their research papers, as a class we focused on classification and census-taking (Rodriguez, 1992; Sandor, 1994), the integration of race, class, and gender (Lorde, 1992), and opportunities for building socially just communities in multicultural societies (Reagon Johnson, 1992).

The Experience of Teaching the Course

From the very start, this course was a work of collaboration. Karen Downing was a marvelous source of support, feedback, and encouragement to restructure my course and focus on interracial issues. I also received enormous assistance from Diana Alvarado who, as a research assistant, developed an extensive bibliography on course topics. As the instructor of the course, my own new reading and learning from this teaching experience began well over a year prior to its offering.

On another level, that of the student make-up and course style, it was also a terrifically exciting and stimulating work of collaboration. Students in the class ranged from first-year undergraduates to advanced Ph.D. candidates. The students ranged widely in their academic backgrounds, their own background in the subject matter of interracial issues, and in their own racial and religious identities.

While I had prepared a well-defined and challenging syllabus, I structured the course and my role in it as one of common exploration and learning. Each person in the course, including myself, was invited to bring his or her own areas of interest and expertise to the course, whether that be from ongoing research as in the case of the graduate students, or new areas of research for required presentations and papers. Certainly I offered my own experience and learning in the field in those sections of the course where I clearly had extensive knowledge and expertise. But the structure of the course, with four books, thirty articles, ten films/documentaries, student presentations, joint research papers, and numerous outside speakers, made for a thrilling and collective venture in learning.

One of my contributions to the course was to work to create an atmosphere that would encourage openness and trust for sharing and collaboration in learning. Our initial discussions and intergroup exercises helped to forge a willingness of intellectual and personal risk-taking in the classroom. Students not only made an intentional decision to think very critically about their own social identities and racial identity development, but to explore the personal, social, and intellectual with their peers.

I have argued elsewhere (Schoem, 1995; 1990) about the intellectual importance and power of taking time to establish a classroom environment that values trust and sharing as a means of students engaging the class content and learning in much deeper ways. I also have argued (Schoem, 1991a; 1991b) for a pedagogy that integrates the theoretical with the personal in such a manner that each serves to inform and enhance deeper understandings of the material. As students take theoretical issues and apply them to personal experiences and vice versa, they are able to analyze, challenge, and critically engage the intellectual content of the course to a degree that is often not realized through study of theory alone or simply through personal exploration and reflection.

The research papers and presentations were a highlight of the course. Early in the semester students identified topics they would study in depth over the course of the term and present to the class in the latter half of the semester. Topics included the following:

- A comparison of U.S. and Latin American understandings of race and mixed racial identities
- A historical review of changes in racial categories in the U.S. census
- The experience of "White-appearing" Blacks and biracial identity
- A comparison of growing up in Greek American and Indian American communities
- An exploration of mixed-race identity at different schooling levels
- A collection and analysis of life stories from interviews of multiracial students
- A comparison of changes in the experiences of women in one family over three generations
- A personal journey to learn about the different racial backgrounds and histories of one's parents

Speakers who were willing to talk openly about their racial experience were invited to the class. A Black/Puerto Rican speaker discussed her acceptance within her family and the questions she faced from the Black community as to whether she was White. A Lebanese/Egyptian/ Irish speaker described how he identified mostly as an Arab and a mixed-race person. A White parent talked about the issues she and her adopted Black children faced growing up in a mixed household. A woman whose mother looks Black and father looks White discussed her own mixed background, including Black/Cherokee/Portugese/ Irish/Chinese/White/Jewish/Ethiopian. A man who is Seminole and Black described his experience of seeing how all or many in Seminole County are mixed-race, but how he grew up among all Whites in a city in Oklahoma. Another speaker of Colombian and Mayan background who was adopted by Whites described growing up as a "White" child.

We heard other voices in the class through films and documentaries. Among these, the class viewed *None of the Above, Skin Deep, True Colors, L.A. Is Burning, American in Black and White, Just Black, Politics of Love in Black and White, Crossing Delancey, School Ties,* and *Gefilte Fish.*

One weekend the class also attended the "Mixed Conference," a conference organized by a group on campus called the Mixed Initiative. The conference featured Maria Root as the keynote speaker and included workshops led by students on campus, including several from this class, on topics such as "Biracism/Multiracism," "Dating/Relationships," "Family Issues," "Transracial Adoptees," "The U.S. Census," and "Identity."

Each week students came to class with new excitement and interest about readings and current news related to race, interracial identity, multifaith issues, etc. The graduate students routinely kept us up-to-date on developments in the design and definitions for the upcoming census or on racial identity issues arising in Latin America and South America. One student used his spring break to make a very personal journey to explore in-depth for the first time the roots of his Native American identity from his father's heritage. The Greek American and South Asian Indian American students who collaborated on their research paper were invited to be the two students honored to speak at the University's Honors Convocation based on the strength of their collaborative research project. While many presentations were more typically formal with handouts and overheads, we were frequently treated to dance, music, poetry, picture albums, and food to help in our understanding.

Where Are the Other Interracial Issues Courses?

Happily, more universities are beginning to offer courses on interracial issues, especially in the West and Southwest. For all the reasons discussed above, the lack of such courses on most campuses represents a gap in the liberal arts learning offered to students in our colleges and universities, and may leave unchallenged in other courses many of the assumptions students hold about the construction and rigidity of racial categories.

The Association of MultiEthnic Americans lists U.C. Berkeley as having a course on "People of Mixed Racial Descent" that has been offered once a year by different instructors since 1980. It also points to a course at Golden Gate University's Law School on "Multiracial, Multiethnic People: The Law and Society."

Among other colleges that have readily identified course listings on interracial issues is Mills College's Ethnic Studies course on "Mixed Race Descent in the Americas." California State Polytechnic University at Pomona offers a course entitled "Multiracial and Hybrid Identities." The History Department at the University of Oregon offers "The History of Interracial Families in the United States." Cal State Sacramento's Ethnic Studies Program offers "Biracial and Multiracial Identity in the U.S." The Asian American Studies Program at the University of California, Davis has a course on "Biracial and Multiracial Asian Pacific American Experience" and the Asian American Studies Program at the University of California, Santa Barbara offers "Multiethnic Asian Americans."

Still other campuses offer content on interracial issues that is embedded in existing courses. These are likely more plentiful than the list above, but are more difficult to locate. Two examples include "Introduction to Chicana Studies" in the Women's Studies Program at the University of New Mexico, and "Race and Ethnicity in the U.S." in the Anthropology Department at the University of Vermont.

Summary

Courses on interracial issues and about interracial people are still scarce in college curricula. Yet the study of interracial issues and interracial people is of significant intellectual importance in our understanding of race, racial identity, and racial categorization. Teaching such a course should give faculty reason to consider an array of instructional approaches in order to maximize student learning. The experience of this one course on interracial issues and people was that of the excitement of intellectual exploration, new understandings and perspectives, discovery and rediscovery of self, others, and social group identities, collaboration, and deep learning.

Notes

Please see Appendix III for a list of works referred to in this chapter. The author wishes to thank Mark Chesler, Karen Downing, and David R. Harris for their comments on earlier versions of this chapter.

Why This Chapter and Why I Am the Author: Why are so few courses taught in our colleges and universities on interracial issues and about interracial people? I ask that question because the explanation, in part, expresses why I, and not someone else, am the author of this chapter. On a certain level I believe I should not be the author of this chapter. In a book written primarily by authors of interracial identity, I am an outsider, an interloper. In the first place, I am not an interracial person as we define the term in the context of U.S. racial categories. And, second, my specific scholarly expertise is not in the area of interracial identity.

Yet here I am. And, indeed, the fact that I, as a mono-racial White man, was invited to write this chapter tells an important story about the place of interracial people in America today. It speaks volumes about the continuing invisibility of interracial people in the United States and in the classrooms of higher education. It teaches us about the enduring boundaries of racial categories and the limited ways in which the public and the scholarly community continue to think about race.

And, yet, there is a story here, too, about the openness of the interracial community to people like myself and the unequaled mentoring and nurturing I have received from many interracial colleagues and students. For that I am deeply thankful and greatly indebted.

In fact, despite all my doubts, I do feel that it is perfectly appropriate that I be the author of this chapter. The challenge to my authorship, I believe, is not whether I should be the author, but why there aren't a great many more faculty to choose from to write this chapter, and where all my colleagues in the social sciences are who have yet to teach this course or others like it. Why is the subject of interracial issues and interracial people still so often ignored, simply an add-on or a supplementary reading, or an unworthy topic for under-graduate, graduate or scholarly study? As for me, I am both honored by the invitation and humbled by the responsibility.

3   Hot Button Issues

Karen Downing and Kelly Webster

This chapter collects resources that address some hot button issues related to interracial people. Hot button issues are those that are frequently researched, but evoke strong and sometimes emotional feelings due to the racial history of our country. Though topics such as interracial dating or parenting are also controversial, these three topics are highlighted here because information about them inspires special attention both within the interracial community, and outside it. The three categories include: appearance-based issues, including how others perceive or misperceive racially mixed individuals; passing, the practice of moving clandestinely from one race to another—most commonly moving from Black to White; and blood quantum, the measurement of American Indian ancestry often used to delineate racial membership. All three of these issues can generate heated discourse and strong opinions. The literature annotated below contains a mixture of personal narratives, scholarly research, and philosophical examinations of these very intense topics.

Appearance Issues and "Fitting In"

Many mixed-race individuals do not physically conform to a stereo-typical idea of a standard phenotype. For this reason, many multiracial people experience, on a regular basis, being misperceived racially by others. The following resources, most of which are personal narratives, show the variety of ways individuals deal with others' reactions to their appearance and how it affects their racial identity. Whether they are perceived as racially ambiguous, monoracial, or the often heard "exotic looking," the authors of the following works stress the importance of appearance in their lives. It is interesting to note that most of the writers in this section are women, reflecting, perhaps, the differential impact that appearance has on women.

Bradshaw, Carla K. "Beauty and the Beast: On Racial Ambiguity." In *Racially Mixed People in America*, edited by Maria P.P. Root. Newbury Park, Calif.: Sage Publications, 1992.

"What are you?" is probably the most common question asked a racially mixed and racially ambiguous-looking person. It is also the launching point for this discussion on physical appearance and how it affects one's life. Bradshaw points out that the institutional effects of racism, including the allocation of resources based on mutually exclusive racial categories, cause racial appearance to have ramifications in both personal and wider social spheres. She also discusses the profound importance of family on one's ability to make sense of our racially polarized environment.

Brand-Williams, Oralandar. "I Just Don't Understand You: In Black and White." *Detroit News*, June 14, 1992.

Brand-Williams, a freelance writer who grew up in a mixed-race family, describes the role appearance played in her life, including the process of identity development, and others' reactions to her race and appearance. The way in which her mother prepared her for these reactions is also discussed.

Chao, Christine M. "A Bridge over Troubled Waters: Being Eurasian in the U.S. of A." In *Racism in the Lives of Women: Testimony, Theory, and Guides to Antiracist Practice*. Binghamton, N.Y.: Haworth Press, Inc., 1995.

This frank discussion of pan-Asian/non-Asian mixing includes topics such as the importance of names to identity, being a mixed "minority of minorities," the ongoing nature of identity development, and how people of all racial groups, strangers included, feel free to "dissect your appearance." Chao also discusses White-appearing mixed-race Asians and "inadvertent passing."

Funderburg, Lise. "I Am What I Say I Am." *Time*, March 26, 2001.

Funderburg gives a detailed description of how other people have perceived her physical attributes as being "White" or "Black." She also describes some of her cultural tendencies that she attributes to her mixed-race upbringing. The author of a ground-breaking book of mixed-race narratives in the early nineties, *Black, White, Other: Biracial Americans Talk about Race and Identity*, Funderburg blends her own story into a discussion of national issues such as the "check all that apply" option on the 2000 census.

Hayes, Janice. "True Blackness." *Essence* 21, no. 12 (April 1991).

Hayes, a light-skinned, biracial author, describes the "unsolicited privilege" she feels she has received since birth. She discusses the opinions of both Black and White acquaintances about her racial identity; the frequent misidentifications (people thinking she is

Italian or Middle Eastern); and her use of "White speech." After struggling through attempts to make herself "Blacker," she realizes that the real issues are those of self-esteem and racial acceptance from within.

Kashef, Ziba. "Black, White, Other." *Essence* 28, no. 4 (August 1997).

Kashef reflects on the difficulties of being a light-skinned woman who is both Black and Persian. Because of her appearance, she feels pressure to identify with her Persian side; however, she grew up in a primarily Black southern community, which strengthened her identification with that side of her heritage. Ultimately, she refuses to choose one part of her identity over the other. Earlier in her life, she allowed the expectations of others to define her, but after much thought and turmoil, she resists, in her words, "the notion of separating parts of myself for someone else's convenience."

Mahdesian, Linda. "It's Not Easy Being Green." *U.S. News & World Report*, November 23, 1987.

The daughter of a Black father and a White mother, Mahdesian describes various events throughout her life in which people judged her based on her light-skinned appearance. Though she endured painful treatment by both Whites and Blacks while growing up, she now believes that her background has been a blessing. Her hardest battle, she writes, was developing and accepting her racial place in the context of American society.

Martin, Antoinette. "It's Not Black and White." *Detroit Free Press Magazine*, October 9, 1994.

This very balanced and substantive discussion reveals the ways in which appearance, family influences, and life experiences have shaped the racial identities of a dozen interracial (Black/White) individuals. Viewpoints range from identifying as being "just Black" to being "mostly White" and everything in between. A very strong national context is also included in the article. This is one of the most in-depth pieces to be found in a newspaper publication.

Richardson, Brenda Lane. "Not All Black and White." *Glamour* 53, no. 5 (August 1992).

Richardson, an African American mother, describes a discussion she had with her four-year-old daughter about skin color and appearance, revealing the values a young child subconsciously picks up in a society based on appearance. She recalls several racially based incidents that took place in front of her young mixed-race daughter, and the subsequent impressions her daughter was left with.

Russell, Kathy, Midge Wilson, and Ronald Hall. *The Color Complex: The Politics of Skin Color among African Americans.* New York: Harcourt Brace Jovanovich, 1992.

This groundbreaking book on issues relating to African Americans and skin color begins with a historical overview of race mixing during the early colonial period, including the different rights and privileges granted to European, Native American, and African American offspring. The narrative jumps to the post-Civil War era through the Harlem Renaissance with a discussion of mulattos and "mulatto elites." At that time, most major cities included residential areas where light-skinned Blacks lived in groups. The authors go on to discuss racial features, dating and marriage, prejudice in the workplace, and how the media helps shape notions around skin color.

Santiago, Roberto. "Black *and* Latino." *Essence* 20, no. 7 November 1989.

This short narrative by a racially mixed Puerto Rican/Black author describes the problems people of all races have accepting his racial identity. He describes skin color issues within the Puerto Rican community and issues of culture intertwining with race and appearance.

Scales-Trent, Judy. *Notes of a White Black Woman: Race, Color and Community.* University Park, Pa.: The Pennsylvania State University Press, 1995.

A beautifully written autobiographical work that incorporates poetry and prose to describe the life experiences of Scales-Trent. The author is a light-skinned Black woman who is often mistaken for being White. She writes of the many instances she has been misidentified and ways in which she internally and externally copes with those situations.

Terry-Azios, Diana. "My Life as a Light-Skinned Mejicana." *Hispanic* 14, no. 5 (May 2001).

In this narrative, Terry-Azios writes about her physical and cultural attributes such as her light skin and her fluency in Spanish, and how these play into how she is racially perceived by Latinos and non-Latinos. Though she has experienced continual challenges to her racial identity, the author is proud of her multiracial heritage. She writes, "My color can't revoke my culture."

Walden-Kaufman, Edie Natalie. *The Unseen Cost of Privilege: The Psychological Experience of African American Women Mistaken as Caucasian.* Ph.D. diss., The Wright Institute, 1999.

This investigation studies how being mistaken for White impacts the racial identity development of African American women. The women who experienced this phenomenon reported feeling rejection from others within their own race. When they are misidentified as being White, they must also deal with White privilege through unintentional passing. Though other studies have measured privilege based on skin color, this study deals specifically with the personal, rather than social, impact. Using in-depth interviews with eight light-skinned African American women, the author found parental and family influences to be important in resolving identity issues, and important in the ability to balance thought and emotion around issues of unintentional passing and fitting in.

Passing

"Passing" or "passing for White" is the term/phrase used to describe light-skinned Blacks, or racially mixed people of Black ancestry, who choose to live as White. These individuals may allow others to assume that they are White in certain situations or throughout an entire lifetime. Some authors have used the term to include any deliberate change in racial status, regardless of the race(s) involved.

The toll that "passing" exacts on individuals is clearly present in most of the literature on the topic. The "tragic mulatto/a" in the literature and films of the early part of the twentieth century always ended poorly; emotionally scarred at best, or dead at worst. Liera-Schwichtenberg states that "passing exacts a high price, for the ability to 'pass' and transgress boundaries and assimilate to 'Whiteness' inevitably leads to death of the self."[1]

Ahmed, Sara. "'She'll Wake up One of These Days and Find She's Turned into a Nigger': Passing Through Hybridity." *Theory, Culture and Society* 16, no. 2 (1999): 87-106.
    Ahmed, a multiracial professor of women's studies, analyzes the subject of passing by examining works including Nella Larsen's *Passing*, Judith Butler's *Gender Trouble* and *Bodies that Matter,* and Gail Ching-Liang Low's *White Skins/Black Masks: Representation and Colonialism*. She is one of very few authors who examines passing outside of the traditional Black-passing-as-White narrative.

Boateng, Osei. "Passing Along Fine." *New African*, no. 377 (1999): 32-34.
    An analysis of the term "passing," which outlines how it has been used from the 1950s to the present. Boateng discusses the overlaying roles that skin-color, features, and class play in the decision to

pass. A number of personal narratives from individuals who have chosen to pass are shared within the article.

Cotter, Holland. "Inside-Out Meditations on the Poison of Racism." *New York Times,* January 8, 1999.

Cotter provides a critical review of the work of Adrian Piper, a light-skinned Black artist who is often mislabeled by others as being White. Piper has included the experience of unintentional passing in much of her art. She helped introduce identity and racial politics into the Conceptualism movement thirty years ago, and her art continues to explore the theme of being "in-between."

Daniel, G. Reginald. "Passers and Pluralists: Subverting the Racial Divide." In *Racially Mixed People in America,* edited by Maria P.P. Root. Newbury Park, Calif.: Sage Publications, 1992.

Daniel defines passing as a "radical from of integration whereby individuals of a more European phenotype and cultural orientation make a clandestine break with the African American community, temporarily or permanently, in order to enjoy the privileges of the dominant White community." He has written an excellent history of passing from the Free People of Color groups founded in the antebellum period, to the Blue-Vein Societies of the early twentieth century. He also covers the little-known scattered groups of racially mixed individuals called "triracial isolates" who lived in groups on the physical and social fringes of larger communities throughout the country.

Derricotte, Toi. *The Black Notebooks: An Interior Journey.* New York: Norton, 1997.

These selections from the poet's journals, which were kept over the course of twenty years, focus on the author's identity as a light-skinned Black woman who is often mistaken for White. Derricotte describes with candor her occasional choice to "pass" for White, as when she was attempting to buy a house in a predominantly White suburban neighborhood in New York, though these episodes resulted in profound discomfort.

Piper, Adrian. "Passing for White, Passing for Black." *Transition*, no. 58 (1992): 4-32.

An emotionally honest essay written by artist Piper, a light-skinned Black woman who grew up in Harlem to the taunts of others calling her "White girl." She describes issues relating to being misperceived by both Blacks and Whites throughout her life, and her struggle to forgive those of her relatives who decided to pass for White. She includes many quotations from literature about interracial experiences throughout the history of the United States.

Wilson, Robin. "At the Racial Dividing Line." *Chronicle of Higher Education* 41 (1995): A17.
This interview with Gregory Howard Williams and Judy Scales-Trent coincided with the publishing of their autobiographical works on growing up interracially. Both Williams and Scales-Trent are academics in the field of law, and both describe how race has impacted their careers and their lives. Wilson supplements the interviews with background information on both authors.

Passing in Fictional Literature

Passing has been a ripe subject in fictional literature for centuries. Sollors' *Neither Black nor White Yet Both* contains an excellent timeline that traces the continuum of interracial literature from the fifth century B.C. through the mid-1990s. The highest volume of passing literature occurred between 1880-1950. Bennett states that "Passing for White captured the imaginations of past writers because it was symbolic of America's contradictions . . ." [2] Passing literature flourished in a time when American legal and social systems were used to create the "separate but equal" laws and mindsets throughout the southern part of the country, and de facto segregation based on race was rampant in the North. Legal cases such as *Plessy v. Ferguson* were brought before state and federal courts, testing the limits of the "one-drop" rule, and the boundaries of fabricated racial lines. With all the attention paid to racial "purity" during this time, it is no wonder that fiction writers took up their pens to illustrate how easy it was to fool those who claimed they could "tell" one's race by looking at them.

Bennett, Juda. "Multiple Passings and the Double Death of Langston Hughes." *Biography* 23, no. 4 (Fall 2000): 670-693.
An exploration of Langston Hughes' theme of "passing for White" is provided in the context of the works of other authors (both Black and White) of the time, including Nella Larsen, Jessie Fauset, and William Faulkner. Bennett contends that Hughes' repetition of this theme revealed his interest in deviation from what was considered normal at the time, and his delight in the "act of transgression."
———. "Toni Morrison and the Burden of the Passing Narrative." *African American Review* 35, no. 4 (Summer 2001): 205-217.
In another interesting reflection on interracial literature as it relates to racial ambiguity and "passing for White," Bennett compares the prevalence of this type of literature in the first half of the twentieth century, and its decline in the latter half of the century. Issues re-

lated to passing are discussed in Toni Morrison's *The Bluest Eye, Tar Baby, Song of Solomon,* and *Jazz,* where "dynamics of crossing the color line are moved from the body to the psyche."

Ginsberg, Elaine K. *Passing and the Fictions of Identity.* Durham, N.C.: Duke University Press, 1996.

This group of essays, collected by the Modern Language Association, addresses the issue of light-skinned Blacks passing for White in written literature. The collection includes a few essays that stretch the common meaning of "passing," including a discussion of White identity in *Black Like Me* by John Howard, and several essays on gender passing.

Johnson, James Weldon. *The Autobiography of an Ex-Colored Man.* New York: Alfred A. Knopf, Inc., 1927. Reprint, New York: Vintage Books, 1989.

One of the few "tragic mulatto" stories to have a male protagonist, *Autobiography* is a compelling classic. Written during the Harlem Renaissance, when the issue of light-skinned Blacks "passing" for White was considered a major issue, it purported to be an actual autobiography rather than a work of fiction. It depicts a man who leaves his Black family to live as a White person, and his resulting conflicts. It was important not only because it launched a trend in literature and film that lasted well into the twentieth century, but also because the book's enormous popularity gave Whites a hard look at the issue from a Black perspective. The Vintage edition has an introduction by Henry Louis Gates.

Larsen, Nella. *Passing.* New York: Modern Library, 2000.

Passing is a classic tragic mulatta story of a beautiful protagonist (Clare) who passes for White, and her light-skinned friend (Irene) who does not. Clare's attempt to move between Black and White society has fatal results. The story is acclaimed for its beautiful writing and honest emotions. Author Nella Larsen, born of interracial parents in 1891, led a somewhat bifurcated life herself. She went to Fisk University and the University of Copenhagen (her mother was of Danish ancestry and her father from the Virgin Islands). This Modern Library edition includes an introduction by Ntozake Shange.

Liera-Schwichtenberg, Romona. "Passing or Whiteness on the Edge of Town." *Critical Studies in Media Communication* 17, no. 3 (September 2000): 371-375.

The author analyzes the phenomenon of passing, drawing on examples from popular media and celebrities while incorporating frameworks from literary theory. She explores themes of "otherness" and "transgressing boundaries," and describes our fascination with, and revulsion to, the idea of passing, or the perceived necessity of it. With equal ease, she quotes Elaine K. Ginsberg, author of *Passing and the Fictions of Identity*, and Selena, the murdered pop singer.

Pfeiffer, Kathleen. "Individualism, Success, and American Identity in *The Autobiography of an Ex-Colored Man*." *African American Review* 30, no. 3 (Autumn 1996): 403-419.

Pfeiffer provides a critical analysis of *The Autobiography of an Ex-Colored Man* through the lens of individualism versus collective racial identity, claiming that the protagonist "embodies the paradox of race and color because he is both legally Black and visibly White." Though *Autobiography* has been viewed as a tale of racial self-hatred, Pfeiffer offers a view of the protagonist as a man who values individualism, is idiosyncratic, and is inclined to improvisation. She also discusses the dissonance of mulattoes' legal and social identities in the context of the protagonist's era.

Sollors, Werner. "Passing; or, Sacrificing a Parvenu." In *Neither Black Nor White Yet Both: Thematic Explorations of Interracial Literature*. Oxford: Oxford University Press, 1997.

Sollors' work is a mainstay of interracial literature. He includes literature "in all genres that represent love and family relations involving Black-White couples, biracial individuals, their descendants, and their larger kin." His chapter on passing provides historical and social analysis of the major works of fiction on the subject.

Sullivan, Neil. "Nella Larsen's *Passing* and the Fading Subject." *African American Review* 32, no. 3 (Autumn 1998): 373-386.

Sullivan, a professor of English, critically examines Larsen's *Passing* as a metaphor for disappearance of the soul and death of the body. She traces the influences of Larsen's interracial childhood experiences of being marginalized within society, and Larsen's family on her writing.

Wald, Gayle Freda. *Crossing the Line: Racial Passing in Twentieth-Century U.S. Literature and Culture*. Durham, N.C.: Duke University Press, 2000.

Wald has written a historical and psychological analysis of a wide body of twentieth-century literature and film pertaining to passing. Her examination reveals the contradictory nature of race.

Blood Quantum

For a variety of reasons, non-Indians often feel comfortable asking those who identify as American Indian such personal questions as "How much?" and "On which side?," which is often followed by "My great-great-grandmother was Cherokee." While many American Indians greet these questions with politeness or amusement, mixed blood individuals are given yet another reminder of the need to justify their Indianness.

American Indians are the only racial group that is still legally defined in the United States; policies that measure what makes a "real Indian" vary from one U.S. government agency to the other. Definitions used are based on an understanding of "blood" that is difficult to grasp. Meeting these requirements has implications for tribal sovereignty, distribution of economic resources, access to social service programs and to health care, and even whether or not a tribe legally exists. Blood quantum is carefully tracked within Native communities also. While individual tribes vary in the way tribal membership is established, many have replaced traditional means with blood quantum policies. Meeting these definitions can impact one's right to hold tribal office, vote in elections, and live on the reservation.

The authors cited in this section examine the political, social and economic implications of blood quantum policies, analyze the flaws in this controversial system, and reveal the personal impact on mixed-race individuals.

Baird-Olson, Karren. "Colonization, Cultural Imperialism, and the Social Construction of American Indian Mixed-Blood Identity." In *New Faces in a Changing America: Multiracial Identity in the 21st Century*. Thousand Oaks, Calif.: Sage Publications, Inc., 2003.
   In this article, Baird-Olson characterizes the use of blood quantum categories as "statistical genocide." She examines historical and contemporary ways of determining American Indian identity and offers a new model to consider. The discussion is supplemented by a list of terms used to label mixed-bloods, a chart showing multiple race combinations that include American Indian with the corresponding data from the 2000 census, and the table used by the Bureau of Indian Affairs to establish a child's degree of Indian blood.

Chadwick, Allen. "Blood and Memory." *American Literature* 71, no. 1 (March 1999): 93-116.
   Chadwick examines the debate in American literary and cultural studies about the concept of "blood memory," used heavily in the works of N. Scott Momaday and developed by many other con-

temporary American Indian authors. The debate is ultimately about who may speak as an "authentic" American Indian author. After reviewing the history of the use of blood quantum standards in the United States, this article traces the theme of "blood memory" through Momaday's works and analyzes various reactions within the literary world to the concept and its implications.

Desjarlait, Robert. "How Much Indian Are You? Blood Quantum v. Lineal Descent." *The Circle* 22, no. 11 (November 2001): 12.

This article describes the politics of American Indian identity and the resulting "eugenic pecking order" that has caused divisiveness in Native communities. The discussion centers on a profile of the case of the Lac Courte Orielles Band of Ojibwe and their attempts to change membership standards from blood quantum to lineal descent.

Garroutte, Eva Marie. "The Racial Formation of American Indians: Negotiating Legitimate Identities with Tribal and Federal Law." *American Indian Quarterly* 25, no. 2 (2001): 224-239.

Garroutte provides an introduction to federal and tribal legal definitions that regulate membership in American Indian communities and the implications of these definitions. She points out that modern definitions are rooted in antiquated notions of race, and gives examples of the complications that can arise from the use of these requirements. She contrasts blood quantum requirements with the "one-drop rule" historically used in racially classifying individuals with any degree of African American ancestry, and points out that almost a third of tribes have rejected specific blood quantum requirements as membership criteria.

"Government Has No Business Deciding What a Person's Ancestry Is: A Move to Determine for Indians Who Their Brothers Are Is Offensive." *Portland Press Herald*, March 1, 2001.

In this editorial, a mixed-blood author gives his point of view on blood quantum requirements used by the Bureau of Indian Affairs and shares what it is like to feel neither Native enough nor White enough to be accepted into a community. The author relates his perceptions of the attitudes of other mixed-blood people he knows, and discusses the racism of current policies.

Hagan, W.T. "Full Blood, Mixed Blood, Generic and Ersatz: The Problem of Indian Identity." *Arizona and the West* 27 (1985): 309-326.

Hagan provides an overview of the history of defining American Indian identity. He describes court cases and federal policy making throughout the nineteenth century, by the end of which tribes were given authority over their own membership criteria. By pointing out periods over the last two centuries in which claims to Indian identity were subject to suspicion, he shows that accusations of "ethnic fraud" are not a new phenomenon. After discussing the many implications for being defined as Indian by a federal agency, the article ends with the example of the Mashantucket Pequot tribe, which gained federal recognition and subsequently large amounts of grant money and land, resulting in a huge increase in membership.

Krouse, Susan Applegate. "Kinship and Identity: Mixed Bloods in Urban Indian Communities." *American Indian Culture and Research Journal* 23, no. 2 (1999): 73-89.

Using formal and informal interviews with urban mixed blood individuals, as well as the research of anthropologists and publications by mixed blood authors, Krouse examines how this group negotiates ethnic identity and the problems that arise from that process. Topics include the process of urbanization for American Indians, physical and cultural characteristics of mixed blood individuals, self-identifying, kinship-based identity, and challenges faced by the mixed blood population.

Meyer, Melissa. "American Indian Blood Quantum Requirements: Blood is Thicker Than Family." In *Over the Edge: Remapping the American West*, edited by Valerie Matsumoto and Blake Allmendinger. Berkeley: University of California Press, 1999.

Meyer traces the history of the changing criteria used by the U.S. government to define American Indian identity and explores how blood quantum has become the most important standard in both federal and tribal policies. She offers theories to explain how most tribes went from using complex kinship systems to determine tribal membership, to a reliance on an understanding of "blood," a concept introduced by federal government to determine U.S. Indian policy. She shows how the understanding of "blood" has changed over time and was often based on nonscientific and racist beliefs. Includes a table showing the blood quantum requirements of tribes.

Pewewardy, Cornel. "Will the 'Real' Indians Please Stand Up?" *MultiCultural Review* 7, no. 2 (June 1998): 36-42.

This article explores the many federal, tribal, and personal definitions of a "real Indian." Pewewardy points out the difficulty of discussing this when even the Bureau of Indian Affairs and other government agencies are unable to agree on a definition. Identifying blood quantum as the principal determinant in these definitions, he discusses how its importance plays out in various settings, emphasizing the racist implications in asking someone about his or her blood quantum to determine "authenticity," a tactic that is not used with other ethnic groups. He concludes that the notion of a "real Indian" is an American social construct. Includes a list of humorous terms used to delineate Indians and non-Indians.

Snipp, C. Matthew. "Some Observations about Racial Boundaries and the Experiences of American Indians." *Ethnic and Racial Studies* 20 (1997): 667-689.

This article focuses on American Indians to illustrate the issues around the future of race in America and the impact of multiracialism on racial classification. Citing urbanization and the lessening of stigma as contributing to the high rate of intermarriage among American Indians, Snipp discusses blood quantum, tribal membership, and self-identification as the standards for defining populations. He describes their use in public policy, distribution of economic resources, employment, and college admissions. The article concludes by drawing parallels between these issues and those that may face multiracial populations in the future.

Taliman, Valerie. "Termination by Bureaucracy." *Native Americas* 19, no. 1/2 (2002): 8.

Taliman describes how the definitions of American Indian identity used by the federal government and individual tribes can impact the lives of mixed blood members in surprising ways. She provides examples from several tribes dealing with enrollment policies and identifies blood quantum standards introduced by the federal government as a tactic meant to reduce the official number of American Indians.

Weaver, Hilary N. "Indigenous Identity: What Is It, and Who Really Has It?" *American Indian Quarterly* 25, no. 2 (2001): 240-255.

Focusing on cultural identity as a reflection of indigenous beliefs, Weaver examines three facets of identity: self-identification, community identification, and external identification. She gives an overview of methods used to measure American Indian identity and discusses their inadequacies and implications. Finally, she shares her reflections on how internalized oppression/colonization impacts identity and its regulation in Native American communities.

Wilson, Terry P. "Blood Quantum: Native American Mixed Bloods." In *Racially Mixed People in America,* edited by Maria P.P. Root. Newbury Park, Calif.: Sage Publications, 1992.

Wilson identifies blood quantum as a thorny issue that preoccupies most people in the Native American community who carefully reveal their own, and scrutinize that of others. She explores the history of African American/American Indian unions, the richness of which is hidden by the use of the "one-drop rule." Wilson's interviews with about one hundred African Americans with Native

American ancestry revealed that most were interested in learning more but would not identify as Native American. Further discussion includes a description of how phenotype plays into identity, anecdotes from students at the author's university, and trends in census data. Some brief biographical information about mixed-blood leaders in history is provided.

Notes

1. Liera-Schwichtenberg, Romona. "Passing or Whiteness on the Edge of Town." *Critical Studies in Media Communication* 17, no. 3 (September 2000): 373.

2. Bennett, Juda. "Toni Morrison and the Burden of the Passing Narrative." *African American Review* 35, no. 4 (Summer 2001): 205-217.

4   Core Historical Literature

Chuck Ransom

Throughout most of the history of the United States "race" usually referred to Black and White. According to Hening and others, the first
Africans were brought to Jamestown, Virginia, in 1619. Not long after
(1630), the first recorded actions against race mixing were recorded. It
was ordered:

> [T]hat Hugh Davis be soundly whipped before an assemblage of Ne-
> groes and others for abusing himself to the dishonor of God and the
> shame of Christians by defiling his body in lying with a Negro, which
> fault he is to acknowledge next Saboth *(sic)* day.[1]

In 1640 it was recorded that "Robert Sweet is to do penance in
church according to the law of England, for getting a negro *(sic)*
woman with child, and the woman to be soundly whipped."[2] In 1662,
Virginia enacted its first law prohibiting intermarriage;[3] seven other
colonies followed suit by 1754.

The Virginia act of 1662 reads:

> Whereas some doubts have arisen whether a child got by an Eng-
> lishman upon a Negro woman should be free or slave, be it therefore
> enacted by this present grand assembly, that all children born in this
> country shall be bound or free according to the condition of the
> mother, and if any Christian shall commit fornication with a Negro
> man or woman, he or she so offending shall pay a fine double the fine
> imposed by the previous act.[4]

With this divisive historical context in mind, it is easy to see how
our modern taboos against interracial relationships and people have
come to pass. This chapter will focus on the early literature relating to
interracial people. The time period of this chapter spans from the earliest colonial American period to 1967, a pivotal year in civil rights history. In 1967 the U.S. Supreme Court ruled on the case *Loving v. Virginia,* ending the anti-miscegenation laws in the United States, if not
the extreme social taboo still associated with interracial marriage.
Much of the early literature, both fiction and nonfiction, focused on the

tragic mulatto, who never fit in and was despised by both African Americans and Whites. Very little was written about relationships between people of other races during this time period. Most of the literature reflects the prevailing racist and eugenic thoughts and practices that characterized U.S. society before the civil rights era.

Resources for this chapter were identified primarily by searching the online catalog of the University of Michigan Library, OCLC's WorldCat database, and a variety of historical indexes. The most useful Library of Congress subject headings include "miscegenation," "racially mixed people," and "race identity." JSTOR and Periodicals Content Index (PCI), two periodical databases that include full text, were also both very useful. For a fuller list of useful subject headings and indexes, see Appendix I.

Fiction

Brown, William Wells. *Clotel; or, The President's Daughter: A Narrative of Slave Life in the United States*. New York: Arno Press, 1969.

This novel by Brown, a runaway slave who fled the United States because of the Fugitive Slave Law of 1850, was published in London in 1853. *Clotel* is generally held to be the first complete novel by an African American. The original edition, *Clotel; or, the President's Daughter*, was not published in the United States until 1969.

In Brown's historical novel President Thomas Jefferson fathers a quadroon slave, Clotel, who is sold for $1,500. Clotel and a friend escape slavery to Ohio posing as a White gentleman and his servant. Clotel is recaptured three times, but escapes each recapture. Her final recapture ends with her committing suicide. Brown is sometimes blamed for institutionalizing the image of the tragic mulatta in early African American fiction. He published three revised versions of the novel with different titles: *Miralda; or, the Beautiful Quadroon* (1860-61); *Clotelle: A Tale of the Southern States* (1864); and *Clotelle; or the Colored Heroine* (1867). Each version was tailored for a different audience. *Clotel* for British Christians, *Miralda* for the American abolition debate, *Clotelle: A Tale of the Southern States* for Union soldiers and *Clotelle, or, the Colored Heroine,* for women readers. These later editions of the novel were published in the United States, with Jefferson replaced by an anonymous senator or a Southern gentleman.

Chesnutt, Charles W. *The House behind the Cedars.* Ridgewood, N.J., Gregg Press, 1968.

Chesnutt, an African American who appeared White, was a tremendous contributor to literature about people on the "color-line." Widely reviewed when it was first published in 1900, this novel told the story of two young biracial siblings who appeared White. First the brother passes for White and establishes himself in White society, then he brings his sister into his life, and helps her pass for White as well.

Johnson, James Weldon. *The Autobiography of an Ex-Coloured Man.* Boston: French & Company, 1912.

The Autobiography of an Ex-Coloured Man resembles other "tragic mulatto" narratives of the day. It depicts, often in sentimental terms, the travails of mixed-race protagonists unable to fit into either racial culture. In Johnson's novel, the unnamed narrator is light-skinned enough to pass for White but identifies emotionally with his beloved mother's Black race. In his youth, he aspires to become a great Black American musical composer, but he fearfully renounces that ambition after watching a mob of Whites set fire to a Black man in the rural South. Though horrified and repulsed by the Whites' attack, the narrator feels an even deeper shame and humiliation for himself as a Black man and he subsequently allows circumstances to guide him along the easier path of "passing" as a middle-class White businessman. The protagonist finds success in this role but ends up a failure in his own terms, plagued with ambivalence over his true identity, moral values, and emotional loyalties.

Jones, J. McHenry. *Hearts of Gold, a Novel.* Wheeling, W.V.: Daily Intelligencer Steam Job Press, 1896. Reprint, College Park, Md.: McGrath Publishing Co., 1969.

First published in 1896, this story revolves around an interracial relationship. The heroine Regina Underwood is the daughter of a White heiress and a fugitive slave. Jones, an African American, self-published his book.

Larsen, Nella. *Passing.* New York: A.A. Knopf, 1929.

Passing is the story of Clare Kendry, a beautiful, fair-skinned African American woman who escapes likely impoverishment by passing for White. She marries a wealthy White man, who assumes that she is also White. Her passage across the color line is completely successful. Clare renews ties with childhood friend Irene Redfield, who has married an African American physician and is living in the upper circles of Harlem. Clare finds herself as attracted to Irene's husband as he is to her. Perceiving Clare as a threat to her own marriage and security, Irene wants Clare to disappear, a wish that comes true when Clare falls, jumps, or is pushed from an open window at a Harlem apartment party just as her husband appears to confront her with his discovery of her African American roots.

Larsen, Nella. *Quicksand.* New York: A.A. Knopf, 1928.

Quicksand, which appeared in 1928, is the largely autobiographical story of Helga Crane, the daughter of an African American man and a Scandinavian woman, who searches in vain for sexual and racial identity. Her quest takes her from a teaching position at a small college in the South to the elite social circles of Copenhagen and New York City, to a backwoods Atlanta community pastored by the illiterate preacher she marries. The marriage fulfills Helga's longing for an uncomplicated existence and for sexual gratification, but it leaves her mired in a life of rural poverty and continual pregnancies.

Smith, Lillian Eugenia. *Strange Fruit.* New York: Reynal, 1944.

A novel about a love affair between an educated African American woman, Noonie Anderson, and a White man, Tracy Dean. Their love results in murder and lynching. Smith presented the couple's sexual relations in graphic scenes which shocked many reviewers. Smith's book was banned in the South and in Boston and Detroit.

Sumner, Cid Ricketts. *Quality.* New York: Bantam Books, 1946.

This novel, on which the film *Pinky* was based, was originally serialized in *Ladies Home Journal.* Pinky is an African American nurse passing for White. She is scheduled to marry a northern White doctor, but the wedding never happens. The story illustrates the main aspects of Black-White relations in a small southern town.

Webb, Frank. *The Garies and Their Friends.* New York: AMS Press, 1971 (reprint of 1857 edition).

First published in London in 1857, this novel was, as critic Arthur P. Davis notes, "the first work of fiction to describe the lives and problems of free Northern Negroes; the first to treat with any appreciable depth the 'mixed marriage,' . . . the first to treat ironically . . . the vagaries of the 'color line'; and the first to make 'passing for White' a major theme in a novel."[5]

White, Walter Francis. *Flight.* Baton Rouge: Louisiana State University Press, 1998.

Originally published in 1926 during the Harlem Renaissance, *Flight* was White's attempt to counter the usual "tragic mulatto" in fiction of the time. He made his protagonist's Black identity questioned "by her own people, to disown." White considered himself

Black, yet he appeared to be White in skin tone and features. He later went on to become head of the NAACP.

Wilson, Harriet. *Our Nig, or, Sketches from the Life of a Free Black, in a Two-Story White House, North Showing that Slavery's Shadows Fall Even There.* New York: Random House, 1983 (reprint, original published Boston: G. Rand & Avery, 1859).

This book was the first novel published in the United States by an African American. *Our Nig* is the story of Frado, the mulatto daughter of Mag Smith, a poor, ostracized White woman and Jim, a free Black cooper. Following Jim's death, Mag remarries and abandons six-year-old Frado to the Bellmonts, a White family in New Hampshire. There Frado is physically and emotionally abused by the racist Mrs. Bellmont, blocked from all but a minimum of formal schooling, severely overworked, and treated as a virtual slave. Eventually, Frado leaves the Bellmonts and moves to Massachusetts, where she marries Samuel, a Black man. Samuel deserts a pregnant Frado to go to sea. After Frado gives birth to a boy, she leaves him in foster care to return to New Hampshire to find work. At the end of the novel Frado's struggle becomes an appeal to the reader to relieve her suffering. In *Our Nig,* we see the tragic mulatta figure as a central thematic element.

Personal and Family Accounts

Allen, William G. *The American Prejudice Against Color, An Authentic Narrative, Showing How Easily the Nation Got into an Uproar.* London: W. and F.G. Cash; 1853. Reprint, New York: Arno Press, 1969.

Allen writes about being run out of town by an angry mob after his marriage to one of his White students. The book was first published in London. Allen graduated from Oneida Institute, studied law in Boston, and then became a professor of Greek and German languages and rhetoric at Central College. He contributed several letters to the *Liberator* and an essay on Placido to the 1853 edition of *Autographs for Freedom.*[6]

Craft, William, *Running a Thousand Miles for Freedom, or, the Escape of William and Ellen Craft from Slavery.* London: W. Tweedie, 1860.

Craft recounts how he and Ellen fled slavery in Macon, Georgia. In December of 1848 they left Macon, with Ellen disguised as a wealthy rheumatic Southern gentleman. Ellen was the child of her White master and her slave mother. William had African features

and Black skin; he posed as her servant. The Crafts fled to England
to avoid recapture under the Fugitive Slave Law. This book was
made into a short film by the Learning Corporation of America in
1972 titled *A Slave's Story: Running a Thousand Miles to Freedom.*

White, Walter Francis. *A Man Called White: The Autobiography of
Walter White.* New York: Viking Press, 1948.
Walter F. White worked for the National Association for the Ad-
vancement of Colored People (NAACP) for more than thirty years.
Less than one-quarter Negro by blood, White had light skin, blue
eyes, and blond hair but chose to remain in the Black society in
which he had grown up. He was able to cross the color line at will
and frequently posed as a White to gather information in his fight
against lynching, segregation, and other forms of discrimination.
His findings and achievements became the basis of several fiction
and nonfiction books. In his autobiography, *A Man Called White*,
he revealed the atrocities against Blacks that he witnessed while
growing up in Black society as well as the progress that was made.

Woods, Frances Jerome. *Marginality and Identity: A Colored Creole
Family through Ten Generations.* Baton Rouge: Louisiana State
University Press, 1972.
Woods traces a "colored Creole" family back to 1767, and identifies 10,147 descendants of Pierre Latoyant, a French soldier and
Marie, a young Black woman. The author points to three factors in
the unity of the family including: familial relation, a common religion (Catholicism), and geographic isolation. Also contributing to
the marginality and identity of the family is the rejection of the
family by Whites, and the family's rejection of non-Creole Blacks
not of the same color.

Early Social and Scientific Studies of
Interracial Matters

Adams, Romanzo Colfax. *Interracial Marriage in Hawaii: A Study of
the Mutually Conditioned Processes of Acculturation and Amalgamation.* New York: Macmillan, 1937.
The Hawaiian Islands have long been a melting pot for various racial and ethnic groups. The islands were a way station in the early
trade with Asia and a wintering point for whalers. The increase in
the production of sugar resulted in the importation of various racial
and ethnic groups, including Chinese, Portuguese, Spanish, Rus-
sians, Germans, Koreans, Blacks from Cape Verde and Puerto

Rico, Japanese, Filipinos, and others. The result of this importation was a considerable amount of racial intermixture. Adams traces the course of racial intermixture and discusses the related social, economic, and political consequences of the mixing.

Barnes, Irene. "The Inheritance of Pigmentation in the American Negro." *Human Biology* 3, no. 1 (September 1929): 321-361.

Barnes analyzes how skin color is inherited in interracial marriages. She concludes that children resemble the parent with the darker skin slightly more often than the parent with the lighter skin.

Barron, Milton Leon. *People Who Intermarry: Intermarriage in New England Industrial Community.* Syracuse, N.Y.: Syracuse University Press, 1946.

Barron studies all of the incidents of racial, ethnic, and religious intermarriage in Derby, Connecticut, in 1930 and 1940. The small African American community and the tiny number of racial intermarriages make his conclusions difficult to evaluate.

Boas, Franz. "The Half-Blood Indian." *The Popular Science Monthly* 45 (1894): 761.

This article compares the physical features, height, breadth of face, birth rate, growth of children, and length of head between "full blooded Indians and Indian-White mixed Indians." Boas concludes that mixed Indians are bigger and have a higher birth rate than full-blooded Indians. Boas sees this difference as being caused by the mix of White blood, rather than environmental factors.

Burma, John H. "The Measurement of Negro 'Passing.'" *American Journal of Sociology* 52, no. 1 (July 1946): 18-22.

This article attempts to find an accurate way to estimate the number of African Americans passing for White. The author states that earlier methods of estimating the number are no longer credible.

Castle, W.E. "Race Mixture and Physical Disharmonies." *Science* 71, no. 1850 (June 13, 1930): 603-606.

This article is a response to the arguments made by H.S. Jennings and C.B. Davenport regarding "physical disharmonies" in racially mixed people. Castle argues that these supposed disharmonies are minor and in many cases do not exist.

———. "Biological and Social Consequences of Race-Crossing." *American Journal of Physical Anthropology* 9, no. 2 (April/June, 1926): 145-156.

A shorter version of this article appears in *The Journal of Heredity* vol. 15, September 1924. These articles reject Dr. J.H. Mjoen's conclusions on race-crossing, which were based on observations of two sets of rabbits crossed with a third set. Dr. Mjoen observed physical deterioration, decreased size, diminished fertility, failure of sexual instinct, and asymmetrical carriage of ears. Castle maintains that social rather than biological factors affect our understanding of race mixing.

Davenport, Charles B. *Heredity of Skin Color in Negro-White Crosses.* Washington, D.C.: The Carnegie Institution of Washington, 1918.

Davenport tries to explain the law of inheritance of skin color in Negro and White crosses. His conclusions included the idea that the offspring of Black/White unions are relatively infertile, their skin color is unpredictable, and there is no correlation between skin color and the curliness of the hair. This book helped to popularize terms for interracial African Americans such as "pure Black," Negro, "Sambo or Mangro," mulatto, quadroon, octoroon, and "mustifee."

————. "The Effects of Race Intermingling." *Proceedings of the American Philosophical Society* 56 (1917): 364-368.

Davenport claims that some of the effects of race mixing are feeble-minded children, children with internal organs too small for their large frames, and overcrowding or wide separation of teeth due to a lack of harmony between the size of the jaw and the size of the teeth. Davenport supported restricting immigration and the use of eugenic ideals in mating.

————. *Race Crossing in Jamaica.* Washington, D.C.: Carnegie Institute of Washington, 1929.

Davenport presents a quantitative study of Blacks, Whites, and mixed-race people in rural Jamaica. Among his findings is the report that those subjects in the racially mixed group have long arms and short legs, hence they have trouble picking things up off the ground. This book was seen as the best study done on racially-mixed people to date.

Day, Caroline Bond. "A Study of Some Negro-White Families in the United States." *Harvard African Studies* 10 (1932).

This study analyzed 346 families' or 2,537 individuals' blood proportions of White and Black, then reported on the results. Day, who was a person of mixed heritage, collected genealogical, sociological, photographic, and anthropometric records on families to determine their exact blood proportions. The study contains photographs and family histories.

Dollard, John. *Caste and Class in a Southern Town.* New Haven, Conn.: Yale University Press, 1937.

This book is based on interviews with African American and White residents in Indianola. It discusses the social, economic, and political implications of race prejudice. Two castes are defined:

upper caste Whites and lower caste Blacks. This structure permits sexual relations between upper caste White males and lower caste Black females.

Drake, St. Clair. "Crossing the Color-Line." In *Black Metropolis: A Study of Negro Life in a Northern City.* New York: Harcourt, Brace and Co., 1945.

This chapter of *Black Metropolis* describes a sociological study of the African American community in Chicago. It covers intermarriage, passing, and sexual relations between races.

Eckard, E.W. "How Many Negroes 'Pass'?" *American Journal of Sociology* 52, no. 6 (May 1947): 498-500.

An article in *Collier's* of August 3, 1946, stated that thirty thousand African Americans pass into the White race per year. This study investigates the thirty thousand number and finds it very inflated. According to Eckard, the number of African Americans passing is closer to two thousand per year.

Embree, Edwin R. *Brown America: The Story of a New Race.* New York: Viking Press, 1931.

Embree proposes that African Americans are forming a new race: a mixture of the three branches of man. According to Embree, the new race has physical differences and a culture distinct from their African ancestry. His views were considered liberal in the 1930s.

Ferguson, George Oscar. "The Psychology of the Negro: An Experimental Study." *Archives of Psychology*, no. 36. New York: Science Press, 1916.

This monograph contains a chapter comparing the sub-classes of African Americans ("pure Negroes" and mulattoes). The subjects in this study were divided into four classes on the basis of racial purity as indicated by color of skin, hair texture, and general facial and cranial conformation, with the main emphasis placed on color. Ferguson's conclusions were that the intellectual performance of the "colored" population was approximately 75 percent of that of Whites, and that as the percentage of White blood goes up so does the intellectual efficiency.

Golden, Joseph. "Facilitating Factors in Negro-White Intermarriage." *Phylon Quarterly* 20, no. 3 (1959): 273-284.

Golden studied fifty African American/White mixed families to examine the factors that contribute to intermarriage. His study cited such factors as the availability of mates in the same racial group, occupational proximity, education, recreation, mutual friends, and participation in organizations with biracial membership.

————. "Characteristics of the Negro-White Intermarried in Philadelphia." *American Sociological Review* 18, no. 2 (April 1953): 177-183.

This study, based on Golden's 1951 dissertation, used a sampling of marriages in Philadelphia from 1922 to 1947. The characteristics studied in the 141 interracial marriages include the physical characteristics of the African American spouse as well as detailed demographic information.

————. "Patterns of Negro-White Intermarriage." *American Sociological Review* 19, no. 2 (April 1954): 144-147.

In this follow-up to the article cited above, Golden is concerned with the marriage itself, rather than the demographic information. He analyzes the public symbolization of the marriage, family relationships, children, relations with the community, and occupational adjustment.

Herskovits, Melville J. "The American Negro Evolving a New Physical Type." *Current History* 24, no. 6 (September 1926): 898-903.

Using physical measurements, Herskovits compares African Americans in 1920s Washington D.C. with what he calls pure Africans. He concludes that a "New Negro" is evolving both physically and socially because of race mixing with Whites, Blacks, and American Indians. Herskovits says "we shall have to think [of] the American Negro not as an African type in which there has been a small amount of White blood, but a mixture which is still continuing and that will continue long enough finally to achieve the absorption of the Negro into the dominant White population."

————. "A Critical Discussion of the 'Mulatto Hypothesis.'" *Journal of Negro Education* 3, no. 3 (July 1934): 389-402.

Herskovits challenged the ideas brought about by earlier research on the effects of race mixing on certain variables, such as intelligence. He concluded that one's ancestry had more of an effect on the variables than race.

————. "Preliminary Observations in a Study of Negro-White Crossing." *Opportunity: A Journal of Negro Life* 3, no. 25 (January 1925): 69-74.

This article describes the preliminary results of Herskovits' study of Negro-White crossing detailed in his book *The American Negro: A Study in Racial Crossing* (Bloomington: Indiana University Press, 1928). The study, begun in 1923, examined race differences and race crossing by observing physical traits such as skin color and head form, plus the role of environment and heredity.

Hoffman, Frederick L. "Race Amalgamation." In *Race Traits and Tendencies of the American Negro*. New York: Macmillan, 1896.

Hoffman was a German-born statistician who became interested in the vital and social statistics of the "colored" population of the United States. Hoffman felt by being a German he could analyze this data "free of the taint of prejudice or sentimentality." Hoffman concludes that race crossing is detrimental to the progress of the Negro, and has increased the mortality of the Negro.

Jennings, Herbert S. "Race Mixture and Its Consequences." In *The Biological Basis of Human Nature*. New York: Norton, 1930.

Jennings covers the advantages and disadvantages of race mixing. Among the advantages he finds are "increased hybrid vigor" and less defective genes passed on to offspring. Among the disadvantages: "offspring may develop combinations of parts that lack complete harmony." For example, "Large teeth, resulting from the genes of one parent, may be crowded in a small jaw that results from the genes of the other parent."

Johnston, James Hugo. *Miscegenation in the Ante-Bellum South*. Chicago: University of Chicago, 1939.

This book is based on Johnston's master's thesis, *The Social Significance of the Intermixture of Races in the Colonial and National Period*, completed in 1925 at the University of Chicago. This is a study of the causes of interracial mixing during the colonial period, and the resulting legislative policies.

Jones, William H. "Negroes Who Pass for White." In *Recreation and Amusement among Negroes in Washington, D.C.: A Sociological Analysis of the Negro in an Urban Environment*. Washington, D.C.: Howard University Press, 1927.

This chapter deals with the problems of people living in two worlds. Jones cites some advantages of passing to the individual and to the African American group including the lowering of the barriers of cultural exclusion. The main disadvantages are lost race loyalty and race consciousness.

Kephart, William M. "Is the American Negro Becoming Lighter? An Analysis of the Sociological and Biological Trends." *American Sociological Review* 13, no. 4 (August 1948): 437-443.

Kephart addresses the three points of Linton's theory (see next page) to refute Linton's claim that the American Negro is disappearing. He argues that the "Negro problem will not solve itself in 200 years either sociologically or biologically."

Linton, Ralph. "The Vanishing American Negro." *The American Mercury* 64, no. 178 (February 1947): 133-139.

Linton predicts that there will not be a "Negro problem" in the United States by the year 2147 because the Negro will not be recognizable. He sees three reasons for this change: the decline in the overall proportion of Negroes to Whites, the distribution of the Negro over the whole country instead of being concentrated in the South, and the lightening of skin tone of American Negroes.

Merton, Robert K. "Intermarriage and the Social Structure: Fact and Theory." *Psychiatry: Journal of the Biology and the Pathology of Interpersonal Relations* 4, no. 3 (August 1941): 361-374.

Merton points out that to understand intermarriage you must take into consideration the cultural orientations and the system of social stratification in society. The social variables affecting intermarriage are group size, sex ratio, age composition, and degree and kind of intergroup contacts. With special reference to the "caste system" involving Blacks and Whites, he shows how structural and functional elements in American society explain the taboo against racial intermarriage in the United States.

Panunzio, Constantine. "Intermarriage in Los Angeles, 1924-33." *American Journal of Sociology* 47, no. 5 (March 1942): 690-701.

This study examines the intermarriage of the principal ethnic minorities in Los Angeles; namely Mexicans, Filipinos, Chinese, American Indians, and Blacks. The study indicates a higher rate of interracial marriage than other comparable areas. Panunzio concludes that the presence of a high proportion of Mexicans, Filipinos, and American Indians, all of whom are permitted by law to intermarry with Whites, led to the higher interracial marriage rate.

Reuter, Edward B. "The Superiority of the Mulatto." *American Journal of Sociology* 23, no. 1 (July 1917): 83-106.

Reuter believes that the mulatto is superior to the "pure Negro." He uses Ferguson's great man's theory[7] to predict the racial makeup of future populations. Reuter believes that the superiority of the mulatto is borne out by the patterns of marriage selection, in which the most talented (eminent) "pure Negro" men married wives of a lighter color, producing lighter-skinned offspring who were superior to their parents.

Laws and Politics

Croly, David G. *Miscegenation: The Theory of the Blending of the Races, Applied to the American White Man and Negro.* New York: H. Dexter, Hamilton, 1864. Reprint, Unionville, N.Y.: Royal Fireworks Press, 1995.

————. *Miscegenation.* 1863. Reprint, Upper Saddle River, N.J.: Literature House, 1970.

————. *Miscegenation and the Republican Party.* New York, 1864. Alternative title: *Miscegenation Endorsed by the Republican Party.* Reproduction (Microfiche), Sanford, N.C.: Microfilming Corporation of America, 1980.

This series of pamphlets was published during the election of 1864 by David Goodman Croly and George Wakeman of the anti-abolitionist *New York World.* The pamphlets were written from the abolitionist viewpoint in an attempt to scare voters away from presidential incumbent Abraham Lincoln. The pamphlets spurred a heated debate on miscegenation. After the South's defeat at Atlanta, the campaign turned in the Republicans' favor, and Democrats published another pamphlet titled *Miscegenation and the Republican Party*, while Croly and Wakeman, posing as Lincoln supporters, tried to get Lincoln's support for the second pamphlet. Croly used the assumed name David Goodman.

Jenks, Albert Ernest. "The Legal Status of Negro-White Amalgamation in the United States." *American Journal of Sociology* 21, no. 5 (March 1916): 666-678.

In 1916, six of the American states prohibited Negro-White marriage in their state constitutions. Twenty-eight states had statute laws forbidding intermarriage. This article contains some of the state statutes. It also explains the differences between the states in defining what constitutes a "negro." For example, "In Alabama the descendant of a negro is forever a negro; in Florida the descendant of a negro is such for only four generations—provided one ancestor in each generation is a White person."

Woodson, Carter G. "The Beginnings of the Miscegenation of the Whites and Blacks." *Journal of Negro History* 3, no. 4 (October 1918): 335-353.

Woodson gives a history of the beginning of anti-miscegenation laws in the United States.

Zabel, William D. "Interracial Marriage and the Law." *Atlantic Monthly* (October 1965): 75-79.

Zabel discusses the illogic of anti-miscegenation laws of the states and gives background information on the *Loving v. Virginia* Su-

preme Court case. The article calls for the United States Supreme
Court to strike down the state laws.

Social Commentary

Asbury, Herbert. "Who is a Negro?" *Collier's* (August 3, 1945): 12.
This popular article made inflammatory claims about the number
of African Americans permanently passing for White. In addition,
it quotes Noah's curse of Canaan that was used as a divine justifi-
cation for slavery.

Baldwin, Louis Fremont. *From Negro to Caucasian: or, How the
Ethiopian is Changing His Skin; A Concise Presentation of the
Manner in Which Many Negroes in America . . . Have Abandoned
Their Affiliation with Negroes.* San Francisco: Pilot Publishing
Co., 1929.
Baldwin published this work for the Society for the Amalgamation
of the Races. The book advocates race mixing, but only by a select
few, and only with the consent of both parties.

Barron, Milton Leon. *The Blending American: Patterns of Intermarriage.* Chicago: Quadrangle Books, 1972.
In this work, Barron begins by establishing a conceptual and theoretical framework for the study of intermarriage. He then explores
such topics as the boundaries of intermarriage, the boundaries dividing nationalities, races and religions, racial and religious intermarriage, and the consequences of intermarriage.

Black, Algernon D. "An Ethical View of Intermarriage." *The Ethical
Outlook* 48, no. 1 (January/February 1962): 40-45.
Black believes if there is true love, common interests, and equality
of intelligence, if a couple is well adjusted and has not been too
damaged by racial attitudes, and if they have a basic sense of values and unified way of seeing life, then interfaith and interracial
couples can have an excellent life together.

"Color Lines among the Colored People." *Literary Digest* 72, no. 11
(March 18, 1922): 42-44.
In this work, African American society is divided into three parts:
Yellows, Browns, and Blacks, with their social hierarchy and im-
portance to be found in this order. The article discusses why a dark
African American man would marry a mulatto woman.

"Famous Negroes Married to Whites." *Ebony* 5, no. 2 (December
1949): 20-21.
This article is a result of the controversy involving the marriage of
NAACP Secretary Walter White to Poppy Cannon, a White

woman. Leading scholars of the day give their opinions on "why Negro leaders often wed Whites."

Fosdick, Franklin. "Is Intermarriage Wrecking the NAACP?" *Negro Digest* 8 (June 1950): 52-55.

In 1950 Walter White, executive secretary of the NAACP, and Leslie Perry, Washington NAACP administrative assistant, both married White women. These two marriages were used by political enemies of White and Perry as the reason for the declining membership of the organization. In his article, Fosdick points out that there were other reasons for the decline in membership. Fosdick called for stronger leadership and positive programs as a way to increase membership, rather than the ousting of White and Perry.

Hoffman, Frederick L. "The Problem of Negro-White Intermixtures and Intermarriage." In *Eugenics in Race and State* (vol. 2 of The Scientific Papers of the Second International Congress of Eugenics). Baltimore: Williams & Wilkins Co., 1923.

Hoffman claims that intermarriage between Blacks and Whites is usually between mentally and physically superior Black men and White women who are mentally, morally, and physically inferior, and that the offspring are more often Black than White. He also suggests that the women in such couples are usually foreign-born workers who do not know the local prejudice against mixed marriage, or do not consider the ramifications of the offspring. He believes that these women do not constitute a social loss to the White race, and considers such marriages to be antisocial.

Holm, John James. *Holm's Race Assimilation, or Fading Leopard's Spots: A Complete Scientific Exposition of the Most Tremendous Question That Has Ever Confronted Two Races in the World's History.* Naperville, Ill.: J. L. Nichols and Company, 1910.

This work contains editorials from Southern newspapers on the anti-miscegenation movement. It also has flyers from the movement. Holm advocates legal interracial marriage.

Jordan, Winthrop D. "American Chiaroscuro: The Status and Definition of Mulattoes in the British Colonies." *William and Mary Quarterly* 10, no. 2 (April 1962): 183-200.

Jordan used the analogy of a chiaroscuro picture (a picture of an object using different tones of the same color) to discuss the history of interracial people.

Klineberg, Otto. *Characteristics of the American Negro.* New York: Harper & Bros., 1944.

This is the last volume in the *Negro in American Life* series and includes two chapters on interracial issues. Chapter three, "The Hybrid and the Problem of Miscegenation," analyzes statistics on Negro-White marriages in Boston. Chapter five, "The Hybrid" covers miscegenation and intermarriage, passing, physical characteristics of mixed-race people, and legal issues.

Mencke, John G. *Mulattoes and Race Mixture: American Attitudes and Images, 1865-1918.* Ann Arbor, Mich.: UMI Research Press, 1979. Mencke uses a psychosexual theme as the main point of his analysis, claiming that mulattoes represent clear evidence of the White man's inability to restrain his sexual interest in African American women.

"Mixed Couples Charge Ban by Both Races; Form Club," *Amsterdam News*, February 22, 1936 and "Scores Seek to Join Club Formed for Mixed Couples," *Amsterdam News*, March 14, 1936. These articles discuss the formation of a club for interracial couples. The Penguin Club was organized to combat the ostracism faced by interracial couples in New York City. Similar organizations were formed in the Midwest called Manasseh Societies.

Park, Robert E. "Mentality of Racial Hybrids." *American Journal of Sociology* 36, no. 4 (January 1931): 534-551. Park analyzes what he calls the "conflict of color" in mixed-race people. This conflict is caused by the "warring ancestry in his veins." Park states that the mind of the mixed-race person is the melting pot in which the lower and higher cultures meet.

Reuter, Edward Byron. *The Mulatto in the United States: Including a Study of the Role of Mixed-Blood Races throughout the World.* Boston: R. G. Badger, 1918. Reuter worried that the infusion of 10 percent African American blood into the population would reduce the intellectual and cultural levels of the country. He wanted to stop race mixing and to establish separate working conditions.

Shannon, Alexander H. *The Racial Integrity of the American Negro.* Nashville, Tenn.: Lamar and Barton, 1925. Shannon, the former chaplain of the Mississippi State Penitentiary, was concerned about mixing of the races. The objective of the book was to promote removal of African Americans to Africa in order to maintain the integrity of the White race.

Stonequist, Everett V. *The Marginal Man.* New York: Charles Scribner's Sons, 1937. Stonequist deals with racial and cultural hybrids in one of the first works to discuss the concept of marginality. Examples of the racial hybrid are the Eurasians of India, the colored people of South Africa, and the mulattoes of the United States. Examples of cultural hybrids are Europeanized Africans, Jews, and Westernized Asians. Stonequist describes the phases in identity development of mulattoes, from being unaware of any social conflict to attempting to adjust to such conflicts.

Thompson, Henry O. "Interracial Marriage and the Bible." *Negro History Bulletin* 34, no. 5 (May 1971): 103-106.

Many racists use the Bible to justify segregation and anti-miscegenation laws. This article discusses many of the interracial marriages in the Bible. It also covers the curse of Ham and what it means. Finally, it raises the idea of Jesus being a product of inter-marriage.

Notes

1. William Waller Hening, *Statutes at Large: Being a Collection of All the Laws of Virginia*, vol. 1 (Richmond, Va.: S. Pleasants, 1809), 146.

2. McIllwaine, H. R. Minutes of the Council and General Court of Colonial Virginia, 1622-1632, 1670-1676, with Notes and Excerpts from Original Council and General Court Records, into 1683, Now Lost (Richmond, Va.: The Colonial Press, 1924), 476.

3. Hening, *Statutes*, vol. 2, p. 280.

4. Hening, *Statutes*, vol. 2, p. 280.

5. Arthur P. Davis, "The Garies and Their Friends: A Neglected Pioneer Novel," *CLA Journal* 13, no. 1 (1969): 27-34.

6. Brawley, Benjamin Griffith, *The Negro Genius* (New York: Dodd, Mead & Company, 1937), 83.

7. Ferguson, George Oscar, "The Psychology of the Negro: An Experimental Study," *Archives of Psychology*, no. 36. New York: Science Press, 1916, chapter 4.

5   The Politics of Being Interracial

Karen Downing

The concept of race, and therefore *inter-race*, is a social and political one. Anthropologists, biologists, and sociologists have known for decades that there is as much variety within so-called races as between them.[1] Yet we also know that throughout the history of this country, being categorized as a member of a non-White race has very real political and socioeconomic consequences. That history includes the legacy of slavery and the "one-drop rule." This "rule" is a uniquely American idea, the result of the power imbalance that led to abuse and rape of African-descended women by European-descended men, and the perceived need to draw a line between that which was "pure White" and not. Henriques (1974) makes the same argument as it relates to Native American women and European men. He points out that the history of race mixing is often discussed through a lens of "racial pollution," and that nearly all Anglo-Saxon colonial communities had laws against interracial unions. Henriques makes reference to writings from 1710, "Nay in almost every village are to be seen a little race of mulattoes, mischievous as monkeys, and infinitely more dangerous."[2] Johnston (1970) labels the theme of miscegenation a "centrally important aspect of (American) race relations."[3]

It is from this enflamed historical context that interracial politics emerged, in an organized manner, with the birth of the mass multiracial movement in the 1980s and 1990s. This loosely organized movement may be characterized as a set of overlapping local, regional, and national interracial groups that include national spokespersons such as Susan Graham from Project Race, Ramona Douglass and Carlos Ferndandez of the Association of MultiEthnic Americans, and hundreds, if not thousands of local and regional interracial support group members. The movement has been strengthened by the growth of the burgeoning Internet throughout the 1990s. The World Wide Web has allowed for greater ease of communication between disparate groups, and gave voice to leaders such as Charles Bryd of *Interracial Voice* and Matt Kelley at the Mavin Foundation.

In the late 1980s and early 1990s, the first widely available research by interracial authors (or those in interracial families) for interracial people and families began to paint a much more balanced picture of interracial issues. Research and narratives illustrated that interracial people and families suffered from the same racism as other non-White groups. When Maria Root (1992) and Paul Spickard (1989) published their groundbreaking works, many interracial people felt they had a voice for the first time

On the political front, throughout the 1990s, the largest gains by multiracial leaders were seen in the number of states that adopted a multiracial category to use on state forms that requested race data. The culmination of this work was the addition of the option to choose "Two or More Races" on Census 2000. While only 6,826,228 people (2.4 percent of the entire U.S. population)[4] chose to identify with more than one race, the movement to fully identify one's parentage was gaining momentum, and making some people of color particularly wary of the potential threat of diluting their own precarious political power.[5]

By the year 2001, there was a backlash developing against the gains of the multiracial movement by authors such as Spencer (1997) and Texeira (in Winters and DeBose, 2003). They countered that "multiracialists" were reducing numbers, and thus political clout and federal funding dollars, used for civil rights purposes from the existing minority groups, and that multiracialism was creating a new racial hierarchy not unlike that seen in South Africa. Finally, in the morphing of this political landscape, some multiracial leaders worried that the multiracial cause was being co-opted by political conservatives such as Ward Connerly,[6] known for his efforts to abolish affirmative action, and others as proof that racial categories are becoming more and more meaningless, and that race data collection should be abolished altogether.

The literature annotated in this chapter falls into three categories: legislation concerning interracial marriage and racial designations; classification, categorization, and enumeration of interracial people; and the multiracial political movement.

Anti-Miscegenation and "Racial Purity" Laws

There is a surprising amount of literature to be found on the history of state and federal laws and constitutional provisions as they relate to interracial marriage and an individual's racial assignment. Within these areas, literature is concentrated on anti-miscegenation laws in the colonial states, and specific landmark cases such as *Loving v. Virginia*, which made anti-miscegenation laws unconstitutional in 1967, *Plessy v. Ferguson*, in which the "one-drop rule" was used to endorse the idea of "separate but equal," *Naim v. Naim*, where the annulment of an interracial marriage resulted in the deportation of a Chinese husband, and many lesser known but important cases. The resources below present a variety of legal, political, historical, and sociological writings.

Applebaum, Harvey M. "Miscegenation Statutes: A Constitutional and Social Problem." *Georgetown Law Journal* 53, no. 1 (Fall 1964): 49-91. (Also reprinted in Finkelman, 1992.)

At the time Applebaum wrote this article, nineteen states still had anti-miscegenation laws on their books. Applebaum provides a very legalistic discussion of individual states' anti-miscegenation laws with references to specific cases. The article discusses ramifications of "miscegenous marriages" such as loss of marital benefits (spousal workman's compensation, testimony in legal trials, legitimacy of children, etc.) and cites relevant case law where each of these situations was adjudicated. This work is prior to *Loving v. Virginia*, thus the discussion on judicial decisions is comprehensive through the early 1960s. Court cases are discussed in the context of the larger issues they covered such as freedom of religion and due process. The article includes extensive notes.

Avens, Alfred. "Anti-Miscegenation Laws and the Fourteenth Amendment: The Original Intent." *Virginia Law Review* 52, no. 7 (November 1966): 1224-1255. (Also reprinted in Finkelman, 1992.)

The author takes the point of view that the Constitution (specifically the Fourteenth Amendment) should be used to decide anti-miscegenation laws. One year later when the Supreme Court ruled on *Loving v. Virginia* that was the exact defense used to prevent the Lovings from going to jail. Here, the author uses the recently decided case of *McLaughlin v. Florida* (which reversed *Pace v. Alabama*) to launch his discussion of anti-miscegenation laws. The point is made that these laws were among the oldest categories of legislation, and were widespread from the time of the Civil War up to the time this was written. There are many quotes from constitutional framers and legislators throughout the history of the country, as well as extensive notes.

Blockson, Charles L. *Black Genealogy*. Baltimore: Black Classic Press, 1991.

A book written to assist African Americans setting out on genealogical searches, *Black Genealogy* includes an excellent chapter on miscegenation. The book was first published just after *Roots* appeared in 1977, spurring both Blacks and Whites to search out their ancestors. Blockson writes that racial mixing was "as much a part of plantation life as slavery itself." Literature throughout the history of race mixing is cited, with attention given to the Jefferson-

Hemings relationship, and the public reaction to it at the time. Blockson advises Black genealogists: "Sooner or later, your family tree will finally reveal a couple of White members."

Colker, Ruth. *Hybrid: Bisexuals, Multiracials, and Other Misfits under American Law.* New York: New York University Press, 1996.
The chapter "Race" discusses the history of anti-miscegenation laws in the United States from the 1896 *Plessy v. Ferguson* case to the present. Throughout the history of these laws, states were concerned with White people mixing with non-Whites, but not concerned with peoples of color mixing with one another. Other chapters in this work are discussed in other sections of this bibliography.

Davis, F. James. *Who is Black? One Nation's Definition.* University Park, Pa .: Pennsylvania State University Press, 1991.
This work is one of the most frank and descriptive discussions of all the delicate and politicized issues concerning who is considered Black in this country. Issues covered include the "one-drop rule," court cases such as Plessy and Phipps (both about White-appearing racially mixed people petitioning the court to be classified as White), census enumeration of Blacks, miscegenation, and racial identity. When this book first appeared in 1991, many of these issues were still considered taboo and not openly discussed; it is a groundbreaking work.

Davis, Timothy, Kevin R. Johnson, and George A. Martinez. *A Reader on Race, Civil Rights, and American Law: A Multicultural Approach.* Durham, N.C.: Carolina Academic Press, 2001.
Readable for non-lawyers, *A Reader on Race* is a very informative collection of essays on legal cases and federal and state laws concerning race, civil rights, and the restrictions placed on people of color throughout the history of our nation. Several chapters specifically address topics of race mixing, including the "one-drop rule," the census, and racial identity ambiguity. Throughout the book there are discussions of multiracial issues embedded in other larger issues such as social construction of race as it relates to the law.

Finkelman, Paul. *The Era of Integration and Civil Rights, 1930-1990.* New York: Garland Publishing, Inc., 1992.
This series of reprints of classic articles on African Americans and the law includes several relevant articles, some of which are annotated separately here (Applebaum, 1964; Avens, 1966; Wadlington, 1966).

Greenberg, David. "White Weddings: The Incredible Staying Power of the Laws against Interracial Marriage." *Slate* (June 15, 1999), http://slate.msn.com/id/30352/.

This persuasive piece was spurred by the 1999 vote in Alabama to repeal the state anti-miscegenation law thirty-two years after *Loving v. Virginia*. The author succinctly discusses the history of U.S. anti-miscegenation legislation including states that repealed their laws early (pre-Civil War), and Lincoln's detractors using the threat of "mongrelization" of the races against him. Greenberg describes Alabama's use of the law until it was repealed in 1999, and includes statistics on interracial marriage.

Hanley-Lopez, Ian Haney. *White by Law: The Legal Construction of Race*. New York: New York University Press, 1996.

A well-argued book about our society's efforts to make every imagined aspect of race (behavior, appearance, etc.) immutable and "scientifically" supported in order to keep "pure Whites" distinct from other races. The author believes the "multiracial" designation on the census form or any government documents just propagates the idea that race is a physically inherited thing. He argues that we are *all* multiracial, and there is no such thing as a pure race, thus the notion of a separate multiracial category just supports the farce.

Henriques, Fernando. *Children of Conflict: A Study of Interracial Sex and Marriage*. New York: E.F. Dutton & Co., Inc., 1974.

The author, a self-described "Black man who grew up in White world and whose major orientation lies with Europe, but who nevertheless can never escape the heritage of his colour, and who is a part of the process of miscegenation that he has tried to describe," is a cultural anthropologist whose family immigrated to London from the West Indies. He has provided a well researched and easily read history of race-mixing and interracial marriage, and the laws against these phenomena in England and France, Africa, the West Indies, and most thoroughly covered, the United States. It is one of the few books to cover the laws and social mores in the context of other countries and continents.

Higginbotham, A. Leon. *In the Matter of Color: The Colonial Period*. New York: Oxford University Press, 1978.

Higginbotham looks at the American legal process for six of the colonies (Virginia, Massachusetts, New York, South Carolina, Georgia, and Pennsylvania) as it related to races during the colonial period. He discusses interracial relationships in terms of White male domination over Black slave women, pointing out that the legal process was tolerant of those relationships, but included harsh penalties for White female/Black male relationships. The discussion is divided by state, and will surprise those who think the North was much more racially tolerant or enlightened.

Johnston, James Hugo. *Race Relations in Virginia and Miscegenation in the South, 1776-1860.* Amherst: University of Massachusetts Press, 1970.

In this reprint of Johnston's 1937 University of Chicago doctoral dissertation, history professor Winthrop Jordan places the work in historical context, explaining in the foreword that in 1937, it was rare and unpopular to write and publish a dissertation on "Negro" history. The volume examines race relations in the South from the American Revolution to the Civil War. Part III of the book addresses miscegenation, the legal reactions, racial identity imposed on mixed-race individuals, and the social fabric between Whites, Black slaves, and indigenous peoples.

Kennedy, Randall. "Marital Color Line." *The Nation* 271, no. 21 (Dec. 25, 2000): 8.

From the author of *Interracial Intimacies*, this earlier article contains an overview of the history of Alabama's laws and social customs relating to interracial marriage. Prompted by Alabama's vote on November 7, 2000, to strike down the nation's last state-based anti-miscegenation law, Kennedy's essay considers the social significance of such laws. He argues that anti-miscegenation laws were an expression of official opposition specifically to Black/White intimacy, and that these latent feelings remain a potent force in American culture today. He also compares the multiple arguments made against interracial marriages in the latter part of the nineteenth century to the similar arguments made today against same-sex marriages.

Moran, Rachel F. *Interracial Intimacy: The Regulation of Race and Romance.* Chicago: The University of Chicago Press, 2001.

Moran, a law professor, is herself biracial, the daughter of a White-Irish father and a Mexican mother. She very clearly explains the different intents and permutations of anti-miscegenation laws throughout the history of the country. She also provides an examination of the legislation for racial mixing beyond Black/White relationships, an area which is neglected in other works on this topic.

Nash, Gary B. "The Hidden History of Mestizo America." *The Journal of American History* 82, no. 3 (December 1995): 941-964.

Nash, a professor of history at the University of California Los Angeles, writes a meticulously researched history of Anglo-American/Native American race mixing from colonial times to the twentieth century. He populates his study with fascinating characters from our nation's history including John Rolfe and Pocahontas (the "embryo of a mestizo United States"), Patrick Henry, Sam Houston, and many others. White/Native American race mixing occurred throughout the country until the early twentieth century when the "new White orthodoxy" depicted mixed-race people as degenerates and mongrels. The White orthodoxy of which Nash writes included the eugenics movement at the early part of the twentieth century, and the "melting pot" ideal which was limited to Americanizing European immigrants, but did not condone race mixing.

Pascoe, Peggy. "Race, Gender, and the Privileges of Property: On the Significance of Miscegenation Law in the U.S. West." In *Over the Edge: Remapping the American West,* edited by Valerie J. Matsumoto and Blake Allmendinger. Berkeley, Calif.: University of California Press, 1999.

Written from a feminist perspective, the intertwining issues of race and gender are discussed by the author. This piece includes an analysis of anti-miscegenation laws throughout the country, especially the West. Pascoe is interested in anti-miscegenation laws that were formed primarily to criminalize White female/Black male relationships, when the vast majority of interracial sex occurred between White males and African or Native American females. The author reports that anti-miscegenation laws were most elaborate in the Western region of the country, and included the non-White racial groups.

Sickels, Robert J. *Race, Marriage and the Law.* Albuquerque: University of New Mexico Press, 1972.

Sickels' comprehensive book includes historical and sociological analyses of the taboo of interracial relationships before and after the historical *Loving v. Virginia* Supreme Court case that overturned anti-miscegenation laws in 1967. He includes information about public opinion polls from throughout the twentieth century, several of the most influential court cases, and the impact and implications of the Loving decision.

Sollors, Werner. *Interracialism: Black-White Intermarriage in American History, Literature, and Law.* New York: Oxford University Press, 2000.

This excellent collection of essays collected by Sollors, a professor of literature and African American studies at Harvard University, traces the history of interracial marriage from the earliest laws in colonial America to current thinking on the topic. It includes essays from early writers such as Charles Chesnutt, Carter G. Woodson, and W.E.B. DuBois, to contemporary scholars such as

Randall Kennedy and Peggy Pascoe. The book is divided into three
sections; the first covers American law as it has intersected race
and interrace, the second traces interracial themes in literature, and
the third examines interracial relationships and American society.

———. "Appendix B: Prohibitions of Interracial Marriage and Cohabi-
tation." In *Neither Black Nor White Yet Both: Thematic Explorations of Interracial Literature*. Oxford: Oxford University Press,
1997.

This sixteen-page appendix traces the history of miscegenation
laws in this country. The timeline begins with the year 1514, in
which a Spanish law explicitly permitted intermarriage with Indians, and ends with the 1987 deletion of the section of the Mississippi state constitution which bans interracial marriage. Along the
way there are many surprises and reminders of our nation's discomfort with interracial unions.

Spickard, Paul. "Appendix A: Summary of the States' Law on Interracial Marriage." In *Mixed Blood: Intermarriage and Ethnic Identity
in Twentieth-Century America*. Madison, Wis.: University of Wisconsin Press, 1989.

This brief appendix lists the states which never had anti-
miscegenation laws, states which had laws but repealed them by
1900, states which kept laws throughout most of their history,
states forbidding other racial mixtures besides Black/White, states
that specify the degree of Black ancestry that excludes one from
marrying a White person, and a list of penalties for interracial marriage.

Wadlington, Walter. "The Loving Case: Virginia's Anti-Miscegenation
Statute in Historical Perspective." *Virginia Law Review* 52, no. 7
(November 1966): 1189-1223. (Also reprinted in Finkelman,
1992.)

A detailed examination of Virginia's anti-miscegenation laws, including laws pertaining to slaves and indentured servants, who
were often White. Laws pre- and post-American Revolution are
described, including an act in 1787 declaring which persons would
be considered "mulattoes." The author explains how courts and
legislatures used "certificates of racial composition" to trace individual families' genealogy. Unique features of this article include
discussions of penalties for miscegenation and intermarriage, arguments supporting the constitutionality of anti-miscegenation
laws, and relevant case law throughout the state's history. It is the
most easily read of the legal articles, and includes extensive notes.

Wallenstein, Peter. "Law and the Boundaries of Place and Race in Interracial Marriage: Interstate Comity, Racial Identity, and Miscegenation Laws in North Carolina, South Carolina, and Virginia,
1860s-1960s." *Akron Law Review* 32 (1999): 557-576.
Wallenstein, author of *Tell the Courts I Love My Wife*, has
amassed a substantial history of the laws governing interstate legal
courtesies, racial identification, and interracial relationships during
the one hundred-year period from just before the Civil War to the
1960s. Wallenstein uses case materials from the Carolinas and
Virginia to explore whether interracial marriages that were performed in one state were legal in states with miscegenation statutes, how people were racially categorized pertinent to defining interrace, and a critical look at the anti-miscegenation laws
themselves.

———. *Tell the Court I Love My Wife: Race, Marriage, and Law: An
American History.* New York: Palgrave Macmillan, 2002.
This work provides the most recent and most extensive discussion
of the history of anti-miscegenation laws throughout the United
States. A very readable and thorough history, its scope includes
pre-American Revolution laws through the period following *Loving v. Virginia*. It is one of the few sources that discuss the climate
immediately following that landmark case. It includes several appendices, including a list of states with anti-miscegenation laws
and the years they were repealed by state action.

Yancey, George A., and Michael O. Emerson. "An Analysis of Resistance to Racial Exogamy: The 1998 South Carolina Referendum."
Journal of Black Studies 32, no. 1 (September 2001): 132-147.
Sociologists from the 1970s to the present have claimed that support for interracial marriage may serve as a proxy measure for
American race relations in general, and can help assess White acceptance of racial minority groups. Yancey and Emerson have analyzed data from the 1998 South Carolina referendum on removing
the prohibition of interracial marriage from the state constitution.
Though the 1967 *Loving v. Virginia* Supreme Court ruling nullified
state statutes, it is clear from the results of the South Carolina election (in which many voted to keep the anti-miscegenation statute)
that a significant amount of resistance continues to exist toward interracial relationships. The authors examine this data and make
meaning of the election returns within a sociological framework,
examining factors such as socioeconomic status, religious affiliation, and others.

Zabel, William D. "Interracial Marriage and the Law." *Atlantic Monthly* 216, no. 4 (Oct. 1965): 75-79.

Written on the eve of the *Loving v. Virginia* argument, Zabel, a practicing lawyer at the time, gives an excellent overview of the status of anti-miscegenation laws as of 1965, and provides a short history of laws pertaining to interracial marriage. He argues that the U.S. anti-miscegenation laws are an outgrowth of slavery in this country, as there was no precedent in British common law or its statutes. He also discusses the definition of who is Black under these laws, along with the penalties for disobeying the laws.

Zack, Naomi. *Race and Mixed Race*. Philadelphia: Temple University Press, 1993.

The chapter entitled "Introduction to the History of Mixed Race" covers the nonscientific nature of defining people by race, how definitions were used to propagate slavery in colonial America, and how those distinctions have influenced the culture today. The chapter entitled "The Law on Black and White" discusses anti-miscegenation laws from the 1600s to *Loving v. Virginia*. In the chapter on "Genocidal Images of Mixed Race," the author outlines many of the reasons that have been used against miscegenation throughout the history of the country including "scientific," religious, and cultural arguments.

Zackodnik, Teresa. "Fixing the Color Line: The Mulatto, Southern Courts, and Racial Identity." *American Quarterly* 53, no. 3 (2001): 420-451.

This extensively researched article examines laws and statutes relating to mulattoes, Whites, and Blacks. The author's main purpose is "to extend our understanding of race and its attendant distinctions between Whiteness and Blackness" by discussing mulattoes in relation to the legal regulation of interracial relationships and as the personal property of Whites. She also addresses the concept of Whiteness as it relates to privilege rather than as a biological concept. This is a very interesting discussion of mulattoes as the "racial borderland" that delineated Blacks from Whites, and why they have been viewed as a threat to White racial privilege.

Classification and Categorization of Interracial People

In the United States, the way in which interracial people have been classified and categorized has been highly politicized since the first census in 1790. Classification, a public and societal function, is often at odds with individual and group identities. The resources here reflect the tension between the public purposes and motivations for categorizing individuals, and the personal wishes of multiracial individuals to categorize themselves in a variety of ways.

Becker, Stanli K. "Mixed Origins." In *All Blood is Red . . . All Shadows are Dark!,* edited by John T. Becker and Stanli K. Becker. Cleveland, Ohio: Seven Shadows Press, 1984.
    "Mixed Origins," written by Stanli Becker, a community college youth educator and a member of an interracial family, discusses the classification of people in America with a lens on the public school system and the rigid categories used in collecting racial statistics (in 1984). She writes about the dilemma that mixed-race students and families face when filling out these forms.

Boyd Krebs, Nina. *Edgewalkers: Defusing Cultural Boundaries on the New Global Frontier.* Far Hills, N.J.: New Horizon Press, 1999.
    Boyd provides a very interesting analysis of those individuals who move between groups of people with ease and comfort. The author's purpose in writing this book is to look at the common traits that allow some people to make these transitions more easily than others. Although many of the individuals interviewed are multiracial, many are not, and there is much to learn from their stories about valuing difference.

Dalmage, Heather M. *Tripping on the Color Line: Black-White Families in a Racially Divided World.* New Brunswick, N.J.: Rutgers University Press, 2000.
    Dalmage, a sociologist, writes about the political and social issues interracial families and multiracial individuals face in our racially polarized society. The chapter "Thinking about the Color Line" gives a nice sociological history of the exclusivity of the "color line" in the United States, along with the common arguments made to force interracial people to choose one race (usually the side of color). She also discusses the media's concentration on Black/White mixing, though this pattern occurs far less often than other racial mixtures. In the chapter "Communities, Politics, and

Racial Thinking" she discusses how formal and informal communities of interracial people have come together. There is a solid overview of several major regional and national groups, a wonderful discussion of categorization of racial groups used in the U.S. census, and an examination of the politics of racial identification (both personal and governmental identification).

Daniel, Reginald G. *More Than Black? Multiracial Identity and the New Racial Order.* Philadelphia: Temple University Press, 2002.

Daniels, a multiracial sociologist at University of California Santa Barbara, has written a unique and thought-provoking contextual analysis of multiracial identity and racial classification throughout the history of the United States. The book is divided into four parts: "White over Black" discusses the historical context for racial separation and hierarchy between Whites/Europeans and others; "Black No More," discusses passing for White, skin color hierarchy within Black communities, triracial isolates, and other topics relating to movement away from Black identification; "More Than Black" discusses multiracial identity as being inclusive of existing racial categories and separate from them; and "Black No More or More Than Black?" covers the continuing significance of color, the current state of the "one-drop rule," and postmodern ideas of racial inclusiveness.

Forbes, Jack D. "The Manipulation of Race, Caste and Identity: Classifying Afroamericans, Native Americans and Red-Black People." *Journal of Ethnic Studies* 17, no. 4 (Winter 1990): 1-51.

This densely argued analysis covers the history of race mixing between African Americans, Native Americans, and European Americans. An anthropologist, Forbes looks at African mixing throughout the Americas and the Caribbean. His use of terminology is quite different from other researchers. He uses the term "caste" or "racial caste" to denote social standing, and he uses the term "American" to denote Native Americans which can be confusing. However, he has made a substantive contribution to the understanding of African race mixing with Native American and European American groups, early race-mixing terminology used by the Europeans in the Americas and Europe, and the ways in which African Americans racially identify themselves in the face of a mono-racially oriented society.

Hickman, Christine B. "The Devil and the One Drop Rule: Racial Categories, African Americans, and the U.S. Census." 95 *Michigan Law Review* (1997): 1161-1265. Reprint, A *Reader on Race, Civil Rights, and American Law: A Multiracial Approach*, edited by Timothy Davis, Kevin R. Johnson, and George A. Martinez. Durham, N.C.: Carolina Academic Press, 2001.

Hickman, a multiracial professor of law at California Western School of Law, gives a substantial and complex analysis of multiracial identity and classification. Hickman has drawn from an incredible range of sources including slave narratives, *Ebony* magazine, Harlem Renaissance literature, and others, to rethink the "one-drop rule" and its implications for the Census 2000. The article contains two parts; part one discusses the origins of the American racial classification system, and part two critiques the movement to allow individuals to chose multiracial or more than one race on the census. The article includes extensive notes with statistical and historical data.

Holmes, Steven A. "The Confusion Over Who We Are." *New York Times,* June 3, 2000.

Holmes, a frequent contributor on issues of race and classification, reports on the conflict between the politics of racial counting and the desire of interracial parents to fully describe their children on census and other forms. He reports on the Clinton administration's decision to count those who identified themselves as multiracial as members of the minority group. Holmes describes the political lobbying on the part of civil rights organizations to insure their numbers do not decrease due to the collection of multiracial data.

Jacobson, Matthew Frye. *Whiteness of a Different Color: European Immigrants and the Alchemy of Race*. Cambridge, Mass.: Harvard University Press, 1998.

This is a wonderful examination of racial inclusiveness and exclusiveness throughout the history of America. The work includes chapters on the fluidity of racial concepts and definitions, discussion of laws, political history, and social mores.

Liu, Eric. "Blood Simple: The Politics of Miscegenation." *Slate* 1996. http://slate.msn.com /id/2398/ [August 22, 1996].

In this editorial piece, Liu describes the political reaction to the proposal for including a multiracial category on the Census 2000 form. He gives context to the political maneuvering by considering past arguments in favor of race mixing (to dissolve race problems) and current statistics on interracial marriage by African Americans, Asian Americans, and Latinos. Liu cautions that multiracial line blurring may not be the answer to America's race problem because "racialism is highly adaptive," and he fears a South African-like system might evolve. Ultimately, Liu believes, in order to rid ourselves of color-consciousness in this country, intermarriage alone is not the answer.

Makalani, Minkah. "A Biracial Identity or a New Race? The Historical Limitations and Political Implications of a Biracial Identity." *Souls* 3, no. 4 (Fall 2001): 73-102.

Makalani analyzes the social science scholarship relating to biracial identity politics, and argues that biracial identification has a negative political impact on African Americans. He criticizes recent scholarship (of the previous fifteen years) for focusing on personal experiences rather than looking more broadly at the societal impact of race and racism as it relates interracial issues.

Morganthau, Tom. "What Color is Black?" *Newsweek* 125, no. 7 (February 13, 1995).

This thoughtful article introduces a special issue of *Newsweek* on race and interrace in the United States. It examines the meaning and implications of race and mixed-race in the United States, and how the politics of identity often pit public and personal identity against one another. Morganthau begins by describing race as an idea, and highlights the American "racialist" way of thinking in the face of immigration, the Bell Curve, race and ethnic census statistics, and the growing "diversity" movement. He writes that growing multiracialism is challenging America's traditional binary race experience, and that Americans are demanding a more flexible view of race and ethnicity. A *Newsweek* poll is included, giving statistics on the public's support for adding a multiracial category to the census.

Mosley, Albert. "Are Racial Categories Racist?" *Research in African Literatures* 28, no. 4 (Winter 1997): 101-111.

Mosley's thought-provoking essay analyzes the debate on whether or not to abolish racial categories. He reviews three recent appeals by Yehudi Webster, Naomi Zack, and Anthony Appiah for abandoning the use of racial categories. They argue that categories have become harmful, actually working against the reasons they were created in the first place, and that they propagate racial exclusion. Mosley examines each writer's arguments, and points out his perceptions of their flaws including his belief that they are "anti-realist." He argues that if we remove the categories, the ramifications of historical difference remain in our society. Blindness to group differences, he believes, is "pernicious" and encourages the status quo.

Pieterse, Jan. "Hybridity, So What? The Anti-Hybridity Backlash and the Riddles of Recognition." *Theory, Culture, and Society* 18, no. 2/3 (April 2001): 219-245.

Pieterse's essay examines "those who straddle or are between and/or combine identities." He describes public recognition of hybridity as a recent phenomenon, and discusses it as it relates to ideas of purity, new and existing notions of hybridity, and delineates the knowledge domains in which hybridity has played a role including science, social science, art, and business. A major portion of the essay includes Pieterse's responses to some of the "anti-hybridity" arguments commonly heard among social scientists.

"Redefining Race in America." *Newsweek* (Special Report) 136, no. 12 (September 18, 2000).

Newsweek revisits its 1995 special issue on race (see Morganthau above) with this excellent follow-up. This issue is devoted to the issues of America's increasingly complicated racial composition. Spurred by Census 2000, the articles in this issue deal with questions of race and interrace. The article entitled "What's White, Anyway?" by Ellis Cose discusses how the boundaries of Whiteness are expanding, and the special privileges of being White are slowly eroding.

Rodriguez, Clara E. *Changing Race: Latinos, the Census, and the History of Ethnicity in the United States.* New York: New York University Press, 2000.

This outstanding contribution to the literature on the history of Latino classification in America also covers arguments relating to all the "social races." Rodriguez begins with the idea of race and its fluidity, describes the U.S. race structure over time, and places Latinos within that structure. Issues relating to the U.S. Census are given special consideration, including the "other" option and Census 2000 changes.

Spickard, Paul R. "The Illogic of American Racial Categories." In *Racially Mixed People in America*, edited by Maria P.P. Root. Newbury Park, Calif.: Sage Publications, 1992.

Spickard, author of *Mixed Blood*, analyzes the history of racial categorization in the United States over the last one hundred years. He asks, and attempts to answer, "What is race? And if we can figure that out, what is a person of mixed race?" He splits his analysis into two areas: race as a biological category and race as a social category.

Warren, Jonathan W., and France Winddance Twine. "White Ameri-
    cans, the New Minority? Non-Blacks and the Ever-Expanding
    Boundaries of Whiteness." *Journal of Black Studies* 28, no. 2 (No-
    vember 1997): 200-218.
    In this examination of U.S. immigration policy, the authors reveal
    how the "White" racial category has expanded over time to include
    new groups that were previously excluded. Many past analyses of
    racial categorization have excluded this phenomenon. The authors
    use the Irish, Italians, and Eastern Europeans as prime examples of
    how the notion of who is "White" has expanded through American
    history.
"What is Race, Anyway?" *Scholastic Update* 127, no. 6 (November 18,
    1994).
    This is a short article on the blurring of race and phenotypes. It
    briefly outlines "dusty old" race theories based on appearance and
    discusses the purpose of government collected race data.

Census Taking and Enumeration of Interracial People

The history and motivations for racially enumerating individuals in the United States is intertwined with institutional racism and politics. Political agendas are reflected in many of the policies used when gathering statistics by race. Sollors (1999) lists the "fractional counting (of slaves) and non-counting (of Indians), counting to see racial peril (of the Chinese), and the use of counts for deportation purposes (of Japanese Americans)" as a few examples of the ways in which counting people by race have been used against them.Writing about the use of race in census-taking, Perlmann and Waters state, "The combination of state power, census, and race has wreaked too much havoc and has produced too many Kafkaesque absurdities to be too naively or carelessly adopted, even for well-intentioned policies." (Perlmann and Waters, 2002, p. 264.) Of particular note are the more recent debates that took place in the media, in Congress, and in the pages of journals and magazines regarding the Census 2000 option of allowing individuals to choose two or more races. The following resources shed light on the political nature of racial enumeration.

Baron, Dennis. "How to Be a Person, Not a Number, on the U.S. Cen-
    sus." *Chronicle of Higher Education* 44, no. 30 (April 3, 1998).
    In one of a plethora of articles anticipating the changes in the way
    the 2000 Census would allow individuals to identify their race,
    Baron, a Bengali/Jewish American, lends a nice historical over-

view of how the Census Bureau came to their 2000 decision. He describes the political maneuvering that occurred on the part of many interested parties. As a multiracial person who was happy with the "other" category, Baron resists the idea of specifying every detail of his racial make-up, preferring to "remain imprecise in the eyes of the government," in order to "remain a person instead of a number." Personal viewpoint aside, he has done a good job of summarizing the arguments used against the previously considered "multiracial" category in favor of the "check all that apply" choice.

Colker, Ruth. *Hybrid: Bisexuals, Multiracials, and Other Misfits under American Law.* New York: New York University Press, 1996.
The chapter "Invisible Hybrids under the U.S. Census" argues that the government should not give up categories all together, rather, that the categories should not be mutually exclusive (or "bipolar," as she designates them). There is a discussion about Directive 15, the government attempt to categorize people by five racial categories in 1977. (See Appendix IV for the full text of Directive 15.)

Davis, F. James. "Census Enumeration of Blacks." In *Who is Black? One Nation's Definition.* University Park, Pa.: Pennsylvania State University Press, 1991.
Davis describes how the Census Bureau "counts what the nation wants counted," and points out that Blacks are the only ethnic group in the United States that has been counted or defined by a "one-drop" standard. He describes the ways in which Blacks have been counted over the course of data gathering, and how self-definition in the 1960s did not change the numbers of Blacks identifying themselves, evidence they were self-subscribing to the one-drop rule.

Etzioni, Amitai. "Surveys and Their Findings, New Issues: Rethinking Race." *The Public Perspective* 8, no. 4 (June/July 1997): 39-48.
This is a solid review of the political and social arguments for and against a new multiracial category on the Census 2000 form. Etzioni includes the results of several national polls conducted by the National Opinion Research Center and the Princeton Survey Research Associates that ask the American public about their thoughts on collecting racial data on the census and whether a multiracial category should be included.

Gillespie, Nick. "Blurred Vision." *Reason* 29, no. 3 (July 1997): 7-8.
In this short history of racial enumeration and categorization, Gillespie contends that additional racial designations will not help the country in any significant way. Evidence is considered from eighteenth-century writings, to the nineteenth-century "one-drop rule,"

to the Census Bureau's recognition that their racial categories "have come under growing criticism from those who believe that the minimum set of categories no longer reflects the increasing racial and ethnic diversity of the Nation's population."

Holmes, Steven A. "New Policy on Census Says Those Listed as White and Minority Will Be Counted as Minority." *New York Times*, March 11, 2000.

Holmes reports how the Office of Management and Budget intends to use the "two or more races" data from the Census 2000. Responding to minority groups' concerns about losing minority numbers, the Clinton administration plans to amalgamate those who identify themselves as White and non-White as being solely non-White. The policy decision was based on the consideration that those who "suffered discrimination in the past should be subject to certain protections."

————. "The Politics of Race and the Census." *The New York Times*, March 19, 2000.

This follow-up article by Holmes gives some background and perspective on how the "check all that apply" option on Census 2000 will work. He reports on the resulting sixty-three racial categories, and how politics, not biology have always played an important role in how we classify people. Holmes discusses the confusion and concern these changes may cause to sociologists, civil rights advocates, and government statisticians.

House Committee on Government Reform. *Federal Measures of Race and Ethnicity and the Implications for the 2000 Census.* Washington, D.C.: Congressional Information Service, Inc., April 23, May 22, July 25, 1997.

This is a massive compilation of testimony, letters, and statements submitted for the record from individuals and groups across the country giving their opinions on whether or not the Census Bureau should change Directive 15, the federal categories for race and ethnicity, and the implications for the Census 2000 data collection. Of special note are testimonies from Ramona Douglass and Carlos Fernandez (both of the Association of MultiEthnic Americans), and statements from Nathan Douglas and Susan Graham, all in favor of changes, while U.S. Representative Maxine Waters and Senator Daniel K. Akaka express concerns. This work is indispensable for those wishing to understand the political positions and arguments taken by groups from every minority community.

Jones, Nicholas, and Amy Symens Smith. *Two or More Races Population: 2000.* Washington D.C.: U.S. Census Bureau, November 2001.

In an excellent special report issued by the Census Bureau on the results of Census 2000, the authors give an overview of the statistics generated by the new "two or more races" categories. The report gives overall numbers for the country and breakdowns for the places with the largest concentrations of individuals claiming two or more races. Includes several charts and tables.

Lee, Sharon. "Racial Classifications in the U.S. Census: 1890-1990." *Ethnic and Racial Studies* 16, no. 1 (January 1993): 75-94.

Lee uses the changing racial categories in the history of the census as a launching point to discuss the importance of racial relations in the United States. She argues that census categories "represent political, legal, and professional authority to the public," which, in turn, influence how we all perceive race. This is a very important primer on the history of racial classification within the U.S. census.

Morning, Ann. "New Faces, Old Faces: Counting the Multiracial Population Past and Present." In *New Faces in a Changing America: Multiracial Identity in the 21st Century*, edited by Loretta I. Winters and Herman L. DeBose. Thousand Oaks, Calif.: Sage Publications, 2003.

Though the term "mixed-race" is recent, Morning points out that mixed-race people have been a part of America since the first European settlers arrived. By obscuring the historic dimensions of American race mixing, it is easy to ignore the lessons of our racial past. By examining the history of census enumeration and scientific estimation of race mixing, we can glean the political thought and sociological conceptions of race and interrace throughout the history of the country. Morning reviews the collection of mixed race data from the earliest census in 1790 through the most recent census in 2000.

Nobles, Melissa. "History Counts: A Comparative Analysis of Racial/ Color Categorization in U.S. and Brazilian Censuses." *American Journal of Public Health* 90, no. 11 (November 2000): 1738-1745.

In this substantial article comparing census racial categories in America and Brazil, Nobles analyzes how race categories have changed over time due to shifting ideas about race, and the "enduring power of those ideas as organizers of political, economic, and social life in both countries." She looks critically at racial categories in the U.S. census in thirty- to seventy-year groupings, analyzing why it was necessary, at any given time, to count race. The Brazilian census is also discussed and compared to the U.S. census. Nobles concludes that the choice of racial categories on both censuses tell us much about the relationship between racial ideas, enumeration, and public policy. They also illustrate that the categories do not "merely capture demographic realities, but rather reflect and help to create political realities and ways of thinking and seeing."

O'Hare, William. "Managing Multiple-Race Data." *American Demographics* 20, no. 4 (April 1998): 42-44.

O'Hare discusses the change in racial data collection for Census 2000 and its implications for change on the private sector, which relies heavily on government statistics for defining and analyzing markets. He outlines how the new categories offer greater detail (a possibility of 128 combined categories as opposed to the previous five), but points out that having more possibilities makes the work of analysis more complicated. He predicts that companies that generate their own population estimates and projections will likely adopt the official classification system.

Peirce, Neal R. "The 'Scientific Nonsense' of the Census." *National Journal* 27, no. 51-52 (December 23, 1995): 3163.

In this conservative editorial piece, Peirce argues that the racial and ethnic categories used in the U.S. Census are "whimsical, changeable, and unscientific." The problem, he contends, is that the categories are not able to capture "the true story of what we are," including immigrants from around the world and increasing numbers of multiracial individuals. Peirce believes that instead of enumerating race, which is unscientific in nature, the government should be collecting demographic data on the poverty level instead, since it is a greater predictor of failure.

Perlmann, Joel, and Mary Waters. *The New Race Question: How the Census Counts Multiracial Individuals.* New York: Russell Sage Foundation, 2002.

This outstanding series of essays on how, why, and if we should count multiracial people in the census includes contributions by noted scholars on this topic. Chapters cover topics such as what we learn from counting multiracials, the implications of race counting policies, and the politics of race numbers. Each chapter includes notes and references.

Sandor, Gabrielle. "The 'Other' Americans." *American Demographics* 16, no. 6 (June 1994): 36-42.

Sandor discusses the ambiguity of current definitions of race and ethnicity as they relate to the census and other demographic collection tools. While the Census Bureau views race and ethnicity as two separate concepts, most people who fill out the forms find the two inseparable. She describes the conflict between demand for detailed data and demand for quality and consistency of race data. She argues that social and demographic characteristics of America's youth and their attitudes toward race and interrace have important implications for demographers.

Schmitt, Eric. "Blacks Split on Disclosing Multiracial Roots." *The New York Times*, March 31, 2001.

Schmitt tells the stories of several African Americans who have come to various decisions on whether or not to disclose their multiracial ancestry on the census. These individuals, for various political or cultural reasons, have chosen different paths when marking their census forms. They have taken into account how they are perceived and treated by society, how they think the multiracial information will be used, and their own sense of racial identity.

————. "Broader Palette Allows for Subtler Census Portrait." *The New York Times*, March 12, 2001.

This collection of stories illustrates the incredible complexity of racial identities and highlights the complex relationship between race, ethnicity, and interrace. Issues such as identification of White and non-White Hispanics and Arabs, and issues related to religion and ethnicity are all revealed through the interviews of many multiracial Americans.

Skerry, Peter. "Many American Dilemmas: The Statistical Politics of Counting by Race and Ethnicity." *The Brookings Review* 14, no. 3 (Summer 1996): 36-39.

Skerry analyzes the concern on the part of many Americans that our "increasingly diverse society is fragmenting along group lines and identities," and the results of a federal government survey that sheds light on this concern. He places this in the context of the government's history of collecting race data since Directive 15 in 1978 (which splits people into five separate racial categories—see Appendix IV for the full text of Directive 15), and discusses the idea of racial and ethnic self-identification.

Spencer, Rainier. "Census 2000: Assessments in Significance." In *New Faces in a Changing America: Multiracial Identity in the 21st Century*, edited by Loretta I. Winters and Herman L. DeBose. Thousand Oaks, Calif.: Sage Publications, 2003.

Spencer analyzes the "four main stakeholders" in relation to the U.S. census: the "federal government, multiracial activists, Afro-American organizations, and the American political right" and discusses the winners and losers in the political haggling over Census 2000's racial data options.

Stanfield, Rochelle L. "Multiple Choice." *National Journal* 29, no. 47 (November 22, 1997): 2352-2355.

Stanfield predicts how the option to choose more than one racial category may affect redistricting, civil rights laws, and eligibility for government programs. She believes it will produce very few changes at first; estimates of how many respondents will choose the option range from 1 to 7 percent. However, the real change will be seen over time as interracial marriage is increasing dramatically. She also discusses how the statistics may be used and manipulated, depending on political intentions.

Winkel, George. "How Many Multiracials?" *The Multiracial Activist.* (April/May 2001).

http://www.multiracial.com/readers/winkel2.html.

This editorial takes the opinion that multiracial people are being "split and minimized" by a federal government that is interested in holding onto the "one race-five option" paradigm. The historical "one-drop rule," the persistence of separating Hispanics into an ethnic category rather than a racial one, and other decisions are discussed in relation to the government's insistence on linking multiracial individuals to one race or another. Links to related resources and several tables are included.

Wright, Lawrence. "One Drop of Blood." *The New Yorker,* July 25, 1994.

In this substantial history of the census, Directive 15, the "one-drop rule," and racial categorization by the federal government, Wright very clearly discusses exactly what is at stake, politically, when changing the census racial categories, such as entitlement programs, legislative districts, and political clout. The author also interviews many influential individuals both for and against including a "multiracial" category on the census.

Multiracial Groups and Movements

Though there is not a lot written on the multiracial movement as a political force, the following books and chapters give a variety of opinions on the impact, motivations, and possible outcomes of the multiracial movement in the United States. From Spencer's ominous warnings that the "new racial movement" is "silently shifting the earth beneath (our) feet" to Brown and Douglass' suggestions for increasing the effectiveness of multiracial organizations, this literature runs the gamut of opinion on the politics of interrace.

Brown, Nancy G., and Ramona E. Douglass. "Evolution of Multiracial Organizations: Where We Have Been and Where We Are Going." In *New Faces in a Changing America: Multiracial Identity in the 21st Century*, edited by Loretta I. Winters and Herman L. DeBose. Thousand Oaks, Calif.: Sage Publications, 2003.

Brown, an interracially married psychotherapist, and Douglass, a long-time civil rights activist and former president of the Association of MultiEthnic Americans, give the recent history of the multiracial movement, highlighting the most influential national and regional groups. They outline what is needed to keep multiracial organizations viable for the future.

Douglass, Ramona E. "The Evolution of the Multiracial Movement." In *Multiracial Child Resource Book*, edited by Maria P.P. Root and Matt Kelley. Seattle: Mavin Foundation, 2003.

Douglass, the former president of the Association of MultiEthnic Americans (AMEA), writes a historical overview of the multiracial movement, including the history of AMEA and other influential groups across the United States. She addresses the multiracial movement's accomplishments and challenges, as well as the future of the multiracial community.

Spencer, Jon Michael. *The New Colored People: The Mixed Race Movement in America.* New York: New York University Press, 1997.

Spencer, director of the African American Studies program and professor of religion at the University of South Carolina, takes a decided stand against the rise of the multiracial movement in the United States. He compares it to the system of racial classification in South Africa, and refers to people in the movement as "multiracialists." His emphasis is on mixed-race Blacks, and he presents arguments for and against categorizing multiracial individuals in this country.

Winters, Loretta I. "Epilogue: The Multiracial Movement: Harmony and Discord." In *New Faces in a Changing America: Multiracial Identity in the 21st Century*, edited by Loretta I. Winters and Herman L. DeBose. Thousand Oaks, Calif.: Sage Publications, 2003.

Winters, associate professor of sociology at California State University, Northridge, divides the multiracial movement into three related but distinct models: the multiracial movement (MM) model, the counter multiracial movement (CMM) model, and the ethnic movement (EM) model. According to Winters, the MM focuses on the individual and their racial identification, CMM focuses on society's construction of race and minority group identity, and EM focuses on ethnicity rather than race. Winters compares and contrasts these models, while placing them in the current sociopolitical landscape, and illustrating each movement with examples of literature supporting each.

Notes

1. Brace (1971), Graves (2001), and many others have looked at biological markers and social behaviors within groups and between groups. They determined that there is as much variation within groups as between them, making distinctive race groups a concept in mind only as opposed to biological reality.

2. Henriques, Fernando, *Children of Conflict: A Study of Interracial Sex and Marriage* (New York: E.F. Dutton & Co., Inc., 1974), 134.

3. Johnston, James Hugo, *Race Relations in Virginia and Miscegenation in the South, 1776-1860* (Amherst: University of Massachusetts Press, 1970), vi.

4. Highlights from the Census 2000 Demographic Profiles. Retrieved on April 19, 2004, from http://factfinder.census.gov/.

5. Testimony given by various individuals and groups opposing the option to allow interracial people to choose more than one race is documented in House Committee on Government Reform. *Federal Measures of Race and Ethnicity and the Implications for the 2000 Census.* Washington, D.C.: Congressional Information Service, Inc., April 23, May 22, July 25, 1997.

6. Connerly, the University of California regent who supported Proposition 209 (which took away the state's ability to use race as a consideration for public hiring, contracting, and university admissions), uses the growing multiracial population as proof of his point that collecting race data should be abolished.

6   Interracial Dating and Marriage

Alysse Jordan

With few notable exceptions, critical explorations of interracial romantic relationships have emerged predominantly from the social and behavioral sciences. From the social structuralist theories of sociologists such as Robert K. Merton to examinations of identity and interpersonal development by psychologists like Maria P.P. Root, the contributions of social science researchers to the body of literature has far surpassed that of other fields. This chapter is therefore intended to provide a review of the literature on the legal and social history of intermarriage in the United States by focusing on research in the areas of cultural anthropology, law and policy, psychology, sociology, and social work. Research that involves couples outside the United States has been excluded, as have biographical, fictional, and sensationalized accounts of interracial relationships.

The literature dealing with the topic of interracial dating and marriage can be divided into a few basic themes: incidence of and legislation surrounding interracial relationships; causal factors and implications of interracial relationships (e.g., social and psychological effects on children; the perceived role of romantic interracial relationships on the Black family and on the dating and marriage prospects of Black women); public opinion of interracial dating and marriage; and the need for a better understanding of the nature of interracial couples among mental health practitioners, clinicians, and society at large. Analysis of selected literature is divided into these four general categories.

Theories of Interracial Dating and Marriage

Perhaps because interracial relationships have confounded researchers and the general public throughout history, the largest body of literature on interracial dating and marriage in the United States is that which deals with the causal factors influencing individuals to become romantically involved with someone of another race. Drawing upon already existing theories from social psychology and social structuralism, this area of research explores the rationale and implications behind endogamy (marriage between members of the same race, ethnicity, and/or class) and exogamy (marriage between members of different races, ethnicities, or classes), and either confirms or refutes outdated (and arguably, sexist and racist) theories of hypergamy (intermarriage into a higher social class) and hypogamy (intermarriage into a lower social class).

Aldridge, Delores P. "Interracial Marriages: Empirical and Theoretical Considerations." *Journal of Black Studies* 8, no. 3 (March 1978): 355-368.
  Aldridge provides an overview of the literature on interracial romantic relationships prior to the 1980s, citing research on causal factors and individual characteristics. She suggests that while the research has concentrated on these areas, more research is needed on the impact of interracial marriage upon Black racial identity and a collective sense of Black consciousness.

Baber, Ray. "A Study of 325 Mixed Marriages." *American Sociological Review* 2 (October 1937): 705-716.
  Though he addresses interfaith and interethnic marriages as well, Baber's study is a must-read for any scholar of interracial marriage. Using terms considered racist or otherwise offensive by today's standards (e.g., "yellow" describing Asian Americans, "Jewess" describing American Jewish women), this article provides contemporary research with an insight into public opinion and prevailing intellectual thought regarding interracial unions in the first half of twentieth-century America. Most likely representing the author's own preconceived notions about intermarried couples, the study found that on average, the happiness rating measurements for such couples was low and inferred that many couples did not feel that they should have children. The author further finds that the children of interracial marriages are "particularly handicapped, for they literally have no race, frequently being rejected by both the races from which they come." For Baber, the question of what would motivate a couple to choose to enter into a relationship so reviled by society is an important one, which he answers by citing case studies of couples who exemplify myths of Black sexual superiority held by the White partner, the perception of the prestige of "marrying up" for the Black partner married to a White spouse, and the myth of Asian Americans as being ideal marriage partners because they are more passive or subservient, when discussing Asian-White unions.

Blau, Peter M., Carolyn Beeker, and Kevin M. Fitzpatrick. "Intersecting Social Affiliations and Intermarriage." *Social Forces* 62, no. 3 (Fall 1984): 585-606.
The authors, interested in the motivations of interracially married persons, seek to explain whether mate selection has more to do with racial preferences or opportunity structures (defined by exposure to and interactions with persons of different races, most often facilitated through residentially or occupationally integrated environments). Their findings show that social affiliations are the single most determining factor in influencing an individual's chances for and desirability of intermarriage.

Cerroni-Long, E. Liza. "Marrying Out: Socio-Cultural and Psychological Implications of Intermarriage." *Journal of Comparative Family Studies* 16, no. 1 (Spring 1985): 25-46.
The author explores factors that influence individuals to outmarry, considering the assumed parameters of social expectations from the presumed and stereotypical to the normalized, and discusses challenges interracial couples face. Implications for maintaining individual identity are discussed.

Crowder, Kyle D., and Stewart E. Tolnay. "A New Marriage Squeeze for Black Women: The Role of Racial Intermarriage by Black Men." *Journal of Marriage and the Family* 62 (August 2000): 792-807.
This article addresses one of the current controversies in interracial marriage: the impact of interracial marriage on the marriage opportunity structure for Black women. Research has shown that Black men of high educational attainment and socioeconomic backgrounds are more likely to marry interracially than Black women of similar backgrounds, having a negative impact on the pool of eligible, heterosexual, and economically attractive marriage partners for Black women. Crowder and Tolnay show a strong correlation between the increasing levels of intermarried Black men and the decreasing rate of marriage among Black women, who are less likely to seek romantic relationships with men of other races.

Davidson, Jeanette R. "Theories about Black-White Interracial Marriage: A Clinical Perspective." *Journal of Multicultural Counseling and Development* 20, no. 4 (October 1992): 150-157.
Davidson discusses theories of what motivates individuals to marry outside their race. Several controversial theories abound, causing many in the mental health profession to assume that interracially married individuals have ulterior motives for their romantic involvement with someone of another race, including the desire to rebel against their families or to "marry up" by marrying a member

of a more prestigious racial/ethnic group or class. Davidson points out the need for practitioners to recognize their own biases when treating interracial couples, and provides suggestions for treating clients who are interracially married.

Fang, Carolyn Y., Jim Sidanius, and Felicia Pratto. "Romance Across the Social Status Continuum: Interracial Marriage and the Ideological Asymmetry Effect." *Journal of Cross-Cultural Psychology* 29, no. 2 (March 1998): 290-305.

This study shows a correlation between social dominance orientation (associated with racial and socioeconomical "high-status" identification and measured by variables such as educational level, income, and number of years living in the United States) and opposition to interracial marriage across groups. "High status" individuals (European Americans) were found to have a higher opposition to interracial marriage than "low status" individuals (Asian Americans, Hispanic Americans, African Americans, and Native Americans).

Fu, Vincent Kang. "Racial Intermarriage Pairings." *Demography* 38, no. 2 (May 2001): 147-159.

Fu's study seeks to explore socioeconomic characteristics of intermarried couples. He finds some evidence consistent with status exchange theories supported by such researchers as Merton and Kalmijn.

Gurak, Douglas T., and Joseph P. Fitzpatrick. "Intermarriage among Hispanic Ethnic Groups in New York City." *American Journal of Sociology* 87, no. 4 (1982): 921-934.

Gurak and Fitzpatrick lay the groundwork for later research which shows a strong correlation between the level of cultural assimilation or acculturation experienced particularly by Asian and Hispanic ethnic groups and their rate of intermarriage. Using data from New York City marriage records in 1975, the authors compare out-group marriage rates among Puerto Ricans, Dominicans, South Americans, and Central Americans, and Cubans. Not surprisingly, Puerto Ricans, the largest Hispanic ethnic group in New York City at the time of the study, had the lowest rates of intermarriage. This seems to confirm Blau's theory of composition, where group size is inversely related to a particular group's rate of intermarriage.

Hwang, Sean-Shong, Rogelio Saenz, and Benigno E. Aguirre. "The SES Selectivity of Interracially Married Asians." *International Migration Review* 29, no. 2 (Summer 1995): 469-491.

Focusing on intermarried Asian Americans, the authors seek to re-examine previous studies of interracial marriage which were based on theories of exchange and assimilation. Hwang, Saenz, and Aguirre pick up where previous research left off and examine gender differences within these frameworks. They found a tendency for Asian American women of lower educational levels and class status to intermarry more frequently with someone from a higher class status, whereas the inverse was found to be true for Asian American men.

————. "Structural and Assimilationist Explanations of Asian American Intermarriage." *Journal of Marriage and the Family* 59, no. 3 (August 1997): 758-772.

The authors discuss the occurrence of Asian American intermarriage within the context of overall status attainment among this population. They found evidence to generally support the previously held assumption that there is a strong correlation between the degree of interracial marriage among Asian American groups and the level at which they have assimilated into mainstream American society.

Kitano, Harry H.L., Diane C. Fujino, and Jane Takahashi Sato. "Interracial Marriage." *Journal of Marriage and the Family* 46, no. 1 (February 1984): 179-190.

Drawing upon marriage data on Asian American ethnic groups in Los Angeles, the authors compare the rates of outmarriage for Chinese, Japanese, Filipino, Korean, and Vietnamese individuals in that region. Their findings support previous studies of Asian American intermarriage, showing a strong correlation between the degree of overall acculturation of a particular ethnic group and that group's rate of outmarriage. It is not surprising, therefore, that Japanese Americans, primarily third-generation, possess the highest rate of intermarriage, while Korean Americans, with relatively less exposure to American culture, account for the lowest rate of intermarriage among Asian ethnic groups.

Lewis, Richard, Jr., George Yancey, and Siri S. Bletzer. "Racial and Nonracial Factors That Influence Spouse Choice in Black/White Marriages." *Journal of Black Studies* 28, no. 1 (September 1997): 60-78.

Negating the popularly held "jungle fever" myth regarding the motivations of interracial romantic partners, the authors find that nonracial factors are more important than racial factors in Black-White marriage. Among the most important deciding factors for Black-White couples were common interests and personal attractiveness, proving that the motivations of interracial couples are no different from those of racially similar couples when it comes to mate selection.

Little, George. "Analytic Reflections on Mixed Marriages." *Psychoanalytic Review* 29, no. 113 (January 1942): 20-25.

Little's analysis of interracial marriages between Blacks and Whites is troubling for the modern day reader, though quite illustrative of the thinking of psychoanalysts in the early part of the twentieth century. Acknowledging that interracial marriage is only of consequence in geographic areas where White supremacist attitudes and ideologies prevail, Little focuses on the nature of intermarriage between Blacks and Whites in the United States. In doing so, he relies upon racist characterizations of men and women, both Black and White, who engage in intimate relations with members of another race. He dismisses the validity of interracial marriages by suggesting that the marriage partners are only motivated by sexual desire for the exotic "other."

Merton, Robert K. "Intermarriage and the Social Structure: Fact and Theory." *Psychiatry* 4, no. 3 (August 1941): 361-374.

Merton asserts that Blacks and Whites are at opposite ends of the racial status continuum. He applies the theory of hypogamy to discuss romantic relations between these two groups. This theory holds that as Blacks occupy a lower status in American society, in order to be perceived as attractive marriage partners to Whites, they must possess another outstanding quality such as a high level of physical attractiveness, income, or educational attainment. Conversely, this theory assumes that Blacks are willing to accept a less wealthy or physically attractive White partner in order to benefit from the status associated with being involved with someone from a higher social class. Most contemporary research negates Merton's theories, finding that, in fact, the majority of interracially married couples come from similar socioeconomic and educational backgrounds.

Porterfield, Ernest. "Black-American Intermarriage in the United States." *Marriage and Family Review* 5, no. 1 (Spring 1982): 17-34.

Porterfield explores demographic trends in outmarriage among African Americans. He ultimately argues in support of Merton's theory of hypogamy and related theories that attempt to dismiss interracial marriage as being motivated by the desire to "marry up," or by lack of suitable same-race marriage partners.

Qian, Zhenchao. "Breaking the Racial Barriers: Variations in Inter-racial Marriage Between 1980 and 1990." *Demography* 34, no. 2 (May 1997): 263-276.

Qian's findings support the findings of other studies showing a strong correlation between educational attainment and interracial marriage. Using census data from 1980 and 1990, this study finds that Asian Americans are more likely to intermarry with Whites, followed by Hispanic Americans/Latinos, with African Americans being the least likely to marry a White partner. While most individuals in interracial couples were found to have comparable levels of educational attainment as their partners, those who did not were married to a spouse of a "higher status" racial group.

———. "Who Intermarries? Education, Nativity, Region, and Interracial Marriage, 1980 and 1990." *Journal of Comparative Family Studies* 30, no. 4 (Autumn 1999): 579-597.

Qian's study supports Blau's theory of composition, which holds that the prevalence of interracial marriage across racial groups differs by region and is dependent upon the racial distribution within a particular region.[1] Thus, the smaller the group size, the higher the prevalence of intermarriage, due to a decrease in opportunities for meeting partners of the same race. Qian's research validates contemporary theories of social and opportunity structure and negates Merton's theory of hypogamy as related to mate selection.

South, Scott J., and Steven F. Messner. "Structural Determinants of Intergroup Association: Interracial Marriage and Crime." *American Journal of Sociology* 91, no. 6 (May 1986): 1409-1430.

South and Messner use Blau's theory of social structure to derive and test their hypothesis that there is a strong correlation between the two seemingly non-related occurrences of interracial marriage and interracial crime. The authors find a positive correlation between the rate of interracial marriage, the degree of socioeconomic parity among the races, and the rate of interracial crime (i.e., crimes wherein the victim and perpetrator are of different races). These factors are strongly related to the degree of residential segregation, concluding that socioeconomic disparities between Whites and people of color breeds distrust, resentment, and negative associations, whereas positive interracial associations increase when there is less of a socioeconomic gap between races.

Spickard, Paul R. *Mixed Blood: Intermarriage and Ethnic Identity in Twentieth-Century America.* Madison: University of Wisconsin Press, 1989.

Focusing on the marriage patterns among African American, Japanese, and Jewish communities, Spickard confirms that individuals are more likely to intermarry in geographic areas where there are fewer opportunities for members of ethnic and racial minority groups to interact socially with people of similar backgrounds. Spickard is therefore critical of Merton's hypogamy theory, arguing that intermarriage occurs most often among middle and upper class individuals of similar socioeconomic status. He also speaks to gender and generational influences, suggesting that with the exception of African Americans, whose rate of intermarriage has traditionally been lower than that of Japanese Americans and American Jews, acceptance of intermarriage is growing with each new generation.

Yancey, George. "Who Interracially Dates: An Examination of the Characteristics of Those Who Have Interracially Dated." *Journal of Comparative Family Studies* 33, no. 2 (Spring 2002): 179-190.

Yancey, who has written extensively on interracial relationships, reexamines the topic, discussing the level of interracial romantic relationships as a measure of the state of race relations in American society. Contemporary singles, argues Yancey, have more opportunities to come into contact with potential dating partners of other races due to increasingly integrated workplaces, neighborhoods, schools, and social environments. In exploring whether a greater degree of interracial social contact has caused people to take a more positive view of interracial dating and marriage, he concludes that European Americans (Whites) are the least likely to date interracially, and that men of all races are more likely to date interracially than women. A strong correlation between integrated schools and interracial dating is also discussed.

Yancey, George A., and Sherelyn W. Yancey. "Black-White Differences in the Use of Personal Advertisements for Individuals Seeking Interracial Relationships." *Journal of Black Studies* 27, no. 5 (May 1997): 650-667.

Using a sample of 439 individuals obtained from *Interrace* magazine's personal ads, the authors discuss characteristics individuals interested in interracial relationships seek in a potential dating partner. Using the frameworks of Robert K. Merton's theory of hypogamy and P.M. Blau's social exchange theory, the authors hypothesize that Whites would be less likely to describe their positive assets and more likely to seek a partner with expressed physical or socioeconomic assets (income, job status, or educational attainment) and that Blacks would be more likely to articulate such assets in order to compensate for their perceived lower social status. The results proved that, to the contrary, Merton's theory of hypogamy cannot be applied to those seeking interracial relationships and that the motivations for individuals to seek out such relationships are complex and do not differ that dramatically from those seeking out relationships with members of the same race.

History and Prevalence of Interracial Relationships

W.E.B. DuBois predicted one hundred years ago that the most salient issue in the twentieth century would be the "problem of the color-line." Indeed, it was not until well after the 1967 *Loving v. Virginia* decision overturning the ban on interracial marriages that interracial marriage became legal in every state in the nation (Alabama was the last state to overturn its ban on interracial marriage in the year 2000 despite the fact that 40 percent of its electorate supported the ban). With the U.S. Supreme Court ruling anti-miscegenation laws unconstitutional came an interracial baby boom and a threefold increase in the proportion of interethnic and interracial marriages in the United States,[2] not surprisingly coinciding with the Civil Rights movement. The following resources provide historical and statistical overviews of interracial relationships throughout American history.

Annella, Sister M. "Some Aspects of Interracial Marriage in Washington, D.C." *Journal of Negro Education* 25, no. 4 (Autumn 1956): 380-391.
  Annella examines trends in interracial marriage in Washington, D.C. from 1940 to 1947, using data collected from the D.C. Marriage License Bureau. Upon contacting many of the interracially married individuals listed in the records for the corresponding years, Annella was granted personal interviews, during which she found that the majority of couples were happily married and experienced a very low rate of divorce. Annella's study also provides useful background data and case studies on interracial marriage prior to *Loving v. Virginia.*

Heer, David M. "The Prevalence of Black-White Marriage in the United States, 1960 and 1970." *Journal of Marriage and the Family* 36, no. 2 (May 1974): 246-258.
  Heer uses data from the 1960 and 1970 decennial censuses of the United States to analyze patterns in marriage between Blacks and Whites, finding a significant increase during this decade, the height of the Civil Rights era. Interestingly, this decade brought an increase in interracial marriages in the regions of the North and the West, yet a decline in the South. As contemporary trends in inter-

racial marriage also reflect, there were more Black men married to White women than Black women married to White men. An important finding of Heer's research is that it does not support Merton's theory of hypogamy, which held that Blacks and Whites are only motivated to marry interracially when there is a financial advantage, perception of status, or other benefit involved.

Hodes, Martha. *White Women, Black Men: Illicit Sex in the Nineteenth-Century South*. New Haven: Yale University Press, 1997.

Relying primarily upon legal documents and testimonies, Martha Hodes provides an adept re-examination of the origins of the "rape myth" concerning sexual relations between Black men and White women. In doing so, she suggests that interracial relationships in the South were often tolerated and rarely met with violent opposition prior to the Civil War. It was the Civil War, she argues, that served as the primary catalyst for the sexual stereotyping and lynching of Black men by White southerners, and which helped to shape the social and political order of the post-Reconstruction South.

Kalmijn, Matthijs. "Trends in Black/White Intermarriage." *Social Forces* 72, no. 1 (September 1993): 119-146.

Kalmijn's is among the many studies that re-examined interracial marriage as an indicator of race relations in the early 1990s, after a period where little attention was paid to the topic. Analyzing data drawn from marriage licenses in thirty-three states from 1968 to 1986 (when race data was still collected in these states), Kalmijn found an unsurprising increase in the number of Black/White interracial marriages once the ban on interracial marriage was overturned by the U.S. Supreme Court in 1967. The study also seems to confirm Merton's controversial theory of hypogamy, finding a significant trend in intermarriage between a member of a "high status" racial group (White) and a "low status" racial group (Black) when the Black partner is of a higher socioeconomic status.

Kennedy, Randall. *Interracial Intimacies: Sex, Marriage, Identity, and Adoption.* New York: Pantheon Books, 2003.

The follow-up to his controversial book, *Nigger*, Kennedy's *Interracial Intimacies* provides a sophisticated critique of American culture through the lens of interracial romantic relationships. Tracing the history of such relationships through an exploration of case law and popular culture mythologies, Kennedy argues that despite the stereotypes and heated social debates surrounding interracial dating and marriage, the fact that the rate of intermarriage continues to grow is a positive outgrowth of our increasingly multicultural society.

Kitano, Harry H.L., Wai-Tsang Yeung, Lynn Chai, and Herbert Hata-naka. "Asian-American Interracial Marriage." *Journal of Marriage and the Family* 46, no. 1 (February 1984): 179-190.

The authors provide a historical overview of the patterns of inter-marriage among various Asian American ethnic groups, concentrating on Korean Americans, Chinese Americans, and Japanese Americans in Hawaii and Los Angeles. Though they found that the ethnic group with the highest proportion of intermarried individuals has shifted through time, the fact that Asian American women tend to intermarry at a higher rate than that of their male counterparts has remained consistent. Factors influencing the rate of intermarriage among Asian Americans include historical factors (i.e., how long a particular ethnic group has been in the United States and under what circumstances), cultural factors (i.e., the level of perceived acculturation of a particular ethnic group), and the receptivity of the dominant group (i.e., how favorably a particular group is viewed).

Liang, Zai, and Naomi Ito. "Intermarriage of Asian Americans in the New York City Region: Contemporary Patterns and Future Prospects." *International Migration Review* 33, no. 4. (Winter 1999): 876-900.

Data from the 1990 Census is used to examine the prevalence of interracial marriage among Chinese Americans, Japanese Americans, Korean Americans, Filipino Americans, and Indian Americans. Though focused on New York City, this is among the broadest studies of intermarriage among Asian Americans due to its comparative nature, acknowledging that intermarriage patterns vary significantly between Asian ethnic groups. The authors do find some commonalities across ethnicities, however. Not surprisingly, U.S.-born Asians of all ethnicities tend to marry interracially at a higher rate than the foreign-born and immigrant populations, and intermarriage is more prevalent among Asian American women than their male counterparts. It is also important to note that Zai and Ito's findings negate Merton's theory of hypogamy, showing that similar socioeconomic and educational backgrounds are a stronger correlate of interracial marriage.

Model, Suzanne, and Gene Fisher. "Black-White Unions: West Indians and African Americans Compared." *Demography* 38, no. 2 (May 2001): 177-185.

Although other studies have explored ethnic differences in interracial marriage among Hispanic and Asian Americans, few studies have explored ethnic differences in Blacks. Model and Fisher use 1990 Census data to compare the prevalence of intermarriage with

Whites among African Americans and Caribbean Americans of British West Indian descent. Interestingly, though studies of Hispanic and Asian Americans have shown substantial differences in the rates of interracial marriage between ethnic groups, this study shows no significant differences between West Indians and African Americans, though there is some evidence presented for gender-based variations.

Monahan, Thomas P. "An Overview of Statistics on Interracial Marriage in the United States, with Data on Its Extent from 1963-1970." *Journal of Marriage and the Family* 38, no. 2 (May 1976): 223-231.

Monahan's analysis of marriage records for the period from 1963 to 1970 shows that the proportion of intermarried males to females varies by state and by race/ethnicity. He finds that states in the North and West have the highest proportion of interracial marriages, and marriages between Blacks and Whites are the most frequently occurring.

Moran, Rachel F. *Interracial Intimacy: The Regulation of Race and Romance*. Chicago: University of Chicago Press, 2001.

Focusing on the notion that racial identity and perceptions of interracial relationships shape one another, Moran provides an overview of two distinct eras in the history of anti-miscegenation legislation in the United States: before and after *Loving v. Virginia*. Arguing that legal and social sanctions on interracial relationships have served to reinforce racial stereotypes and hierarchies over time, Moran sees social problems such as residential and occupational segregation as having a residual impact on the rate of intermarriage in the United States. Herself the daughter of a Mexican mother and Irish father, Moran's historical analysis seems motivated by her own agenda at times. To her credit, however, she provides a broader discussion of race-based legislation than do previous works on the topic. She addresses the rationale behind the disparate treatment of Native Americans, Latinos, Asian Americans, and African Americans throughout history with regard to marriage law.

Rosenblatt, Paul C., Terri A. Karis, and Richard Powell. *Multiracial Couples: Black and White Voices*. Walnut Creek, Calif.: Sage Publications, 1995.

The authors, two of whom are themselves an interracial couple, use narratives from interviews with twenty-one Midwestern couples to explore the impact of race and racism upon interracially married individuals and their relationships. Though strictly qualitative in nature, and therefore not especially interested in critical analysis of the couples' responses or looking at the experiences within any particular theoretical framework, this work is enlightening nonetheless. Unlike more scholarly works that address the nature of interracial romance within the context of external forces that affect the relationship as an entity, this study indeed gives voice to the individuals, allowing them to explore how their involvement in an interracial relationship affects their own racial identities.

Sollors, Werner, ed. *Interracialism: Black-White Intermarriage in American History, Literature, and Law.* Oxford: Oxford University Press, 2000.

A professor of English Literature and American History at Harvard University, Sollors places the American legal and cultural history of interracial romantic relationships into the larger context of American social progress over time. This volume of critical essays provides a historical overview of real-life and literary portrayals of intermarriage between African Americans and Whites in the United States, arguing that the legislation and taboo surrounding these unions is strictly an American phenomenon.

Suro, Roberto. "Mixed Doubles." *American Demographics* 21, no. 11 (November 1999): 57-62.

Suro discusses new trends among interracially married couples. In contrast to previous studies, current census data shows that interracial couples are increasingly young, well educated, and upwardly mobile. The author attributes this shift to an overall shift in ideas about marriage in the general population, where nontraditional families, relationships, and lifestyles are just as commonplace as the nuclear family household was in the 1950s.

Tucker, M. Belinda, and Claudia Mitchell-Kernan. "New Trends in Black American Interracial Marriage: The Social Structural Context." *Journal of Marriage and the Family* 52, no. 1 (February 1990): 209-218.

Acknowledging that national statistics on intermarriage can be misleading, this study finds significant regional differences in the rates of interracial marriage, and examines the underlying structural correlates of outmarriage, specifically among African-Americans. While this study agrees with previous studies which have found that Black men intermarry at a higher rate than Black women, the authors find that demographic factors associated with intermarriage among Blacks, such as education, income, and occupation, are equal for both genders.

Wallenstein, Peter. *Tell the Court I Love My Wife: Race, Marriage, and Law. An American History.* New York: Palgrave, 2002.
Quite possibly the best history of interracial marriage in the United States to date, Wallenstein's book adeptly explores the intersections of sex and race in American case law. Rather than provide the reader with another look at *Loving v. Virginia*, he uses the Loving case as a foundation for exploring shifting attitudes and public opinion about race and intimacy in a segregated society. Appealing to academics and general readers alike, Wallenstein delivers a work that is well researched and as impassioned and moving as its title.

Racial Attitudes and Public Opinion

White authors often explored issues pertaining to Black/White unions, almost completely to the exclusion of other interracial and interethnic pairings in order to address the nature of what was thought of as the societal problem of miscegenation. For this reason, much of the early literature focused on unions between individuals of African and European descent, and discussed such relationships mostly in a negative context, in terms that have come to be identified as racist or White supremacist, such as "miscegenation" and "race mixing." Later research still focused on interactions between these two groups, reasoning that persons of African descent and European descent still represent polar opposites along the race continuum as well as within the social hierarchy in the minds of most Americans. Indeed, according to Ernest Porterfield, "No other mixture touches off such widespread condemnation as Black/White mixing."[3] The following resources discuss attitudes toward interracial relationships from both in-group and out-group perspectives.

Fears, Darryl, and Claudia Deane. "Biracial Couples Report Tolerance." *Washington Post*, July 5, 2001.
The findings of a national survey on interracial marriage and dating sponsored by the *Washington Post*, the Henry J. Kaiser Family Foundation, and Harvard University are discussed. Participants in the survey were 540 adults married to or living with someone of another race. Included also are results from a companion survey of racial attitudes from interviews with 1,709 randomly selected adults. Overall, the former survey finds that approval of interracial marriages is increasing, with disapproval the highest in White communities. Two-thirds of couples in Black-White partnerships

reported that a set of parents initially objected, and a half of Black-White couples reported that interracial union "makes marriage harder." The survey of racial attitudes found that acceptance of interracial marriages is more likely to be found in Black families than White families.

Gaines, Stanley O., Jr., and William Ickes. "Perspectives on Interracial Relationships." In *Handbook of Personal Relationships: Theory, Research, and Interventions,* edited by Steve Duck. New York: John Wiley & Sons, 1997.

The focus of this chapter is an important addition to the body of literature on interpersonal relationships. Gaines and Ickes examine the distinction between in-group and out-group perceptions of race and racism with regard to interracial relationships, finding that while those involved in interracial relationships view their differences as primarily cultural, from the outside, others are quick to define their differences as color or race-based.

Garcia, Stella D., and Semilla M. Rivera. "Perceptions of Hispanic and African-American Couples at the Friendship or Engagement State of a Relationship." *Journal of Social and Personal Relationships* 16, no. 1 (1999): 65-86.

Garcia and Rivera's study speaks to the complexities surrounding perceptions and public opinion about interracial couples. Comparing perceptions of romantically involved interracial couples and interracial couples who are friends, the researchers found that perceptions varied between men and women and were based on the perceived level of intimacy between the couple, with romantically involved couples being perceived more negatively than interracial pairs of friends.

Johnson, Walton R., and Dennis M. Warren. *Inside the Mixed Marriage: Accounts of Changing Attitudes, Patterns, and Perceptions of Cross-Cultural and Interracial Marriages.* Lanham, Md.: University Press of America, 1994.

The authors present the personal accounts of interracially married couples from a broad range of socioeconomic backgrounds. The couples surveyed, primarily consisting of a Black partner and a White partner, discuss the challenges they confronted prior to getting married, as well as the external forces that continue to shape their relationship as a married couple. Johnson and Warren are careful in their presentation of the narratives to make a clear distinction between how interracial couples view themselves, and how those outside their relationship view them.

McNamara, Robert P., Maria Tempenis, and Beth Walton. *Crossing the Line: Interracial Couples in the South.* Westport, Conn.: Praeger, 1999.

Much like *Multiracial Couples* (Rosenblatt, et al.), *Crossing the Line* derives its qualitative analysis from interviews with a small group of Black/White interracial couples. Though the couples in this study candidly express similar experiences with racism and hostility as do those in Rosenblatt's study, McNamara, Tempenis, and Walton attempt to highlight the geographic differences in attitudes toward interracial relationships by focusing on interracially married couples in the South. Interestingly, the authors specifically choose to conduct interviews in South Carolina, one of two states that continued to prohibit interracial marriage well after the *Loving v. Virginia* decision. Not surprisingly, the authors discover that these couples face more overt opposition than do their northern counterparts, and are more likely to be employed by the military and turn to religion as a coping mechanism.

Mills, Jon K., Jennifer Daly, Amy Longmore, and Gina Kilbride. "A Note on Family Acceptance Involving Interracial Friendships and Romantic Relationships." *Journal of Psychology* 129, no. 3 (May 1995): 349.

Based on responses to their Assessment Scale of Interracial Relationships from a mixed group of 142 undergraduate students at a small Midwestern university, the authors found that there was no significant gender or racial difference in the overall perception of interracial relationships. The results showed that men and women, as well as Blacks and Whites, held equally negative views toward interracial relationships and indicated that their families would not support their involvement in such relationships. These findings conflict with other studies that have found interracial marriage approval ratings were higher among White females. The small sample size, median age of respondents, and the racially homogenous environment in which this study took place may provide an explanation for the attitudes of the respondents.

Root, Maria P.P. *Love's Revolution: Interracial Marriage.* Philadelphia: Temple University Press, 2001.

Root discusses the attitudes of the post-Civil Rights generation toward interracial marriage. She examines this group, which holds the highest approval rating for interracial marriage, and how this newfound tolerance still conflicts with the ideas of many American families who don't share in their desire to welcome an individual of another race into their inner circle. Perhaps the most striking distinction between Root's work and other similar explorations of interracial marriage is that Root includes heterosexual as well as same-sex couples in her discussions.

Snowden, Lonnie R., and Alice M. Hines. "A Scale to Assess African American Acculturation." *Journal of Black Psychology* 25, no. 1 (February 1999): 36-47.

Though not specifically focused on the topic of interracial marriage, this study finds that the desirability of interracial marriage and positive attitudes toward such unions are among the most reliable measures used to assess the level of acculturation among Blacks.

St. Jean, Yanick. "Let People Speak for Themselves: Interracial Unions and the General Social Survey." *Journal of Black Studies* 28, no. 3 (January 1998): 398-414.

St. Jean asserts that previous findings regarding attitudes toward intermarriage (which relied upon data from the General Social Survey) are problematic due to the limited nature of the survey, which only asks two questions addressing the topic. St. Jean proposes, therefore, that the focus group approach is a more appropriate method of collecting information on such a complex issue. Focus groups allow people to describe their attitudes in their own words, rather than answering simple yes or no questions written in the language of the researcher.

Zebroski, Sheryline A. "Black-White Intermarriages: The Racial and Gender Dynamics of Support and Opposition." *Journal of Black Studies* 30, no. 1 (September 1999): 123-132.

Whereas public opinion of racially mixed couples was mostly negative in the pre-Civil Rights period due to ideas of White racial superiority and the negative effects of miscegenation with Blacks, contemporary ideas about such unions differ by race and gender and the combination of these two characteristics. Current negative perceptions of interracial couples often have less to do with the notion of a racial hierarchy and more to do with perceptions of what someone else's interracial marriage means for others' chances for dating and marriage. Zebroski finds that support for interracial marriage differed not as much by race as by gender, with White women being the most tolerant and White men being the least tolerant. Not surprisingly, she also found that individuals who were interracially married felt the most opposition from persons of the same race and opposite gender as themselves.

Psychology and Interpersonal Development

Given that interracial relationships were not assumed to be "natural," before the civil rights era, the early research often centered on questioning the motivations of individuals in such relationships. Researchers often hypothesized that the primary reasons a person would have for making what was then thought of as a poor social decision, often with legal and even deadly consequences, included mental illness, lack of identification with one's own ethnic group, a desire to rebel against one's family or society, a strong curiosity or desire to engage in taboo, and other negative personal attributes. While it is impossible to deny that some interracially paired persons do, in fact, match one or more of these descriptions, current research finds that Americans who are interracially married or partnered are healthy, productive individuals, who possess strong senses of individual ethnic and racial identities. The following resources represent a growing body of literature that recognizes the normalcy of interracial relationships and seeks to provide tools for understanding the strengths and challenges involved with interracial intimacy.

Biever, Joan L., Monte Bobele, and Mary Wales-North. "Therapy with Intercultural Couples: A Postmodern Approach." *Counseling Psychology Quarterly* 11, no. 2 (June 1998): 181-188.
   The authors discuss the impact of cultural differences and societal disapproval on the stability of interracial marriages, acknowledging that external pressures and opinions often compound already existing marital difficulties. Although much has been written by social and behavioral scientists about counseling and therapy with multicultural clients (i.e., clients whose race and/or ethnicity differs from that of the therapist), the authors observe that little attention has been given specifically to therapeutic interventions with interracial couples, adding to the lack of understanding and mechanisms for treating such couples. This particularly challenging issue is discussed within a framework of postmodernist ideas such as social constructionism, which, according to the authors, "suggests that what we know as reality is constructed through interactions with others."

Brown, John A. "Casework Contacts with Black-White Couples." *Social Casework* 68, no. 1 (January 1987): 24-29.
   The author acknowledges the multidimensional nature of interpersonal conflict in interracial relationships. He provides techniques for identifying racist attitudes as well as a model for addressing race as one issue, but not the primary issue of dealing with interracial couples in therapy.

Chan, Anna Y., and Elaine Wethington. "Factors Promoting Marital Resilience among Interracial Couples." In *Resiliency in Native American and Immigrant Families*, edited by Hamilton McCubbin, Elizabeth A. Thompson, et al. Thousand Oaks, Calif.: Sage Publications, 1998.

Chan and Wethington are critical of previous studies that have explored treatment of interracial and intercultural couples in therapy from strictly a conflict-based model. Those previous studies discussed interracial marriage primarily as a stressor. Chan and Wethington suggest a more appropriate model, focusing on marital resiliency by taking a strengths-based approach. The authors cite the most common conflicts between interracial marriage partners including family opposition and differing cultural expectations regarding gender roles. They also find that in order to combat these stressors, resilient couples must have strong social support networks and live in communities where their relationship is accepted.

Foeman, Anita Kathy. "From Miscegenation to Multiculturalism: Perceptions and Stages of Interracial Relationship Development." *Journal of Black Studies* 29, no. 4 (March 1999): 540-557.

Foeman seeks to discover the ways in which interracial couples communicate and negotiate their social and interpersonal interactions, assuming that romantic interactions come more easily for intraracial couples who are already familiar with each other's cultural norms and communication strategies. Foeman provides an overview of the history of interracial relationships in the United States as well as the myths surrounding them. She then outlines a theory of the stages of development for Black/White couples, including racial awareness, coping with social definitions of race, identity emergence, and maintenance stages.

Gaines, Stanley O., Jr. "Communalism and the Reciprocity of Affection and Respect among Interethnic Married Couples." *Journal of Black Studies* 27, no. 3 (January 1997): 352-364.

Criticizing Black psychologists who have refused to see the validity and importance of research on interracial couples, Gaines seeks to explore the relationship processes of intermarried couples in order to fill what he sees as a gap in the literature. He discusses various models of interpersonal resource exchange.

Gaines, Stanley O., Jr., Cherlyn S. Granrose, Diana I. Rios, et al. "Patterns of Attachment and Responses to Accommodative Dilemmas among Interethnic/Interracial Couples." *Journal of Social and Personal Relationships* 16, no. 2 (April 1999): 275-285.

This study highlights positive and healthy interactions between interracially romantically involved individuals. The majority of the participants in the study, which included 103 couples, demonstrated that they were "securely attached" versus "insecurely attached." The study proves the researchers' hypothesis that interracial couples are capable of emotional commitment and intimacy, as opposed to having a purely physical or sexual interest in pursuing a relationship with someone of another race or ethnicity.

Hill, Miriam R., and Volker Thomas. "Strategies for Racial Identity Development: Narratives of Black and White Women in Interracial Partner Relationships." *Family Relations* 49, no. 2 (April 2000): 193-200.

Employing the racial identity development theories of social constructionism and feminism, Hill and Thomas explore women's racial identities within the context of interracial relationships. The authors also discuss coping strategies and defense mechanisms that Black and White women employ to set appropriate boundaries against the racism that is often directed at them due to their relationship status with a partner of another race. The authors also engage in an interesting discussion about their methodology. They employ methodology that argues for the validity of researchers in this area to disclose bias and personal experience with their topic in order to make readers aware of their "in-group" status and therefore gain credibility.

Ho, Man Keung. *Intermarried Couples in Therapy.* Springfield, Ill.: Charles C. Thomas, 1990.

Filling a void in the psychotherapy research on couples and marital conflict, Ho lays forth a framework for couples' therapy with racially and culturally different spouses. Ho suggests that intermarried couples have more external stressors to their marriage and are more sensitive to the ethnic background of the therapist than most monoracial couples are. Ho further suggests that the practitioner must therefore possess an additional skill set for helping these couples to address the impact of race, racism, and culture upon their relationships.

Killian, Kyle D. "Reconstituting Racial Histories and Identities: The Narratives of Interracial Couples." *Journal of Marital and Family Therapy* 27, no. 1 (January 2001): 27-42.

Killian's findings from separate and joint interviews with ten Black/White interracially married couples show that Blacks in interracial marriages tend to be more acutely aware of society's negative perceptions of such relationships than their White partners due to their individual experience of racism. Killian discusses the ways in which interracial couples identify as individuals and as couples within the construct of race, as well as effective therapeutic interventions with interracial couples.

Bibliography

Aldridge, Delores P. "Interracial Marriages: Empirical and Theoretical Considerations." *Journal of Black Studies* 8, no. 3 (March 1978): 355-368.

Annella, Sister M. "Some Aspects of Interracial Marriage in Washington, D.C." *Journal of Negro Education* 25, no. 4 (Autumn 1956): 380-439.

Baber, Ray. "A Study of 325 Mixed Marriages." *American Sociological Review* 2, no. 5 (October 1937): 705-716.

Biever, Joan L., Monte Bobele, and Mary Wales-North. "Therapy with Intercultural Couples: A Postmodern Approach." *Counseling Psychology Quarterly* 11, no. 2 (June 1998): 181-188.

Blau, Peter M., Carolyn Beeker, and Kevin M. Fitzpatrick. "Intersecting Social Affiliations and Intermarriage." *Social Forces* 62, no. 3 (March 1984): 585-606.

Brown, John A. "Casework Contacts with Black-White Couples." *Social Casework* 68, no. 1 (January 1987): 24-29.

Cerroni-Long, E. Liza. "Marrying Out: Socio-Cultural and Psychological Implications of Intermarriage." *Journal of Comparative Family Studies* 16, no. 1 (Spring 1985): 25-46.

Chan, Anna Y., and Elaine Wethington. "Factors Promoting Marital Resilience among Interracial Couples." In *Resiliency in Native American and Immigrant Families*, edited by Hamilton McCubbin, Elizabeth A. Thompson, et al., 71-87. Thousand Oaks, Calif.: Sage Publications, 1998.

Crowder, Kyle D., and Stewart E. Tolnay. "A New Marriage Squeeze for Black Women: The Role of Racial Intermarriage by Black Men." *Journal of Marriage and the Family* 62, no. 3 (August 2000): 792-807.

Davidson, Jeanette R. "Theories about Black-White Interracial Marriage: A Clinical Perspective." *Journal of Multicultural Counseling and Development* 20, no. 4 (October 1992): 150-157.

Fang, Carolyn Y., Jim Sidanius, and Felicia Pratto. "Romance Across the Social Status Continuum: Interracial Marriage and the Ideological Asymmetry Effect." *Journal of Cross Cultural Psychology* 29, no. 2 (March 1998): 290-305.

Foeman, Anita Kathy, and Teresa Nance. "From Miscegenation to Multiculturalism: Perceptions and Stages of Interracial Relationship Development." *Journal of Black Studies* 29, no. 4 (March 1999): 540-557.

Fu, Vincent Kang. "Racial Intermarriage Pairings." *Demography* 38, no. 2 (May 2001): 147-159.

Gaines, Stanley O., Jr. "Communalism and the Reciprocity of Affection and Respect among Interethnic Married Couples." *Journal of Black Studies* 27, no. 3 (January 1997): 352-364.

Gaines, Stanley O., Jr., Cherlyn S. Granrose, Diana I. Rios, et al. "Patterns of Attachment and Responses to Accommodative Dilemmas among Interethnic/Interracial Couples." *Journal of Social and Personal Relationships* 16, no. 2 (April 1999): 275-285.

Gaines, Stanley O., Jr., and William Ickes. "Perspectives on Interracial Relationships." In *Handbook of Personal Relationships: Theory, Research, and Interventions*, edited by Steve Duck, 197-220. New York: John Wiley & Sons, 1997.

Garcia, Stella D., and Semilla M. Rivera. "Perceptions of Hispanic and African-American Couples at the Friendship or Engagement Stage of a Relationship." *Journal of Social and Personal Relationships* 16, no. 1 (February 1999): 65-86.

Gurak, Douglas T., and Joseph P. Fitzpatrick. "Intermarriage among Hispanic Ethnic Groups in New York City." *American Journal of Sociology* 87, no. 4 (January 1982): 921-934.

Heer, David M. "The Prevalence of Black-White Marriage in the United States, 1960 and 1970." *Journal of Marriage and the Family* 36, no. 2 (May 1974): 246-258.

Hill, Miriam R., and Volker Thomas. "Strategies for Racial Identity Development: Narratives of Black and White Women in Interracial Partner Relationships." *Family Relations* 49, no. 2 (April 2000): 193-200.

Ho, Man Keung. *Intermarried Couples in Therapy*. Springfield, Ill.: Charles C. Thomas, 1990.

Hodes, Martha. *White Women, Black Men: Illicit Sex in the Nineteenth-Century South*. New Haven, Conn.: Yale University Press, 1997.

Hwang, Sean-Shong, Rogelio Saenz, and Benigno E. Aguirre. "The SES Selectivity of Interracially Married Asians." *International Migration Review* 29, no. 2 (Summer 1995): 469-491.

———. "Structural and Assimilationist Explanations of Asian American Intermarriage." *Journal of Marriage and the Family* 59, no. 3 (August 1997): 758-772.

Johnson, Walton R., and Dennis M. Warren. *Inside the Mixed Marriage: Accounts of Changing Attitudes, Patterns, and Perceptions of Cross-Cultural and Interracial Marriages.* Lanham, Md.: University Press of America, 1994.

Kalmijn, Matthijs. "Trends in Black/White Intermarriage." *Social Forces* 72, no. 1 (September 1993): 119-146.

Kennedy, Randall. *Interracial Intimacies: Sex, Marriage, Identity, and Adoption.* New York: Pantheon, 2002.

Killian, Kyle D. "Reconstituting Racial Histories and Identities: The Narratives of Interracial Couples." *Journal of Marital and Family Therapy* 27, no. 1 (January 2001): 27-42.

Kitano, Harry H.L., Wai-Tsang Yeung, and Lynn Chai. "Asian-American Interracial Marriage." *Journal of Marriage and the Family* 46, no. 1 (February 1984): 179-190.

Kitano, Harry H.L., Diane C. Fujino, and Jane Takahashi Sato. "Interracial Marriages: Where Are the Asian Americans and Where Are They Going?" In *Handbook of Asian American Psychology*, edited by Lee C. Lee and Nolan W.S. Zane, 233-260. Thousand Oaks, Calif.: Sage Publications, 1998.

Lewis, Richard, Jr., George Yancey, and Siri S. Bletzer. "Racial and Nonracial Factors That Influence Spouse Choice in Black/White Marriages." *Journal of Black Studies* 28, no. 1 (September 1997): 60-78.

Liang, Zai. "Intermarriage of Asian Americans in the New York City Region: Contemporary Patterns and Future Prospects." *International Migration Review* 33, no. 4 (Winter 1999): 876-900.

Little, George. "Analytic Reflections on Mixed Marriages." *Psychoanalytic Review* 29, no. 113 (January 1942): 20-25.

McNamara, Robert P., Maria Tempenis, and Beth Walton. *Crossing the Line: Interracial Couples in the South.* Westport, Conn.: Greenwood Press, 1999.

Merton, Robert K. "Intermarriage and the Social Structure: Fact and Theory." *Psychiatry* 4, no. 3 (August 1941): 361-374.

Mills, Jon K., Jennifer Daly, and Amy Longmore. "A Note on Family Acceptance Involving Interracial Friendships and Romantic Relationships." *Journal of Psychology* 129, no. 3 (May 1995): 349-351.

Model, Suzanne, and Gene Fisher. "Black-White Unions: West Indians and African Americans Compared." *Demography* 38, no. 2 (May 2001): 177-185.

Monahan, Thomas P. "An Overview of Statistics on Interracial Marriage in the United States, with Data on its Extent from 1963-1970." *Journal of Marriage and the Family* 38, no 2 (May 1976): 223-231.

Moran, Rachel F. *Interracial Intimacy: The Regulation of Race and Romance.* Chicago: University of Chicago Press, 2001.

Porterfield, Ernest. "Black-American Intermarriage in the United States." *Marriage and Family Review* 5, no. 1 (Spring 1971): 17-34.

Qian, Zhenchao. "Breaking the Racial Barriers: Variations in Interracial Marriage Between 1980 and 1990." *Demography* 34 (1997): 263-276.

———. "Who Intermarries? Education, Nativity, Region and Interracial Marriage, 1980 and 1990." *Journal of Comparative Family Studies* 30, no. 4 (Fall 1999): 579-597.

Root, Maria P.P. *Love's Revolution: Interracial Marriage.* Philadelphia, Pa.: Temple University Press, 2001.

Rosenblatt, Paul C., Terri A. Karis, and Richard D. Powell. *Multiracial Couples: Black and White Voices.* Thousand Oaks, Calif.: Sage Publications, 1995.

Snowden, Lonnie R., and Alice M. Hines. "A Scale to Assess African American Acculturation." *Journal of Black Psychology* 25, no. 1 (February 1999): 36-47.

Sollors, Werner. *Interracialism: Black-White Intermarriage in American History, Literature, and Law.* Oxford: Oxford University Press, 2000.

South, Scott J., and Steven F. Messner. "Structural Determinants of Intergroup Association: Interracial Marriage and Crime." *American Journal of Sociology* 91, no. 6 (May 1986): 1409-1430.

Spickard, Paul R. *Mixed Blood: Intermarriage and Ethnic Identity in Twentieth-Century America.* Madison, Wis.: University of Wisconsin Press, 1989.

St. Jean, Yanick. "Let People Speak for Themselves: Interracial Unions and the General Social Survey." *Journal of Black Studies* 28, no. 3 (January 1998): 398-414.

Suro, Roberto. "Mixed Doubles." *American Demographics* 21, no. 11 (November 1999): 57-62.

Tucker, M. Belinda, and Claudia Mitchell-Kernan. "New Trends in Black American Interracial Marriage: The Social Structural Context." *Journal of Marriage and the Family* 52, no. 1 (February 1990): 209-218.

Wallenstein, Peter. *Tell the Court I Love My Wife: Race, Marriage, and the Law. An American History.* New York: Palgrave, 2002.

Yancey, George. "Who Interracially Dates: An Examination of the Characteristics of Those Who Have Interracially Dated." *Journal of Comparative Family Studies* 33, no. 2 (Spring 2002): 179-190.

Yancey, George A., and Sherelyn W. Yancey. "Black-White Differ-
  ences in the Use of Personal Advertisements for Individuals Seek-
  ing Interracial Relationships." *Journal of Black Studies* 27, no. 5
  (May 1997): 650-667.
Zebroski, Sheryline A. "Black-White Intermarriages: The Racial and
  Gender Dynamics of Support and Opposition." *Journal of Black
  Studies* 30, no. 1 (September 1999): 123-132.

Notes

1. Blau, P.M., *Inequality and Heterogeneity* (New York: Free Press, 1977).

2. Gaines, S.O., Jr., and W. Ickes, "Perspectives on Interracial Relationships." In *Handbook of Personal Relationships*, 2nd. ed., edited by Steve Duck (Chichester, England: Wiley, 1997).

3. Porterfield, Ernest, "Black-American Intermarriage in the United States." *Marriage and Family Review* 5, no. 1 (Spring 1971): 17-34.

7 Interracial Families

Renoir Gaither

Interracial families in the United States are significant in number. According to the 2000 U.S. Census, the householder and spouse in 6 percent of married couple households in the United States are of different races. The rate doubles for opposite-sex unmarried-partner households.[1] Highest numbers of mixed-race households are found in the West. Individuals who identify themselves as being of two or more races comprise 2.4 percent of the U.S. population or 6.8 million people, exceeding the American Indian and Alaska Native population.[2]

Scholarly interest in interracial families has mostly been in the areas of racial and ethnic identity formation and parental effects on child socialization. Aside from sociological and psychological research, there is also a considerable body of literature in the fields of clinical counseling and social services.

Frequently and understandably, materials that discuss interracial families include content surrounding issues of marriage or dating, identity, and transracial adoption. While it is difficult to separate these issues from the larger context of the family, these topics are treated in greater depth elsewhere in this volume. With this caveat, the scope of this chapter is narrowed to those resources that substantially contribute toward an understanding of the interracial family as a whole, including its dynamics and influence within larger social structures.

Books, periodical literature, dissertations, and digital information sources are included, with material from both scholarly and popular sources. All resources listed below are nonfiction and published in the last decade.

These resources were located by searching library catalogs and a host of databases including PsycINFO, Social Sciences Index, Family & Society Studies Worldwide, SocioFile, Ethnic Newswatch, Lexis-Nexis Academic, ProQuest Research Library, Dissertation Abstracts, and OCLC's WorldCat.

Alperson, Myra. *Dim Sum Bagels and Grits: A Sourcebook for Multi-cultural Families.* New York: Farrar, Straus & Giroux, 2001.

Written to an audience of adoptive families, Alperson's book cele-brates cultural diversity in myriad ways that focus on balancing the needs of family members within accommodating, diverse commu-nities. The book is a thoughtful introduction for those seeking to start or those who are in the process of starting intercultural fami-lies, and its keen blend of stories from experienced parents and professionals make for an upbeat how-to manual. Two chapters are devoted to resources such as publications, support organizations, websites, and culture camps.

Amlani, Alzak. "Exploring Cultures: Family Values in Interracial Cou-ples." *India Currents* 16, no. 5 (April 2002): 30.

Psychotherapist Amlani contributes insight into the impact of fam-ily values and culture on the dynamics of decision making among interracial couples from both South Asian and North American families of origin. Amlani finds that Westerners and Easterners are often nurtured by their complementary differences in regards to feelings of personal freedom, deference to extended family, and verbal expressiveness. A significant point of difference, Amlani stresses, may be couples' appreciation for cultural and religious traditions, and this is especially so for couples with children.

Breaux-Schropp, Anissa. *Parenting Biracial and Biethnic Children.* Ph.D. diss., Texas Woman's University, 2003.

This descriptive study surveys biological and adoptive parents of biracial and biethnic children to determine their sense of the chil-dren's unique needs and issues. Some research questions guiding this study ask how parents perceive their children's identity, how parents cope with issues of racial identification and diversity, and what classroom resources parents want to be available. Findings indicate that parents of biracial and biethnic children believe that it is important for their children to know and understand their dual heritages. These parents stress open communication about race and ethnicity. Also, parents in the study feel that schools need to attend to the needs of biracial/biethnic families and children.

Chow, Calire S. "Raising Children Biculturally." *A. Magazine: The Asian American Quarterly* 13, no. 7 (July 1998): 48-53.

Assuming the veracity of growing research suggesting that positive ethnic and cultural identity results in psychological well-being, Chow relates ways in which parents of biracial Asian American children can assist in helping their children develop positive feel-ings about identity. Chow asserts, "Unless parents make a con-scious commitment to helping children develop that part of their identity [Asian], chances are it won't happen." Chow suggests that ideally, parents should have positive, flexible ethnic identities, and discuss traditional activities and customs that they feel are important for their child. Chow also discusses early language training and time spent with extended family.

Dalmage, Heather M. *Tripping on the Color Line: Black-White Multiracial Families in a Racially Divided World*. New Brunswick, N.J.: Rutgers University Press, 2000.

Wife and mother in a multiracial family, author Dalmage explores how multiracial families contend with the color lines operating in America. Chapter 1 examines how multiracial families negotiate discrimination; chapter 2 inspects housing discrimination and its ramifications for multiracial families; chapter 3 scrutinizes racial identity among multiracial family members; and chapter 4 focuses on how individuals and families challenge racial categories. In Dalmage's words, "Ultimately, this book explores the ways in which multiracial family members' identities, politics, and communities both shape and are shaped by the color line."

Farmer, Robin. "A Family's Racial Journey." *Richmond Times Dispatch*, December 17, 2000.

The first installment of a seven-part series profiling interracial families in the Richmond, Virginia, area entitled "Crossing Color Lines," this article recounts the life of Rebecca McSween, a single White mother of a biracial son, Ben, and two other sons, both White, from a previous marriage. McSween relates painful experiences of family rejection from her parents and siblings, and her family's determination to remain close-knit despite troubling incidents in the community involving Ben. Her relationship with Ben's estranged father is noted, as well as its impact on Ben, currently a teacher and baseball coach, as well as a parent in an interracial family.

———. "Pastor's Lessons Reach Home." *Richmond Times Dispatch*, December 24, 2000.

Second of a seven-part series on interracial families in the Richmond, Virginia, area, this article profiles African American Reverend Joe Ellison's efforts to adopt foster child Donna, a White thirteen-year-old living precariously in their community. Farmer depicts Donna's troubled past living with her grandmother, and her eventual path toward a loving, stable relationship with Rev. Ellison and his wife. An interesting aspect of this article is its description of Donna's appropriation of a Black racial identity and the consequences for her in school and among her peers.

Fletcher-Stephens, Barbara J. *An Ethnographic Study of Interracial Couples, Mediating a Family Identity, and Cohesive Personal Identity Development in Their Biracial Children.* Ph.D. diss., Union Institute, 1998.

Using an ethnographic research approach, Fletcher-Stephens interviews interracial couples to study how their shared family identity is developed and maintained. The couples acknowledge the importance of educating their children about their biracial identity and presenting a balanced view of both parental families. They believe that passing on both positive and negative aspects of their families to children helps nurture a more satisfying self-identity. The study also finds that both parents are protective in shielding their children from negative societal views based on race. In addition, the study reveals that biracial children experience less identity conflict and have a greater ability to mediate social marginality when parents present balanced views of family.

Haizlip, Shirlee Taylor. *The Sweeter the Juice.* New York: Simon & Schuster, 1994.

Haizlip writes a wonderfully engaging family memoir that takes readers on a journey through the lives of her Black and White ancestors. Haizlip discovers the legacy of miscegenation and "passing" in her family, as she recounts the desertion of her "mulatto" grandfather in Washington, D.C., and its effects on her mother and siblings. She intelligently explores American notions of race and skin color through examination of census records, letters, and personal reflections from family members. Photographs are included.

Hickey, Gorden. "Turning Home into a Haven." *Richmond Times Dispatch*, December 31, 2000.

Hickey profiles Myung and Ryan Franz, an interracial couple raising three children. Myung, born in Korea, was adopted and brought to the United States at the age of four. Much of the article focuses on Myung, who was raised in a White, middle-class neighborhood, and the couple's ideas about choosing not to discuss issues of race or ethnic or cultural customs with their children. In contrast to Myung's experience, the Franz's express their desire to raise their children in a diverse environment, one where racial differences are more readily accepted. This profile illustrates a family taking an assimilation approach as a strategy for social integration, as well as the challenges associated with such an approach.

Kaeser, Gigi and Peggy Gillespie. *Of Many Colors: Portraits of Multiracial Families.* Amherst, Mass.: University of Massachusetts Press, 1997.

This collection of forty family portraits was published to accompany a traveling photo-text exhibit sponsored by Family Diversity Projects, Inc. It includes brief excerpts from interviews and Black and White photographs. Multiracial two-parent, gay, and single-parent families are presented in first-person narratives. Narratives from both parents and children offer a variety of observations, advice, and biographical material. Each selection has a sidebar with a single, direct quote taken from a family member. The exhibit is also available online at http://www.familydiv.org/ofmanycolors.

Kouri, Kristyan Marie. *Multiracial Families: Issues of Race, Culture Ideology and Identity.* Ph.D. diss., University of Southern California, 1994.

This study examines interracial couples' beliefs about marriage, family life, and their role in supporting their children's self-identity. The researcher interviewed twenty couples: ten Black women married to White men and ten White women married to Black men. Each couple had at least one natural child. Results show that "Black mothers and White fathers were more likely than White mothers and Black fathers to be sensitive to issues of identity" and to report racist incidents involving their children. Also, parents held similar beliefs in understanding their children's identities and helping them mediate discrimination.

Lazarre, Jane. *Beyond the Whiteness of Whiteness: Memoir of a White Mother of Black Sons.* Durham, N.C.: Duke University Press, 1996.

A Jewish novelist and teacher of African American autobiography, Lazarre writes a cogent memoir about raising her two biracial sons as they—and she—come to terms with their identities vis-à-vis a pervasively racist society. This memoir is as much a meta-cognitive survey of White attitudes toward race as it is a topical examination of race consciousness through the eyes of her sons, family members, and friends. Lazarre's feminist perspective adds depth to the loose narrative, a structure woven together with anecdotes, literary allusions, and passages of self-revelation.

Majete, Clayton. "What You May Not Know about Interracial Marriages." *Interrace*, no. 44 (March 1999): 8.

Majete describes his study of interracial couples with Black and White partners regarding family of origin reactions to their interracial relationship, and their children's racial identity. While some reported open hostility toward the relationship from both Black and White families of origin, Majete notes that nearly three-quarters of Black families do not express concern. Overall, 75 percent of families are at least open to the relationship. Over half of the couples report that their parents were "hesitant" about the relationship because of the impact on children. Most parents, Majete says, say they find no adequate label to describe their child's race, and that labeling itself was a societal imposition. Parents, for the most part, perceive that their children are comfortable with their biracial identity.

McBride, James. *The Color of Water: A Black Man's Tribute to His White Mother.* New York: Riverhead Books, 1996.

McBride writes a compelling, heartwarming memoir as one of twelve siblings born to a Jewish mother and an African American father. McBride describes growing up in Brooklyn, New York, during the 1960s and 1970s. His father died just before his birth, and his mother struggled to keep the family together during turbulent times. Chapters alternate between two narratives: his mother's life as a Polish immigrant living with an abusive father and handicapped mother in Suffolk, Virginia, then her eventual escape to New York and marriages to a Baptist minister and laborer; and the author's struggles forging an identity as an African American whose roots include Orthodox Judaism.

McFadden, John. "Intercultural Marriage and Family: Beyond the Racial Divide." *Family Journal* 9, no. 1 (January 2001): 39-42.

In this article directed at family counselors, McFadden briefly summarizes the research literature on interracial marriages from 1995 to 2000, including ethnographies, abbreviated histories, biographies, and empirical studies. The focus is on the dynamics of intercultural marriages and family and social relationships, taking into account both limiting and supportive factors that have an impact on multicultural families. The article includes an illustration depicting stages of individual and family acceptance of intermarriages, as well as a list of strategies for empowerment.

Melwani, Lavina. "The Changing Indian American Family: Beyond Black, White and Brown." *Little India* 6, no. 4 (April 1996): 10.

This article probes the experiences, challenges, and insights faced by interracial couples with one partner of Asian Indian descent and their families. Academics, writers, and filmmakers are among the couples whose perceptions are examined. Of particular concern to interracial families of Indian descent are questions of culture, gender roles, extended family ties, and children's religious affiliation. Successful, long-lasting relationships often hinge on humor, mutual respect for culture, commitment to marriage, and the degree to which a partner is accepted into an Indian family. The article includes comments from author Bharati Mukherjee, David Rathod, producer of the comedy *West is West*, and film director Gitanjali.

Minerbrook, Scott. *Divided to the Vein: A Journey into Race and Family.* New York: Harcourt Brace, 1996.

Framed by the story of the author's attempts to reconcile himself with his estranged, White family in Arkansas, this memoir is a chronicle of journalist Minerbrook's often turbulent life as the son of a woman of Scottish-Irish descent from a poor, working-class family in southern Arkansas and a troubled, Black middle-class man from Chicago. Growing up in the 1950s and 1960s, Minerbrook candidly describes his struggles negotiating the social boundaries of race and class as a biracial child while searching for love and affirmation from his parents and community. Sifting through the turbulence of his parents' marriage, racism harbored by his mother's family, and the intellectual and political battles centered on race during his years as an undergraduate at Harvard University, Minerbrook carves an ever-tenuous identity, strengthened by tolerance and reconciliation. Includes photographs.

Nakazawa, Donna Jackson. *Does Anybody Else Look Like Me? A Parent's Guide to Raising Multiracial Children.* Oxford: Perseus, 2003.

In this guidebook, Nakazawa combines anecdotes from her own experiences raising her two Japanese/White children, research on child development and educational philosophy, and information from interviews with sixty multiracial families. Chapters cover issues from the preschool years through adolescence and include topics such as healthy identity development, dealing with reactions from a child's peers and friends, and issues that arise in school settings. Includes lists of recommended books for children and teens.

Nero, Collette Leyva. *Interracial Children and Families: A Study of Biracial Ethnic Identity and Ethnic Socialization Processes.* Ph.D. diss., Texas A&M University, 2001.

Nero examines the racial identity of biracial children, parental ethnic socialization processes, and psychological adjustment of biracial children. Twenty families completed questionnaires of demographic data and ratings of emotional functioning of biracial children; interviews with parents were used to gather information about socialization patterns. Results suggest that the subject biracial children are not experiencing emotional or behavioral difficulties. Nero proposes that the children's healthy development is due to their being raised to identify with both sides of their ethnic heritage.

Niemann, Yolanda Flores. "Nurturing Antiracism: A Permeation of Life." In *Everyday Acts against Racism*, edited by Maureen T. Reddy, 31-39. Seattle, Wash.: Seal Press, 1996.

Niemann, who is Mexican American, shares her successes and failures as the mother of two biracial children in helping to promote antiracist attitudes in her children, spouse, and students. Niemann relates incidents of racism in her children's lives that provided teaching moments. She also gives insightful examples of times when her Anglo-American husband is made aware of the subtle aspects of White privilege. This brief, self-reflective essay is one in a collection of pieces focusing on pedestrian acts against racism.

Okun, Barbara F. *Understanding Diverse Families: What Practitioners Need to Know.* New York: Guilford Press, 1996.

Okun's guide for therapists provides an excellent starting source for information on sociologically diverse families in the United States with three chapters that treat the subject of multiracial families. Chapter 8, "About Multiraciality: The Participants," provides a historical context of race relations, reviews dominant theories of interracial marriages, and presents issues regarding transracial adoption, interracial relationships, and families of origin. Chapter 9 entitled, "Multiraciality Across the Life Span," highlights racial, biracial, and multiracial identity development theories; identity formation models of interracial couples; and parenting issues across life spans. Chapter 10 discusses treatment implications for therapists working with multiracial clients.

Orbe, Mark P. "Communicating about Race in Interracial Families." In *Communication, Race, and Family: Exploring Communication in Black, White, and Biracial Families*, edited by Thomas J. Socha and Rhunette C. Diggs, 167-180. Mahwah, N.J.: Lawrence Erlbaum Associates, Inc., 1999.

Descriptive rather than theoretical, this essay examines four ways interracial families approach their communication about race or racial identity, and attention is devoted to how parents communicate such topics to their biracial or multiracial children. The approaches are listed as (1) embracing the Black experience; (2) assuming a commonsense approach; (3) advocating a colorblind society; and (4) affirming the multiethnic experience. Orbe concludes that many factors inform these perspectives, including gender, age, spirituality, socioeconomic status, family structure, and geographic location.

Oriti, Bruno, Amy Bibb, and Jayne Mahboubi. "Family-Centered Practice with Racially/Ethnically Mixed Families." *Families in Society* 77, no. 9 (November 1996): 573-582.

This article presents brief clinical case studies of multiracial families adapting to sociopolitical forces of oppression within their families and communities. The authors advocate a strengths perspective, rather than pathological, for family care practitioners helping mixed-race/ethnic families manage life experiences. Some suggestions include recognizing and articulating multiple identities, choosing ethical and moral stances toward diversity, and addressing divisive issues openly. Practitioner guidelines are included.

Prentiss, Suzanne M. *A Qualitative Investigation into the Experiences of Parenting Biracial (Black-White) Children.* Ph.D. diss., University of Tennessee, 2002.

This qualitative study examines the experiences of ten parents, African American or Caucasian, of eleven biracial children to gather information regarding their interracial romantic relationships, family reactions to the relationship, and the rewards and challenges they faced rearing their children. Topics involving parenting of biracial children include preparation for prejudice, racial self-identity, and racist incidents. Also, parents share advice on parenting biracial children.

Radina, M. Elise, and Teresa M. Cooney. "Relationship Quality between Multiracial Adolescents and Their Biological Parents." *American Journal of Orthopsychiatry* 70, no. 4 (October 2000): 445-454.

Authors compare single-race White and minority adolescents to multiracial adolescents in terms of the quality of the relationship with their parents. Three relationship dimensions are examined: interaction, communication, and emotional closeness. Interviews were conducted with 1,870 (69.5 percent) single-race White, 534 (20 percent) single-race minority, and 284 (10.5 percent) multiracial adolescents. Findings indicate that overall, few differences exist between multiracial and single-race adolescents in quality of parent-adolescent relationships. Multiracial boys report significantly lower levels of relationship quality with fathers, in terms of communication and emotional closeness, than did White adolescent boys. Also, multiracial girls report greater behavioral contact with mothers than did White girls, and more contact with fathers than did their single-race peers.

Root, Maria P.P. "The Color of Love." *The American Prospect* 13, no. 7 (April 2002): 54-55.

Root examines the behavior of families who have members in racially mixed marriages and asks "What differentiates those families who can welcome someone racially different from those families who cannot?" Root views families as open or closed systems of relationships. She finds open families accepting of intermarriage; closed or monarchical families less tolerant or hostile. An interracial marriage in closed families, says Root, is often seen as "disloyal," a rejection of "filial obligation." Closed families often have strict criteria for acceptance of marriage partners, and the rigidity of standards often arises from prejudices or unrealistic expectations. Root notes also that opposition to interracial marriage often reflects fears about lost traditions and treatment of children in a racist society.

Segal, Josylyn Cahn. *Shades of Community and Conflict: Biracial Adults of African-American and Jewish-American Heritage.* Ph.D. diss., Wright Institute, 1997.

Eighteen biracial adults of African American and Jewish American heritage participated in this study of racial/ethnic identity and parental closeness. The following hypotheses were supported: (1) the biracial adult phenotypically perceived as African American is more likely to identify as such; the biracial adult phenotypically perceived as White, however, is more likely to identify as either White or "mixed'; (2) it is not necessary that the biracial child be close to the African American parent to identify with African American heritage; (3) it is necessary that the biracial individual be close to the Jewish parent to identify with Jewish heritage, although this is not a sufficient condition; and (4) for those identified as "close" to their Jewish parent, the degree of closeness is related to the degree to which they identify as Jews.

Twine, France Winddance. "Transgressive Women and Transracial Mothers: White Women and Critical Race Theory." *Meridians: Feminism, Race, Transnationalism* 1, no. 2 (2001): 130-153.

This astute essay, informed by feminist and critical race theory, examines how White mothers of biracial children with Black fathers are punished through forms of surveillance and social exclusion similar to Black mothers. Using examples of mothers in Great Britain, Twine asserts that "transracial motherhood is considered a deviation from idealized motherhood," and is often considered by family of origin members and the community as a "transgressive act." Hospitals and unwed mothers' homes are "sites of surveillance," contends Twine, institutions where White transracial mothers risk loss of control over reproductive choice and abusive treatment. Further, such mothers are often met with threats of family expulsion or public displays of racist abuse. Includes photographs.

Wardle, Francis. *Tomorrow's Children: Meeting the Needs of Multiracial and Multiethnic Children at Home, in Early Childhood Programs, and at School.* Denver, Colo.: Center for the Study of Biracial Children, 1999.

Directed at an audience of parents, social workers, and educators, Wardle's book addresses aspects such as identity, stereotypes, and adoption issues for multiracial children. Chapters include supporting multiracial children in school, ideas and activities for the home, and parenting strategies. A partner in an interracial marriage, Wardle includes personal experiences and academic studies in this book that advocate the psychological and political well-being of interracial families. Lists of resources such as books for parents and children, organizations, and websites are provided.

———. "What about the Research?" *Interrace*, no. 41 (March 1998): 16.

In this article, Wardle attacks some of the negative assumptions he sees in the research literature on biracial children and their families. Wardle asserts that biased assumptions guided by a notion that biracial children are essentially dysfunctional and maladjusted have historically been and continue to be used. He debunks what he sees as faulty research methods: poor sampling procedures, statistical error, and inadequate models, such as single-race personality models used to support research in biracial and multiracial identity development. Another central claim here is that researchers themselves approach the subject of interracial families with biases that may alter experimental results. Wardle also asserts that researchers often ask the "wrong questions," and therefore misinterpret the results.

Wehrly, Bea, Kelly R. Kenney, and Mark E. Kenney. *Counseling Multiracial Families.* Thousand Oaks, Calif.: Sage Publications, 1999.

Especially helpful for multicultural counseling professionals and social workers, Wehrly's book provides historical and contemporary perspectives on issues associated with interracial families, as well as counseling interventions. Chapter 1 provides a historical overview of multiracial social and legal experience in the United States, and a brief outline of associated myths and stereotypes. Chapter 2 emphasizes parenting and child rearing by contemporary interracial couples, including gay and lesbian couples. Implications for counseling interracial couples are examined. Chapter 3 discusses issues of multiracial individuals across the lifespan. Multiracial identity models and recent research on identity and mental health are explored. Chapter 4 addresses issues surrounding transracial adoption and foster home placement. Chapter 5 presents recent counseling approaches, interventions, and strategies for working with multiracial populations. Chapter 6 provides five case studies.

Wright, Marguerite A. *I'm Chocolate, You're Vanilla: Raising Healthy Black and Biracial Children in a Race-Conscious World.* San Francisco, Calif.: Jossey-Bass Publishers, 1998.

A guide for parents and educators, Wright's book offers a developmental assessment of how Black and biracial children acquire racial awareness. Wright addresses how children come to understand race, acquire racial attitudes, and negotiate the racial impact on self-esteem and stereotyping from early childhood to adolescence. A developmental psychologist, Wright supports her assertions with a wide range of scholarly and popular sources, interviews with children, and personal anecdotes. Checklists are numerous; examples include "Things to Consider When Planning to Send Children to an Afrocentric School" and "Questions for Teachers to Consider When Selecting Books, Poems, Songs, and Videos." A chart, "Stages of Race Awareness," is included as an appendix.

Websites

Interracial Families in Friendship. http://www.simplyliving.org/ifif/index.htm [May 19, 2003].

This organization offers support to interracial families through social networking. Families are based throughout the mid-Ohio region. The site includes an extensive list of links to various transracial adoption sites, as well as sites with interracial themes. The site includes a photo album of member families and friends and a link to the organization's electronic list.

Interracial Family Circle. http://interracialfamilycircle.org [May 19, 2003].

Founded in 1984, the Washington, D.C.-based Interracial Family Circle (IFC) strives to "recognize, advance, and protect the rights of interracial and multicultural individuals, unions, and families." The IFC holds roundtable discussions, public forums, and living room chats on issues surrounding multiracial families. While membership is not exclusive to individuals living in the Washington, D.C. area, many of the events announced at the site, including day trips, book club meetings, and playgroups, involve local area participation. The site includes resources such as book reviews, archived articles of members' life experiences, a bibliography of children's books, and other articles such as legal rulings and commentaries of interest to interracial families.

Multiracial Family Circle. http://www.cdiversity.com/mfc/ [May 19, 2003].

Based in Kansas City, Missouri, the Multiracial Family Circle's mission is two-fold: "to provide opportunities for education, support, and socialization for multiracial individuals, families, and people involved in interracial relationships" and to "educate the public and policy-makers about the existence and worth of multiracial people and families." The organization sponsors monthly meetings and social events around the area. The website includes information resources for both parents and adolescents. Also included is a geographic listing of support organizations nationally.

Swirl, Inc. http://www.swirlinc.org/ [May 19, 2003].

Founded in 2000, Swirl, Inc., is a national non-profit organization that "aims to build mixed race communities while providing support to mixed adults, mixed families, transracial adoptees, and inter-racial/cultural couples." Swirl has chapters in New York City, Arkansas, San Francisco, Boston, Long Island, Los Angeles, Minneapolis, Philadelphia, and South Florida. Monthly events include dining out, writers' circles, book club sessions, and film screenings. The organization also has an electronic list for its membership.

Notes

1. Tavia Stephens and Martin O'Connell, "Married Couple and Unmarried-Partner Households: 2000." U.S. Census Bureau, U.S. Government Printing Office, Washington, D.C., 2003.

2. Hobbs, Frank, and Nicole Stoops, "Demographic Trends in the 20th Century." U.S. Census Bureau, Census 2000 Special Reports, Series CENSR-4, U.S. Government Printing Office, Washington, D.C., 2002.

8   Transracial Adoption

Darlene Nichols

There is no data on the number of transracial adoptions that take place each year in the United States, though scholars believe the number to be very small. And yet a vast number of pages have been written to address this highly controversial practice. There is no lack of research, commentary, personal essays, news reports, letters, and web pages devoted to advocating for, or arguing against transracial adoption. Very few take a middle road.

The Early Days: Optimism and Hope

Transracial adoption (often abbreviated TRA) is a relatively recent phenomenon. Standard American adoption placement practices prior to about the mid-1960s focused on matching children to prospective parents on the basis of physical characteristics, ethnicity, and sometimes religion. Attempting to hide the adoption by masking it with physical similarities was assumed to make adjustment easier for children and their adoptive parents. War triggered a change. Asian children of American servicemen from Korea, Japan, Vietnam, and elsewhere were typically rejected by the homogeneous societies into which they were born. Many of them were abandoned by both mother and father. Other Asian-born children, separated from their families by war and labeled "orphans" even if a family existed, also earned awareness and concern in the United States. Thus, the 1950s saw the beginning of movements to promote transracial adoption of children from Asia.

Social movements of the 1960s stirred a romantic idealism that racial differences were near an end. Some White adoptive parents saw transracial adoption as a way to break down racial barriers and promote integration. Others simply wanted a child to rear, and African American children were more readily available as the numbers of healthy White children decreased. Much of the writing during this period expressed hope that transracial adoption would mean placements for the many non-White children waiting for adoption. A number of advice books for adoptive or prospective adoptive parents were written to describe the process of negotiating a transracial adoption and how to help the children adjust once they arrived in their new homes (almost invariably middle class, White homes). Some advice for social workers involved in transracial adoption placements appeared as well. The sources below are representative of those optimistic expectations.

Anderson, David C. *Children of Special Value: Interracial Adoption in America.* New York: St. Martin's Press, 1971.

> The first part of this book recounts the personal experiences of several families with transracially adopted children. The remainder of the book discusses adoption in general, such as issues related to the process of adopting, interacting with agencies, children's questions about their birth origins, and adoptees' efforts to search for birth parents. The author concludes with a brief chapter on the controversy surrounding TRA.

Bullough, Vern L. "Interracial Adoption." *Humanist* 28, no. 2 (1968): 10-11.

> An adoptive father of children of several races wrote this brief essay in support of transracial adoption. He describes the social environment of the day that he feels makes TRA a viable choice for parents seeking to adopt and counters arguments against it. He takes a very rosy-eyed view of the state of race relations in the United States and offers his outlook for future change. This article illuminates the ongoing controversy that continues into the twenty-first century.

de Hartog, Jan. *The Children: A Personal Record for the Use of Adoptive Parents.* New York: Atheneum, 1968.

> Jan de Hartog, father of two daughters from Korea, presents frank advice to potential adoptive parents of his day. His advice is drawn not only from his own experiences, but from many other adoptive parents of Korean and Vietnamese children with whom he communicated. He discusses numerous practicalities including the process of adoption, cultural differences that may make children who are not infants confused or distressed, managing families that already have biological children, and dealing with race-related issues. This book gives some insight into how international adoptions were carried out in the 1960s as well as an early perspective on interracial adoption.

Doss, Helen Grigsby. *The Family Nobody Wanted.* Boston: Little, Brown, 1954.

> When, during the Depression, Californians Helen and Carl Doss learned they would never conceive children, they naively pursued

adoption expecting it to be quick and easy. But as a theology student, Carl Doss had very little money to live on and he and his wife were repeatedly rejected as suitable candidates as adoptive parents. Helen Doss was very determined, however, and, before their story ended, they had not one, but twelve children, most of them of mixed-race heritage. While most of the book focuses on family life, Helen Doss does address race and the reactions of social workers, family, and strangers. Transracial adoption was rare before the 1960s, making this book an interesting view of a family that was in the vanguard of the transracial adoption trend. Other accounts of the Doss family appeared in popular magazines such as *Life* (November 12, 1951, January 14, 1952), *Reader's Digest* (August 1949), and *McCall's* (September 1954).

Fanshel, David. *Far from the Reservation: The Transracial Adoption of American Indian Children.* Metuchen, N.J.: Scarecrow Press, 1972.

In the 1960s the federal government's Bureau of Indian Affairs and the Child Welfare League of America jointly ran a program called the Indian Adoption Project. Indian children deemed in need of new families were placed in adoptive homes. In most cases, their new families were White. Fanshel's research on ninety-seven families into which Indian children had been placed spanned the decade. This book reports his findings about both the parents and the children.

Fricke, Harriet. "Interracial Adoption: The Little Revolution." *Social Work* 10, no. 3 (1965): 92-97.

The author, case director of the Lutheran Children's Friend Society in Minneapolis, describes her early experiences with the placement of African American children into White homes. While done with some misgivings, the social workers involved all felt that the outcome was ultimately positive. This is an example of an early, optimistic view of the potential of TRA.

Jones, Edmund D. "Transracial Adoption of Black Children." *Child Welfare* 51, no. 3 (1972): 156-64.

Originally presented as a speech to the Open Door Society, an organization that promoted transracial adoption, in 1971, this is one of the earliest essays by a Black writer arguing against TRA. He questions White parents' ability to truly instill a Black identity in an adopted child, the impact of TRA on the adoptive parents' relationships with others, the tendency to focus on the needs and desires of the White parents rather than those of the children, the social and cultural assumptions of established social welfare practices, and other issues that remain a concern even into the twenty-first century.

Lyslo, Arnold. "Adoptive Placement of American Indian Children with Non-Indian Families." In *Readings in Adoption*, edited by I. Evelyn Smith, 231-236. New York: Philosophical Library, 1963.

The director of the Indian Adoption Project, established in 1958 as a cooperative effort of the federal government's Bureau of Indian Affairs and the Child Welfare League of America, briefly describes the social context, goals, and outcomes of the project.

Mitchell, Marion M. "Transracial Adoptions: Philosophy and Practice." *Child Welfare* 48, no. 10 (1969): 613-619.

Mitchell briefly describes the history of transracial adoption in North America prior to 1969. She describes for placement workers the philosophy and practice of TRA. Mitchell addresses issues associated with the placement workers' commitment, how to conduct the home study, and concerns about the healthy development of a child's racial identity. After providing a detailed case study, she concludes with a description of some organizations for parents who have adopted transracially.

Sellers, Martha G. "Transracial Adoption." *Child Welfare* 48, no. 6 (1969): 355.

Sellers describes the criteria used in her adoption placement agency to determine the appropriateness of placing a Black or mixed child with White adoptive parents. Among the qualities sought in prospective parents are meaningful experience with various racial groups, relatives who accept the non-White child as a family member, and the ability to allow the child to accept his racial identity.

Contention Arises

Everything changed in 1972. In that year the National Association of Black Social Workers (NABSW), a young organization founded in 1968 during a turbulent period of racial unrest and conflict, issued a statement labeling transracial adoption of African American children by White families nothing short of "racial genocide." This statement, of course, did not have the force of law, but many social workers, policy makers, and state legislatures heard, and the adoption of African American children by White parents quickly became much more difficult, if not illegal, in some states in the 1970s and 1980s. Then, in 1978, Congress passed the Indian Child Welfare Act, severely restricting adoption of American Indian children by non-Indian families. At least in part stimulated by the negative voice of NABSW, a number of researchers began to examine the impact of transracial adoption, and numerous works published after 1972 described the results of these research projects. Virtually all concluded that transracial adoption was detrimental neither to the children nor to their families. On the other side of the fight were articles challenging that research on the basis of methodology, cultural assumptions, and fundamental philosophies. Personal accounts continued to appear as well, but with more political awareness than those of earlier decades. Most of the sources below are scholarly publications, indicating the heightened interested among researchers and academics in the TRA controversy.

Andujo, Estela. "Ethnic Identity of Transethnically Adopted Hispanic Adolescents." *Social Work* 33, no. 6 (1988): 531-535.
Andujo compared the ethnic identities of transracially adopted Mexican American children and those adopted by Mexican American families in California in the 1970s. The adoptees were between twelve and seventeen at the time of the study. The study included interviews with the adoptees and their parents as well as adoptee responses to several self-concept questionnaires. While all of the adoptees had similar levels of self-esteem, the transracially adopted children were less likely to have a Hispanic identity. Recommendations for placement workers and parents are included.

Chimezie, Amuzie. "Bold but Irrelevant: Grow and Shapiro on Transracial Adoption." *Child Welfare* 56, no. 2 (1977): 75-86.
Grow and Shapiro were among the first to systematically study the impact of TRA on children and parents. Chimezie was one of the first to examine their research and critique both methodology and findings. Chimezie concluded that the Grow-Shapiro study did not seriously address the issue of Black identity. Suggestions for a more meaningful study design are presented.

———. "Transracial Adoption of Black Children." *Social Work* 20, no. 4 (1975): 296-301.
Writing in a decade of great upheaval, change, and challenge in transracial adoption practices, the author lays out arguments against the transracial adoption of African American children by White families.

Duling, Gretchen A. *Adopting Joe: A Black Vietnamese Child.* Rutland, Vt.: C.E. Tuttle Co., 1977.
Duling, an adoptive mother of a Black-Vietnamese child, describes her personal experiences during her first year with her son, adopted at age three. In addition to describing the general experience of

adopting a child from abroad, she also talks about the reactions of family, friends, and even strangers to their mixed family.

Grow, Lucille J., and Deborah Shapiro. *Black Children, White Parents: A Study of Transracial Adoption.* New York: Research Center, 1974.

This study, conducted by the Child Welfare League of America and sponsored by the Office of Child Development of the U.S. Department of Health, Education, and Welfare, was completed not long after the National Association of Black Social Workers formally stated its opposition to the practice of TRA. Over one hundred children aged six and over were evaluated along with their families. The researchers concluded that about 77 percent of the adoptions were "successful"—a figure then comparable to those found in studies with in-race adoptions. A chapter is devoted to the problem of defining success, which was judged on multiple dimensions including responses to personality tests, emotionality tests, views of adults in their lives, interactions with peers, and attitudes toward "Blackness." Though somewhat difficult to navigate and clearly based on 1970s assumptions of what is "normal," this is a trail-blazing work in the study of transracially adopted people and their families.

Howard, Alicia, David D. Royse, and John A. Skerl. "Transracial Adoption: Black-Community Perspective." *Social Work* 22, no. 3 (1977): 184-189.

Researchers surveyed 150 African American households in Dayton, Ohio, to determine their attitudes toward TRA. Their research showed that most respondents did not support the position of the National Association of Black Social Workers, which militantly opposed TRA. When institutionalization or permanent foster care was presented as the alternative, an even higher percentage of respondents felt that TRA was acceptable.

Johnson, Penny R., Joan F. Shireman, and Kenneth W. Watson. "Transracial Adoption and the Development of Black Identity at Age Eight." *Child Welfare* 66, no. 1 (1987): 45-55.

The authors report on a longitudinal study of forty-two TRA placements and forty-five in-race placements in the Chicago area in the 1970s. Parents were interviewed shortly after the placement and then again along with the children when the children were four and eight. The children were reported to be well-adjusted with a positive Black identity, at least through the elementary school years, but concern was expressed by authors that the parents seemed to be moving away from teaching a strong Black identity to a "human race" identity. Children were also less in contact with other Black people as they grew older.

Ladner, Joyce A. *Mixed Families: Adopting across Racial Boundaries.* Garden City, N.Y.: Anchor Press/Doubleday, 1977.

Ladner, a Black sociologist, worked with 136 families made up of White parents and adopted Black children. She interviewed the parents and, in some cases, the children (both adopted and biological), other family members, friends, and neighbors. She also spoke with adoption workers and policy makers. She describes the very complex nature of TRA in the 1970s, examining the motives parents have for adopting transracially, the feelings of the children about their environments, and the roles of placement workers in a period where policies were shifting from supporting TRA to virtually eliminating it.

The Pendulum Swings: Transracial Adoption and the Law

The landscape for transracial adoption changed again in 1994 with Congressional passage of the Multiethnic Placement Act (MEPA) which specifically restricted the use of race as a factor in adoption placements. The provisions of the Indian Child Welfare Act remained intact, however, as the 1994 Act states: "Nothing in this section shall be construed to affect the application of the Indian Child Welfare Act of 1978." It was followed in 1996 by clarifying legislation, the Removal of Barriers to Interethnic Adoption Provision, which was tacked onto the end of the Small Business Job Protection Act of 1996. Despite the passage of these laws, arguments in the literature have remained heated, though legal realities are, in some cases, grudgingly acknowledged.

Research and writing on TRA continued to expand in the late 1980s and 1990s, producing an enormous wealth of material, including further research, commentary, and discussion by academic observers as well as practitioners.

Alexander, Ralph, Jr., and Carla M. Curtis. "A Review of Empirical Research Involving the Transracial Adoption of African American Children." *Journal of Black Psychology* 22, no. 2 (1996): 223-235.

Alexander and Curtis conducted a critical review of the research literature on transracially adopted Black children. They describe the numerous studies conducted over the previous two decades and summarize the results. In all of these studies, the children were found to be similar to children adopted in-race, both in terms of adjustment and intelligence. While the studies seem to overwhelmingly suggest that Black children of White adoptive parents fare well, the authors question the methodology and biases of the researchers, most of whom were White. Recommendations for policies and research are included. The May 1996 issue of the *Journal of Black Psychology* includes several reactions to Alexander and Curtis' article. Some of the reactions appear in this list.

Baden, Amanda L., and Robbie J. Steward. "A Framework for Use with Racially and Culturally Integrated Families: The Cultural-Racial Identity Model as Applied to Transracial Adoption." *Journal of Social Distress and the Homeless* 9, no. 4 (2000): 309-337.

To frame their Cultural-Racial Identity model, the authors provide an excellent overview of the theoretical foundations of and research literature on identity development in general, in racial minorities, and in adoptees. They also review theory and research specific to identity formation in transracial adoptees prior to proposing their own model. This model allows for both a cultural identity and racial identity, blending these to produce sixteen potential cultural-racial identities, each of which is described. Each distinct identity represents the degree to which the adoptee expresses a sense of belonging to a parent's racial groups or self-identified groups. This model is theoretical and not supported by research within the article. A later article (Baden, "The Psychological Adjustment of Transracial Adoptees: An Application of the Cultural-Racial Identity Model," *Journal of Social Distress and the Homeless* 11, no. 2, April 2002) is the first empirical study of the model, producing positive but not statistically significant conclusions about the model's validity.

Bausch, Robert S., and Richard T. Serpe. "Negative Outcomes of Interethnic Adoption of Mexican American Children." *Social Work* 42, no. 2 (1997): 136-143.

This study focuses on the attitude of Mexican American adults toward transracial adoption of Mexican American children by White families. Respondents, all California residents, were asked to indicate their level of agreement with the following possible outcomes of interethnic adoption: (1) the child may have an ethnic identity conflict; (2) the child may forget his or her Latino background; (3) the child's participation in Latino cultural events may be limited; and (4) the child may not acquire the skills to cope with racism. They were also asked to describe their own level of cultural participation (e.g., celebrating cultural holidays such as Cinco de Mayo) and provide demographic information such as income and educational level. Correlations between these characteristics and respondent attitudes are described. Respondents were also asked about perceived barriers to adoption for Hispanic American families. Overall, about half of the respondents felt that TRA would have a negative impact on Mexican American children adopted into White families.

———. "Recruiting Mexican American Adoptive Parents." *Child Welfare* 78, no. 5 (1999): 693-716.

This study of 591 Mexican Americans in California assesses perceived structural and cultural barriers to Mexican American families adopting children. Structural factors such as lack of information or inadequate finances are considered by respondents to be more significant than cultural factors such as machismo and familism. Finally, the authors present a set of recruitment strategies to encourage Mexican American adoption of Mexican American children based on responses of survey participants.

Bowman, Jennifer. "Teaching Tolerance." *Raising Black and Biracial Children* 6, no. 3 (2002): 36.

Bowman gives advice to White parents considering adopting a Black or biracial child. The author is a Black adoptee of White parents.

Bradley, Carla, and Cynthia G. Hawkins-Leon. "The Transracial Adoption Debate: Counseling and Legal Implications." *Journal of Counseling and Development* 80, no. 4 (2002): 433-440.

The authors challenge the conclusions drawn in numerous studies of transracial adoptees and examine the flaws and implicit assumptions of the research, including the often-cited longitudinal study conducted by Simon and Altstein. They describe relevant federal laws passed in the 1990s, and discuss the implications of the Multiethnic Placement Act (1994), Removal of Barriers to Interethnic Adoption Provision (1996), and the Adoption and Safe Families Act (1997). Finally, they offer recommendations for social workers and counselors working with transracially adoptive families.

Brandt, Joshua. "How Jews Blend Three Cultures with Asian Adoptions." *Jewish Bulletin* 104, no. 33 (2000): 1A.

Brandt describes the experiences of several Jewish families and single women who have adopted children from China. Overall their experiences have been positive but they are faced with the challenge of integrating three cultures: Chinese, Jewish, and American.

Brooks, Devon, Richard P. Barth, Alice Bussiere, and Glendora Patterson. "Adoption and Race: Implementing the Multiethnic Placement Act and the Interethnic Adoption Provisions." *Social Work* 44, no. 2 (1999): 167-178.

> The members of the Adoption and Race Work Group of the Stuart Foundation summarize their two-year analysis of racial matching and child welfare services. The article describes the controversy over TRA, particularly in the context of the Multiethnic Placement Act of 1994 (Public Law 103-382 Sections 551-553). Authors describe problems raised by MEPA, such as lack of funding to support it and vague wording, which leaves considerable room for interpretation. The article focuses on proposed policies, or "principles," for carrying out the requirements of the MEPA, despite its problems.

Curtis, Carla M. "The Adoption of African American Children by Whites: A Renewed Conflict." *Families in Society: The Journal of Contemporary Human Services* 77, no. 3 (1996): 156-165.

> This article includes a concise review of the literature addressing the arguments for and against TRA over the past three decades. The author places the controversy in the context of the Multiethnic Placement Act of 1994 and describes related legislation and legal cases. The author offers policy recommendations for managing the placement of African American children.

Forde-Mazrui, Kim. "Black Identity and Child Placement: The Best Interests of Black and Biracial-Children." *Michigan Law Review* 92, no. 4 (1994): 925-967.

> This note reviews case law on race matching as an adoption practice in the context of child's best interests. The author concludes that a race matching placement policy in adoption is not generally in the best interests of Black and biracial children nor is it in the best interests of the African American community as a whole.

Goddard, Lawford L. "Transracial Adoption: Unanswered Theoretical and Conceptual Issues." *Journal of Black Psychology* 22, no. 2 (1996): 273-281.

> Goddard responds to the critical literature review by Alexander and Curtis (1996) cited earlier. He points out some weaknesses and problems of social science research in general, particularly in the failure to adequately recognize and value cultural differences. Social scientists, who assume cultural homogeneity as do most researchers on the outcomes of TRA, fail to recognize that meanings of concepts are not necessarily equivalent across cultures. Goddard calls for Black researchers to develop theoretical frameworks in which to conduct research on child development and TRA.

Gordon, Linda. *The Great Arizona Orphan Abduction.* Cambridge, Mass.: Harvard University Press, 1999.

In the late nineteenth and early twentieth centuries thousands of poor urban children, who may or may not have actually been orphans, were sent by "orphan train" to live with rural American families. In 1904, 57 Irish American Catholic children from New York were sent by orphan train to live with Mexican American Catholic families in Arizona. The primarily Protestant White neighbors of the Mexican American families were outraged to the point of using vigilante tactics to "rescue" the children and place them with White families. The events caught some media attention and ended with court intervention. Some accounts contemporary to the event appeared in the *New York Times* on October 13, October 16, and November 5, 1904.

Herman, Bobby E. "It Takes a Whole Village." *Raising Black and Biracial Children* 5, no. 1 (2000): 21.

Author Herman, initially opposed to TRA, describes his interactions with some White parents of transracially adopted children and how he has come to believe that TRA can work.

Hollinger, Joan H., and ABA National Resource Center on Legal and Court Issues. *A Guide to the Multiethnic Placement Act of 1994: As Amended by the Interethnic Adoption Provisions of 1996.* Washington, D.C.: The Resource Center, 1998.

This guide was designed to help placement workers understand and meet the requirements of the Multiethnic Placement Act of 1994 and the Removal of Barriers to Interethnic Adoption Act of 1996. Includes the text of both acts and other relevant documents.

Hollingsworth, Leslie Doty. "Promoting Same-Race Adoption for Children of Color." *Social Work* 43, no. 2 (1998): 104-116.

Hollingsworth briefly describes the history of TRA in the United States. She then argues that culturally-sensitive recruitment strategies, eligibility standards, and post-adoption support and services would increase the number of prospective African American adoptive parents. She also suggests that other options should be considered for placement of minority children, such as kinship foster care (subsidized child care) as permanent placements. She recommends that adoption placement agencies address the inequities she sees inherent in the policies and practices.

———. "Sociodemographic Influences in the Prediction of Attitudes toward Transracial Adoption." *Families in Society: The Journal of Contemporary Human Services* 81, no. 1 (2000): 92-100.

A national opinion poll conducted three years prior to the passage of the Multiethnic Placement Act of 1994 showed that most of the

916 respondents to the telephone survey approved of transracial adoptions. Significant differences appear, however, when race, age and gender are considered: the most accepting viewpoints were by African American men and Caucasian women, and younger people tended to be more approving than those over fifty-five. Other variables were also considered. The impact of media portrayals of TRA are discussed briefly.

————. "Symbolic Interactionism, African American Families, and the Transracial Adoption Controversy." *Social Work* 44, no. 5 (1999): 443-453.

Hollingsworth offers a well-considered explanation for the opposition of some African Americans to TRA. Opening with a brief historical review of the TRA controversy, the primary thrust of the article is to frame the arguments against TRA in a cultural context, indicating the meaning of family and children to people of African descent and the importance of socializing African American children in that context. The author also includes an overview of relevant legislation from the late 1970s. Recommendations for a research agenda conclude the article.

"Home Front: Is Love Enough?" *Black Child* 2, no. 2 (1996): 12.

The anonymous author of this article summarizes arguments for and against TRA and describes some state legislation as well as the federal Multiethnic Placement Act of 1994. After describing the experiences of some transracially adopted people, using quotes from the adoptees to support his arguments, the author concludes that TRA is ultimately in the best interest of children and should not be a political issue.

Kearns, Maureen. "Whites Raising Blacks." *Black Child* 2, no. 2 (1998): 23.

Kearns gives advice to White parents on some ways to arm their African American adopted children against racism.

Koenig, Karen. "Interracial Adoption Extends the Family but Can Also Divide It." *Jewish Bulletin* 102, no. 50 (1998): 7.

In this brief personal account of a Jewish single mother of a Korean-born son, Koenig recounts her experiences as a Jewish woman and the mixed feelings of her family when she chose to adopt interracially.

Lovett-Tisdale, Marilyn, and Bruce Anthony Purnell. "It Takes an Entire Village." *Journal of Black Psychology* 22, no. 2 (1996): 266-269.

Lovett-Tisdale and Purnell respond to the article by Alexander and Curtis (1996) cited above. The authors discuss informal adoption in the African American community and how it can be encouraged and supported. They also offer additional comments on problems with the Eurocentric viewpoint of much of the research done on TRA.

MacEachron, Ann E., Nora S. Gustavsson, Suzanne Cross, and Allison Lewis. "The Effectiveness of the Indian Child Welfare Act of 1978." *Social Service Review* 70, no. 3 (1996): 451-463.

The 1978 Indian Child Welfare Act sought to minimize the number of Native American children placed in non-Native families as part of an effort by the federal government to increase tribal self-determination and preservation. The authors evaluated the effectiveness of the act by reviewing several sources of data on placements, including information from the Bureau of Indian Affairs and the Association of American Indian Affairs. Their research suggests that the number of placements of Native American children declined significantly between 1978 and 1986, when it reached a level comparable to placements of non-Native children.

McPherson, Carolyn Flanders, and Jeremy Mario Minton. *Our Native American Child.* Southfield, Mich.: Spaulding for Children, 1994.

This introduction to adoption of Native American children by non-Native families is designed to encourage families to consider adoption. Spaulding for Children is an adoption organization that aims to promote the adoption of "special needs" children. This book is one in a series on adoption in different religious communities. Available at the publisher's website, http://www.spaulding.org.

McRoy, Ruth G., Zena Oglesby, and Helen Grape. "Achieving Same-Race Adoptive Placements for African American Children: Culturally Sensitive Practice Approaches." *Child Welfare* 76, no. 1 (1997): 85-104.

Although there is evidence that many African American couples are open to considering adoption, actual numbers of completed adoptions to African American couples are small. The authors describe some of the factors that may present barriers for prospective African American adoptive parents, such as the preponderance of White female placement workers in adoption agencies, lack of cultural competencies and understanding among placement workers, requirements based on middle-class White standards, and high fees. The authors describe programs by two agencies to successfully recruit Black adoptive families.

Miller, Jim. "Adopting the Black Child: Is It for You?" *Raising Black and Biracial Children* (October 31, 2001): 15.

A White father of two Black children describes the interracial adoption scene, including a brief review of the controversy and some of the problems of the American system of adoption. He offers straightforward advice to White prospective adoptees of Black children.

Patton, Sandra Lee. *Birthmarks: Transracial Adoption in Contemporary America.* New York: New York University Press, 2000.

Patton makes extensive use of interviews with African American and biracial adults who had been adopted into White families as children in her examination of transracial adoption. She encourages interviewees to articulate their own identities, both as racial minorities and as adoptees. She also addresses the socio-political, cultural, and economic contexts of TRA. An adoptee herself, though in-race, she incorporates discussions of issues common to all adoptees such as having no blood ties with one's family in a culture that values such ties; searching for, visualizing or fantasizing about birth families; creating an understanding of origins or roots; and achieving an understanding of self and personal identity. All of this is kept within the context of transracial adoption. This "adoptee" focus represents a unique perspective in the literature on TRA. Many adoptees will find their own voice in this highly readable book.

Penn, Michael L., and Christina Coverdale. "Transracial Adoption: A Human Rights Perspective." *Journal of Black Psychology* 22, no. 2 (1996): 240-245.

Penn and Coverdale respond to the article by Alexander and Curtis (1996) cited above. They place transracial adoption of African American children by White families in the context of the United Nations Convention on the Rights of the Child (1989), in particular principles that state children deprived of their family environment must be protected by the state and due regard paid to the child's "ethnic, religious, cultural and linguistic background" in providing their care. They also challenge the methodologies and cultural assumptions of the researchers who have studied the effect of transracial adoption on adopted minority children.

Rojewski, Jay W., and Jacy L. Rojewski. *Intercountry Adoption from China: Examining Cultural Heritage and Other Postadoption Issues.* Westport, Conn.: Bergin & Garvey, 2001.

This book developed out of the authors' efforts to assemble practical information to enhance their parenting of their adopted, Chinese-born daughters. They discuss the social context of adoption from China, how parents can reconcile the differences between themselves and their children, how parents can respond to prejudice and discrimination, how children develop racial and ethnic identities, and other issues both social and personal. They also summarize research done on intercountry adoption.

Rosenberg, Shelley Kapnek. "A Jewish Rainbow: Transracial and Transcultural Adoption." In *Adoption and the Jewish Family: Contemporary Perspectives*, 298. Philadelphia: The Jewish Publication Society, 1998.

This chapter describes some of the unique challenges both Jewish adoptive parents and their transracially and transculturally adopted children face and offers advice to parents on how to raise children who are able to incorporate both their birth heritage and their Jewish heritage into a positive self-image.

Rush, Sharon. *Loving across the Color Line: A White Adoptive Mother Learns about Race.* Lanham, Md.: Rowman & Littlefield Publishers, Inc., 2000.

A White mother of a Black daughter recounts her own personal growth in understanding the dynamics of race in America as she parents her young child. The experience of adopting transracially has given Rush a new perspective on race and racism in America. She also strongly demonstrates the advocacy role that White parents must play for their Black children.

Shiu, Anthony. "Flexible Production: International Adoption, Race, Whiteness." *Jouvert* (Fall 2001). http://social.chass.ncsu.edu/jouvert/ v6i1-2/con61.htm.

Shiu examines international adoption, particularly of children from Asian countries, in terms of racial politics and White entitlement and privilege. He looks at the legal environment in the United States, which he believes is at least as much about the maintenance of majority entitlement and access to the child as commodity as it is about the best interests of the children. He also describes the process by which American adoptive parents idealize America as the only route to salvation for children from what they perceive as clearly lesser countries. This article is from a journal that is only available via the web.

Simon, Rita James, and Howard Altstein. *Adoption across Borders: Serving the Children in Transracial and Intercountry Adoptions.* Lanham, Md.: Rowman & Littlefield Publishers, Inc., 2000.

Simon and Altstein are prominent researchers on the impact of TRA. This book provides an overview of TRA as well as intercountry adoptions, summarizing some of the points of controversy, the legal perspective, and the empirical research on these adoptions. One chapter describes their study of Jewish families that have adopted transracially or internationally.

————. *Adoption, Race, and Identity: From Infancy to Young Adult-hood.* 2nd ed. New Brunswick, N.J.: Transaction Publishers, 2002.

Simon and Altstein have conducted the longest-running longitudi-nal study of transracially adopted children and their families. This study is cited by almost every writer on TRA. The project began in 1971 and concluded in 1991 as the children were entering young adulthood. This second edition of the book summarizes all of their research related to this study over the years, each stage of which was also previously published separately.

————. "The Case for Transracial Adoption." *Children and Youth Ser-vices Review* 18, no. 1-2 (1996, special issue): 5-22.

Simon and Altstein outline and counter arguments against TRA, then discuss the state of the laws at both national and state levels in 1996. Finally, they summarize their frequently-cited study of trans-racially adopted people and their families that began in 1971 and spanned two decades. According to their research, transracially adopted people raised in White families are well-adjusted with a secure racial identity. Neither White nor non-White children showed a White racial preference and there were no statistical dif-ferences in behaviors between adopted and biological children.

Simon, Rita James, and Rhonda M. Roorda. *In Their Own Voices: Transracial Adoptees Tell Their Stories.* New York: Columbia University Press, 2000.

Part I of this book briefly describes the history of TRA and the cur-rent legal conditions, offers some statistics, and summarizes the controversy. The remainder of the book contains the edited tran-scripts of interviews with twenty-four adult transracial adoptees, most in their twenties. Very brief biographical information is in-cluded about each interviewee. Although the questions in each in-terview varied, most of the interviewees talk about their experi-ences growing up, especially those centering on racial issues, what their families and communities were like, what they consider their racial identity, and their opinions on TRA. The short summary at the end offers little in the way of interpretation or understanding of the interviews, though some reference is made to Simon's longitu-dinal study of TRA families. The purpose of this book is simply to give transracially adopted people a chance to tell their own stories.

Smith, Janet Farrell. "Analyzing Ethical Conflict in the Transracial Adoption Debate: Three Conflicts Involving Community." *Hypatia* 11, no. 2 (1996): 1-33.

In this essay, Smith addresses the political and ethical issues brought to light by the controversy over TRA. She sees TRA as the symptom of social inequality (the maintenance of White privilege);

conflicting values, such as the value of Black community stability versus the value of a child's timely placement into a permanent home; and American society's inability or unwillingness to preserve Black families, community, and culture. She offers no resolutions to the conflict but provides a thought-provoking piece. She concludes with observations on White adoptive parents' responsibilities toward the non-White child, his or her birth parents, and the racial/ethnic community of origin.

Smolowe, Jill. "Adoption in Black and White." *Time* 146, no. 7 (August 14, 1995): 50.

This news account describes a White couple's effort to adopt two African American children they had fostered for several years. Though favoring TRA, the author does explain some of the arguments against it.

Tessler, Richard C., Gail Gamache, and Liming Liu. *West Meets East: Americans Adopt Chinese Children.* Westport, Conn.: Bergin & Garvey, 1999.

The authors report on their survey of 526 adoptive parents of Chinese-born children (largely daughters). In most cases the children were still young. Parents were beginning to face decisions regarding how to incorporate Chinese culture into their and their children's lives, how to create an accepting social environment for their visibly different children, and how they interact with people, including family members, who show bigoted attitudes. The authors also discuss the social and political contexts of adoption from China in the 1990s.

Vonk, M. Elizabeth, Peggy J. Simms, and Larry Nackerud. "Political and Personal Aspects of Intercountry Adoption of Chinese Children in the United States." *Families in Society* 80, no. 5 (1999): 496-505.

The authors explain the social conditions in the United States and in the People's Republic of China that have led to a significant increase in the number of U.S. couples adopting children from China. The article includes information on the process for Chinese adoptions. Also addressed is the impact of international and intercultural adoption on the families, including the birth families, and the children. The authors conclude with recommendations for social workers interacting with families who have adopted internationally.

Williams, Nancy. "Existing Children in Transracial Adoption." *Interrace* 43 (1998): 24.

This is a short article on how White parents can begin to prepare and educate their biological children when the parents are considering transracial adoption.

Willis, Madge Gill. "The Real Issues in Transracial Adoption: A Response." *Journal of Black Psychology* 22, no. 2 (1996): 246-253.

Willis responds to the article by Alexander and Curtis (1996) cited earlier, striving to take the critique of research on transracially adopted Black children even further than they did. She focuses her arguments on the studies of racial identity and identifies several problems with prior research. She then "constructs" transracial adoption from an African-centered worldview, considering cultural differences, politics ("scientific colonialism," the redefining of a group under study in order to maintain control over that group), and African understandings of family and children that influence the way in which children are socialized in African American families.

Searching for Additional Literature

"Transracial adoption" and "interracial adoption" are the most frequently used terms in catalogs, indexes, and online databases. "Transethnic adoption" and "interethnic adoption" also appear in the literature and sometimes reveal sources otherwise missed in keyword searching. Some bibliographic resources do not have a standardized phrase for adoption across racial lines. Searching for works on adoption can often lead to references on that topic combined with race or racial issues. Searching electronic sources provides the option of using two terms, such as "race" and "adoption" and other related words to find articles covering both. Researchers will probably not find it difficult to find material in major sources, particularly in the literature of psychology, sociology, and social work as well as, to some extent, law and political science. Resources that cover alternative presses, particularly left or ethnic presses, may produce less scholarly research, but do provide a wide array of valuable perspectives. The mainstream media sources, especially newspapers, often pick up and report on specific cases, such as stories of White foster parents suing to adopt their Black foster children.

9   Books for Children and Young Adults

Darlene Nichols

We use books to entertain, educate and encourage our children. Parents of mixed-race children can find it affirming to introduce books that reflect their own family, particularly if their children see few other models of mixed-race families and people. Until the 1990s, mixed-race families saw very little of themselves in children's literature and those portrayals that existed were difficult to find. Now there are a growing number of books at all levels, from picture books to young adult reading. The books listed below are a sample of books found through searching various electronic databases and scouring printed sources, libraries, and book stores. It is not a comprehensive list by any means, nor is it intended to represent the "best" books since what is best for any given family will vary. Methods for searching out additional materials are described below.

Picture books are often children's first introduction to books and reading. Some of the picture books listed here introduce ideas of racial difference and blending, such as *You Be Me, I'll Be You*, by Phil Mandelbaum. But many of the picture books show interracial families going about their daily lives, playing, working, and just being a family. These books often make no mention of race at all and readers learn about the nature of the family through the illustrations.

This light touch on issues of race is not the case in books for older children, especially young adult fiction. As is common in young adult literature, the principal characters are faced with a personal crisis, but in the books listed here, the crises are tinged with overtones of racial issues. Frequently the main characters are in early adolescence, at a point when their awareness of their place in their communities is maturing along with their physical and emotional selves. Often the characters are experiencing broken relationships with friends, family, or even themselves. Race is not always the primary issue in these books, but it does always exist at least in the background.

Books can provide a safe way to teach life lessons that parents and teachers sometimes can not. Books featuring interracial characters can provide positive role models for all children but especially for children of mixed-racial heritage.

Finding Literature on Interracial Families and People for Children

Most of the books here were harvested from the OCLC WorldCat database, which is a listing of millions of items owned by hundreds of libraries in North America. This database is widely accessible in American libraries, and often made available for public access. In the 1990s the Library of Congress introduced the subject headings, "Racially mixed people" and "Racially mixed children" which are used to describe books about people of mixed-race backgrounds. (Subject headings, discussed in greater detail in the Access chapter and Appendix I, are standardized terms intended to be consistently applied in describing the contents, or subject, of a book or other item owned by a library. In a library catalog this means that items on a particular subject will all show up together when that subject heading is included in the search.) Using these subject headings in the WorldCat database, or other catalogs that use Library of Congress Subject Headings, will lead to books on that topic. Since some records in these databases include notes with keywords such as "juvenile," "elementary," or "junior high," adding these to a keyword search can be helpful. Despite the recent addition of these subject headings, there is still a measure of serendipity in finding what is out there. Older books in particular, which are often still listed without the current subject headings, might be missed. There are also printed and web-based bibliographies to help guide parents to these elusive materials as well. Several such resources are listed at the end of this chapter.

Picture Books

Adoff, Arnold. *Black is Brown is Tan*. New York: HarperCollins Publishers, 2002.
　　A colorful new edition of the original 1973 publication, *Black is Brown is Tan* is a poem that describes the different skin colors within one multiracial family. It depicts a White father, Black mother, mixed-race kids, aunts, grandparents, and other family members.

Adoff, Arnold. *Hard to Be Six.* New York: Lothrop, 1991.

It is hard to be six when you have a ten-year-old sister, but this youngest child of an African American father and a White mother learns how much his family loves him just as he is.

Bradman, Tony, and Eileen Browne. *Through My Window.* Morristown, N.J.: Silver Burdett, 1986.

Jo, daughter of a Black mother and White father, wakes one morning feeling sick and can't go to school. Her mother heads off to work while dad stays home with Jo, who spends the day watching through the window of her apartment for her mother's return. While she's waiting she interacts with neighbors, the letter carrier, and other people from this multiethnic neighborhood.

Cheng, Andrea. *Grandfather Counts.* New York: Lee & Low Books, 2000.

Helen is angry when her mother's father comes from China to live with them and takes over her room. He speaks no English, and she and her brothers, whose father is Caucasian American, speak no Chinese. But Helen develops a bond with her grandfather when she sees how much he, too, loves to watch the trains that go past the house. Together they begin to teach each other, first by counting the train cars in Chinese and then English.

Davol, Marguerite W. *Black, White, Just Right!* Morton Grove, Ill.: Whitman Publishing, 1993.

In verse we learn about a little girl and her parents—her mother is African American and her dad is White. The book describes the things they all enjoy together.

Friedman, Ina R. *How My Parents Learned to Eat.* Boston: Houghton Mifflin, 1984.

A young girl tells the story of her parents' courtship in Japan. Her dad is a White American sailor in Japan and her mom is Japanese. Both fear the other's rejection because of the different ways they eat. Each finds someone to teach them how to use the utensils of the other's culture. Now living in America, the family uses both.

Garland, Sarah. *Billy and Belle.* New York: Penguin, 1992.

Billy and Belle are the children of an African American father and White mother. The story tells the tale of one exciting day when Belle gets to go to school with her big brother while mom and dad head to the hospital to deliver baby Adam.

Johnson, Angela. *The Aunt in Our House*: New York: Orchard Books, 1996.

Two children, whose mother is African American and whose father is European American, enjoy the off-beat aunt who comes to stay with them at their house.

Little, Mimi Otey. *Yoshiko and the Foreigner.* New York: Farrar,
    Straus & Giroux, 1996.
    This tells the true story of the courtship of a young Japanese
    woman and an American soldier in Japan. The story is written by
    their daughter.
Mandelbaum, Phil. *You Be Me, I'll Be You.* Brooklyn, N.Y.: Kane Mill
    Book Publishers, 1990.
    A little girl and her White dad "trade places" with the use of a little
    flour, coffee grounds, and other accessories, to surprise her mom,
    who is Black. They decide that mom is coffee, dad is milk, and the
    little girl is a blend of the two: coffee milk.
Monk, Isabell. *Hope.* London: Lerner Publishing Group, 1996.
    While visiting her African American aunt, Hope, whose mother is
    Black and father is White, overhears her aunt's friend say some-
    thing unkind about Hope's mixed ethnicity. Her aunt reminds
    Hope of how special she is and tells her the meaning of her name:
    that it represents her parents' faith in a better future.
Senisi, Ellen B. *For My Family, Love, Allie.* Morton Grove, Ill.: Albert
    Whitman, 1998.
    Allie, about age six, wants to make something all by herself for the
    family gathering where aunts, uncles, cousins, and grandparents
    will come together for a meal. Her mother, who is White, and her
    father's mother, who is African American, find a recipe for peanut
    butter treats that Allie is able to make and share with everyone.
    The story is illustrated with photographs.
Vigil-Piñón, Evangelina. *Pablo Torrecilla.* Houston, Tex.: Piñata
    Books, 2001.
    In this brightly illustrated picture book readers meet Marina, her
    grandmother from Hawaii, and her grandfather from Mexico. Ma-
    rina and her grandmother go shopping to find a muumuu that
    makes Marina think of her grandmother's island home. Text is in
    English and Spanish.
Walker, Pamela. *Tiger Woods.* New York: Children's Press, 2001.
    A biography of the multiracial golf star, Tiger Woods. Includes
    many color photos.
Williams, Garth. *The Rabbits' Wedding.* New York: Harper, 1958.
    A little White rabbit and a little Black rabbit enjoy each other's
    company so much that they decide to get married. This book was
    banned in parts of the United States when it was published.

Williams, Vera. *"More More More" Said the Baby: 3 Love Stories.*
New York: Greenwillow Books, 1990.

A beautifully colorful picture book of babies/toddlers with their
grown-ups, including a light-skinned grandmother with her African
American grandchild.

Wing, Natasha. *Jalapeno Bagels.* New York: Atheneum, 1996.

Pablo wants to bring something special from his family's bakery
for his school's International Day. After thinking about *empana-
das, pan dulce*, bagels, and challah, he chooses jalapeno bagels, a
mixture of both his Jewish father's and his Mexican mother's cultures: "Just like me," he says.

Early Readers

Collins, David R. *Tiger Woods: Golf Superstar.* Gretna, La.: Pelican,
1999.

This book tells the story of Tiger Woods' childhood and earliest
professional successes.

Kandel, Bethany. *Trevor's Story: Growing up Biracial.* Minneapolis:
Lerner Publications, 1997.

Trevor and his sisters are children of an African American father
and a White mother. In this brief autobiography, ten-year-old
Trevor talks about his life and shares what he likes and does not
like about being biracial.

Mayer, Mercer, and Gina Mayer. *Just a Little Different.* New York:
Golden Books, 1998.

This book is one in Mercer Mayer's series of *Little Critters* books.
When Zack moves into the neighborhood, most of the kids don't
like him because he seems so different: his mother is a rabbit and
his father is a turtle. But Zack's Little Critter neighbor makes
friends with him and eventually all of the other critters in the
neighborhood come to see that Zack is just another kid like themselves, just a little different.

Wyeth, Sharon Dennis. *Ginger Brown: The Nobody Boy.* New York:
Random House, 1997.

While visiting on the farm of her White grandparents, Ginger
Brown, age seven, whose father is White and whose mother is African American, befriends a sad little boy whose parents are going
through a divorce, just as her parents did the previous summer. A
sequel to *Ginger Brown: Too Many Houses.*

————. *Ginger Brown: Too Many Houses.* New York: Random House, 1995.

Ginger's parents have divorced. She and her mother, who is African American, leave their old house and move in with Ginger's grandparents. Her dad, who is White, has also found a new place to live. She also spends time with her father's parents while her mother is looking for a new home. Young Ginger doesn't like having so many houses but eventually adjusts to her new life.

Fiction for Older Children

Danziger, Paula. *It's an Aardvark Eat Turtle World.* New York: Delacorte Press, 1985.

Divorced since Rose was young, Rose's mother is starting a new life with the divorced father of Rose's best friend. Rose expects this to be a wonderful new life, but everything is not perfect when her best friend becomes her stepsister. This book discusses the difficulties of blended families as well as confronting the solitude that Rose, whose father was African American, experiences as the only non-White person in her new family.

Dorris, Michael. *The Window.* New York: Hyperion Books for Children, 1997.

When ten-year-old Rayona's Native American mother enters a treatment facility, her estranged father, a Black man, finally introduces her to his side of the family, who are not at all what she expected.

Ernst, Kathleen. *Trouble at Fort La Pointe.* Middleton, Wis.: Pleasant Company Publications, 2000.

Suzette is the twelve-year-old daughter of a French voyageur and an Ojibwe mother and has friends with the same background. Her father wants to stay with his family year-round and hopes to win money to pay off his debt to the fur-trade company for which he works. But when he is accused of stealing, Suzette calls upon her knowledge of French and Ojibwe and her familiarity with both cultures to find who actually stole the missing furs.

Garland, Sherry. *The Song of the Buffalo Boy.* New York: Harcourt, Brace, Jovanovich, 1992.

Ostracized by her Vietnamese community because her father was a White American soldier, seventeen-year-old Loi is determined to escape their rejection by running away with the one young man who cares for her. When they arrive in Saigon, she is offered the opportunity to go to America. She has to choose between the dream of finding her father in America and staying in Vietnam with the young man she loves.

————. *Valley of the Moon: The Diary of Maria Rosalia De Milagros.* New York: Scholastic, 2001.

Thirteen-year-old Maria barely remembers her Native American mother, who died from smallpox, and never knew who her father was at all. Though the wealthy Mexican family for which she and her little brother work is very kind to them, she wants desperately to find out everything she can about her parents. The story, written in the style of a diary, describes the life of Mexicans in California from 1845-1846. The backdrop is the war between Mexico and the United States, during which California became part of the United States.

Gaskins, Pearl Fuyo. *What Are You? Voices of Mixed-Race Young People.* New York: Henry Holt, 1999.

The short essays in this book were written by eighty young adults and teenagers of mixed racial backgrounds. They write about their families, friends, racial identity issues, dating, racism, appearance, and much more in these moving, touching, and sometimes humorous firsthand accounts of what life is like growing up mixed in America.

Hamilton, Virginia. *Arilla Sun Down.* New York: Dell Publishing, 1976.

Twelve-year-old Arilla struggles to develop self-understanding and identity as a mixed African American/Native American girl in a small Midwestern town.

————. *Plain City.* New York: Blue Sky Press, 1993.

Twelve-year-old Buhlaire knows almost nothing about her "back time"—her personal history—which has been kept concealed from her by her family. She feels out of place in her family and community and, so, decides to look for her long-missing father and find out her true past.

Little, Kimberley Griffiths. *Enchanted Runner.* New York: Avon Books, 1999.

Kendall's Acoma Indian mother had promised she would take him to her childhood home when he turned twelve. Although she is now deceased, Kendall's White father and maternal great-grandfather to try fulfill that promise. As he discovers a culture only heard about from his mother, Kendall is finally able to discover the magic within him that drives him to run.

————. *The Last Snake Runner.* New York: Alfred A. Knopf, 2002.
	Fourteen-year-old Kendall, White and Acoma Indian, is the last of the Snake clan of the Acoma. Shaken by his father's impetuous second marriage, he runs away to his mother's childhood town. He is drawn by the magic that drives him to run but also knows he must face a great evil that is taking over the mesa. This is a sequel to *Enchanted Runner.*

Meyer, Carolyn. *Jubilee Journey.* New York: Harcourt Brace and Company, 1997.
	Middle schooler Emily Rose, whose mother is African American and whose father is White, travels from her home in Connecticut to Texas with her mother and brothers to visit their mother's birth place and celebrate Juneteenth, both for the first time. While there she learns the history of her family and the Black community in Texas, and learns some painful lessons about racism and bigotry from both Black people and White people they encounter there.

Murphy, Rita, and Glenn Harrington. *Black Angels.* New York: Dell Yearling, 2002.
	It is 1961, and Celli, age eleven, lives a peaceful life on the White side of town, cared for by her African American housekeeper, Sophie. As the Civil Rights Movement begins to grow in their small Georgia town, Celli becomes unwillingly involved through Sophie and through her grandmother, whom she has never met, and who carries a remarkable family secret.

Okimoto, Jean. *Talent Night.* New York: Scholastic, 1995.
	Rodney Suyama, of Japanese and White heritage, wants to be a rap star and win the attention of his beautiful classmate (who is Filipino/African American). This is the story of his efforts to achieve both goals through the school's talent show. This is also a story of his own self-discovery.

Rosenberg, Maxine. *Living in Two Worlds.* New York: Lothrop, Lee & Shepard Books, 1986.
	A photo essay about biracial children from a variety of backgrounds. Some also come from bicultural families as well. The book addresses the positive aspects of their lives as well as some of the difficulties they experience.

Sanders, Dori. *Clover.* Carrboro, N.C.: Algonquin Books of Chapel Hill, 1990.
	After her father dies within hours of being married to a White woman, a ten-year-old Black girl learns with her new mother to overcome grief and to adjust to a new life in their rural Black South Carolina community.

Schwartz, Virginia Frances. *Send One Angel Down*. New York: Holiday House, 2000.

Eliza is the daughter of a slave mother and the cruel plantation owner. As she grows up she comes to understand the pain of slavery, though her older cousin and other family members try to protect her. As a beautiful, fair-skinned, blue-eyed teen, she has to endure the hostility of the master's daughters who do what they can to take out their hatred on her.

Skurzynski, Gloria. *Escape from Fear*. Washington, D.C.: National Geographic Society, 2002.

Thirteen-year-old Forrest Winthrop IV is the biracial birth child of a Black woman from the Virgin Islands and a White American who had died trying to help Haitians flee their country. Adopted as a baby by an American diplomat, Forrest has run away from his parents to find his birth mother and warn her of danger he discovered inadvertently through his father's connections. The Landon family, also traveling to the Virgin Islands, takes the solo traveler under their wings and tries to help him as much as they can.

Taylor, Mildred D. *Let the Circle Be Unbroken*. New York: Bantam Books, 1981.

The story of a Black family in the south of the 1930s. In the first part of the book they contend with the loss of their friend, TJ, tried and convicted for a murder he did not commit. Then their cousin, daughter of their uncle and his White wife, comes to visit. When she tries to pass for White, serious problems arise for the family.

———. *The Land*. New York: Phyllis Fogelman Books, 2001.

This is the prequel to *Roll of Thunder, Hear My Cry* and takes place in the latter half of the nineteenth century. It starts with Paul-Edward, age nine, the son of a southern White landowner and one of his slaves, now free. He dreams of becoming a landowner like his father, and the book tells the story of his growth to manhood and the pursuit of his dream.

Woodson, Jacqueline. *The House You Pass on the Way*. New York: Delacorte Press, 1997.

Staggerlee is the daughter of an African American father and a White mother. Alienated from family members as well as from their predominantly Black southern community, they live isolated on a farm outside of town. In her fourteenth summer, Staggerlee is visited for the first time by a White cousin, close in age. That summer she begins to question her identity, including her sexual orientation, for the first time.

Wyeth, Sharon Dennis. *The World of Daughter McGuire.* New York: Delacorte Press, 1994.

Daughter McGuire, an eleven-year-old African-Jewish-Irish-Italian American, and her siblings move into a new town after their father and mother split up. She struggles with making new friends, adjusting to the change in the family, and dealing with bullies and name-callers.

Yep, Laurence. *The Cook's Family.* New York: Putnam Publishing Group, 1998.

Robin, aged eleven, and her younger brother, seldom see their parents because of the many hours they must work to make ends meet. When they are at home, her parents seem to be constantly bickering. So, when she and her grandmother are asked to pretend to be a lonely cook's long-lost family while on an excursion to Chinatown, Robin finds that she enjoys her pretend family more than her real one. But when her parents, a Chinese American women and a European American man, seem on the verge of splitting up, Robin and her grandmother try to find a way to patch things up again. (Sequel to *Ribbons.*)

————. *Ribbons.* New York: Putnam Publishing Group, 1999.

Eleven-year-old Robin is something of a ballet protégé, but her dreams are cut short when her parents are unable to afford both ballet lessons and the cost of bringing Robin's grandmother to San Francisco from Hong Kong. Robin's Chinese American mother and European American father struggle with issues of responsibility to family and the needs of individual members.

Nonfiction for Older Children

Boyd, Aaron. *Tiger Woods.* Greensboro N.C.: Morgan Reynolds, 1997.

A biography of Tiger Woods; includes black-and-white photos.

Collins, David R. *Tiger Woods: Golf Superstar.* Gretna, La.: Pelican, 1999.

This book tells the story of Tiger Woods' childhood and earliest professional successes.

Katz, William Loren. *Proudly Red and Black: Stories of African and Native Americans.* New York: Maxwell Macmillan International, 1993.

Brief biographies of people of mixed Native American and African ancestry who, despite barriers, made their mark on history, including trader Paul Cuffe, frontiersman Edward Rose, Seminole leader John Horse, and sculptress Edmonia Lewis.

Lanier, Shannon, and Jane Feldman. *Jefferson's Children: The Story of One American Family*. New York: Random House, 2000.
Describes the reunion of the African American and White American descendants of Thomas Jefferson and how their story came to be shared with the public.

O'Hearn, Claudine C. *Half and Half: Writers on Growing up Biracial and Bicultural*. New York: Pantheon Books, 1998.
Eighteen writers of mixed ethnic and racial backgrounds write essays describing their life experiences.

Savage, Jeff. *Tiger Woods*. Minneapolis, Minn.: Lerner Publications Co., 1998.
The life story of Tiger Woods through his winning of the Master's championship in 1997. Includes some color photos.

Teague, Allison L. *Prince of the Fairway: The Tiger Woods Story*. Greensboro: Avisson Press, 1997.
A biography of Tiger Woods through age twenty-one. Includes some black-and-white photos.

Bibliographies of Multicultural Children's Books

Braus, Nancy, and Molly Geidel. *Everyone's Kids' Books: A Guide to Multicultural, Socially Conscious Books for Children*. Brattleboro, Vt.: Everyone's Books, 2000.

Darby, Mary Ann, and Miki Pryne. *Hearing All the Voices: Multicultural Books for Adolescents, Scarecrow Resource Guide Series; No. 2*. Lanham, Md.: Scarecrow Press, 2002.

Helbig, Alethea, and Agnes Perkins. *Many Peoples, One Land: A Guide to New Multicultural Literature for Children and Young Adults*. Westport, Conn.: Greenwood Press, 2001.

Miller-Lachmann, Lyn. *Global Voices, Global Visions: A Core Collection of Multicultural Books*. New Providence, N.J.: R.R. Bowker, 1995.

Muse, Daphne. *The New Press Guide to Multicultural Resources for Young Readers*. New York: New Press. Distributed by W.W. Norton, 1997.

Websites for Children's Books on Interracial Families and People

Association of Multiethnic Americans (AMEA). http://ameasite.org
/biblio.asp
Book Reviews and Recommended Readings Association of Multiethnic Americans.

Smith, Cynthia Leitich, and Greg Leitich Smith. http://www.cynthia
leitichsmith.com/newmultirace.htm
Children's and Young Adult Books with Interracial Family
Themes. Also Interracial Children's Literature Bibliographies.

10   Multiracial Identity Development

Kelly Webster

This chapter collects selected resources on multiracial identity development. It presents a range of resources from scholarly to popular, including literature reviews and anthologies of essays by mixed-race authors. Many useful resources are not included in order to keep the list from becoming unmanageable, so a description of how to access more related resources is included below.

In addition to the resources described above, this list also includes several autobiographies by mixed-race authors. There has been a surge in the publication of such works in the last decade. Autobiographies are relevant to an examination of identity development in that they reveal to readers the great diversity of life experiences among mixed-race people and the variety of influences on the shaping of identity. These writings also show the variety of options multiracial people choose from when developing an ethnic identity. Furthermore, reading these memoirs challenges readers to rethink stereotypes and assumptions about interracial couples and mixed-race people, resulting in a better understanding of the complex issues surrounding this topic.

While it is important to recognize this diversity, there is also a fairly large body of scholarship in the fields of sociology and psychology that examines what multiracial people do have in common. The databases *PsycINFO*, *Sociofile*, and *Wilson Indexes* provide access to a wealth of resources of this type. ProQuest's *Digital Dissertations* (the online version of *Dissertation Abstracts International*) is another helpful tool since many important works on this topic, including proposed models for multiracial identity development, are only available as unpublished dissertations. Dissertations are a good source for data from surveys, interviews, and demographic studies, along with useful descriptions of methodology. Many of these are available through interlibrary loan. Copies of most dissertations can also be purchased from ProQuest directly.

When searching for memoirs or autobiographical essays by multiracial authors, in addition to using various subject terminology and keywords in searching databases, it is useful to check anthologies that focus on one racial group. Skimming the table of contents and contributor biographies may reveal contributions that address mixed-race topics. I have tried to include several examples in this chapter of essays that would not be readily found using traditional searching methods.

Arboleda, Teja. *In the Shadow of Race: Growing Up as a Multiethnic, Multicultural, and "Multiracial" American*. Mahwah, N.J.: Lawrence Erlbaum Associates, 1998.
    Arboleda describes the many ways that his racial makeup and heritage have shaped his life experiences. In relating the racial mixing in his family tree, the many challenges in his childhood and college years, and his relationships with people of other races, he gives great insight into the search for a cultural "home." He ends his memoir with quotes about race and ethnicity from people he met while he performed his play, *Ethnic Man!* all over the country.

Blustain, Sarah. "The New Identity Challenge: Are You Black or Are You Jewish?" *Lilith* 21, no. 3 (1996): 21-26.
    Journalist Blustain writes about the experiences of Black/Jewish biracial adults who were born in the 1960s to activist parents. Using numerous quotations from interviews, she describes the common experiences of this group through their childhoods and college years. She gives a historical and social backdrop of the 1960s, examines the history of relations between Jewish and Black communities, and describes the issues that their offspring deal with now.

Brown, Ursula M. "Black/White Interracial Young Adults: Quest for a Racial Identity." *American Journal of Orthopsychiatry* 65, no. 1 (January 1995): 125-130.
    In this study of the racial identity development of 119 young adults with one Black and one White parent, Brown found that maintaining different public and private identities is a frequently used coping mechanism. She constructed an interview process to collect demographic information as well as data about ethnic self-identification, identity conflict, coping strategies, and social influences. These interviews also explore racial labeling, acceptance of identity choice by peers, quality of family relations, and exposure to culture. Results show that the path to identity resolution varies greatly and is a multidimensional process. The compartmentalization of public and private identities helped individuals to preserve their self-perception as racially mixed, while conforming to societal pressures to identify as Black.

———. *The Interracial Experience: Growing up Black/White Racially Mixed in the United States.* Westport, Conn.: Praeger, 2001.

Psychotherapist Brown explores the way interracial people negotiate their identities within societal frameworks. She analyzes interviews to provide an in-depth look at issues such as family, school, community, and dating. In-depth descriptions of three of the subjects exemplify the key patterns found in the interviews. Discussion includes coping strategies used by subjects, ways that families, mental health professionals, and society can support mixed-race individuals, and factors that predict positive identity resolution. Includes a list of support/advocacy groups by state.

Brunsma, David L., and Kerry Ann Rockquemore. "The New Color Complex: Appearances and Biracial Identity." *Identity: An International Journal of Theory and Research* 1, no. 3 (2001): 225-246.

This study examines the role that phenotype plays in the racial identity choices and self-understanding of Black/White biracial individuals. The authors use data from a survey of 177 subjects, basing their questions on Rockquemore's model (1999) of four biracial identity options. Results show that a biracial individual's understanding of how others perceive his or her appearance affects the resolution reached in biracial identity development.

Buxenbaum, Kim Una. "Racial Identity Development and Its Relationship to Physical Appearance and Self-Esteem in Adults with One Black and One White Biological Parent." Ph.D. diss., Rutgers University, 1996.

Using an identity interview, questionnaire, and self-esteem inventory of her own creation, Buxenbaum examines the identity development of adults with one Black and one White parent. Data from twenty-six subjects aged eighteen to fifty-five are presented, along with seven in-depth case studies. Discussion of results suggests that subjects' identity choices change not only over time, but according to situation as well. About one-third of the subjects maintain different public and private racial identities.

Camper, Carol, ed. *Miscegenation Blues: Voices of Mixed Race Women.* Toronto: Sister Vision, 1994.

This anthology includes poetry, essays, and group dialogues by more than forty mixed-race Canadian women. The collection strives to end isolation and promote self-understanding, providing a forum for women to document their lives, talk about the challenges they face, and feel part of a community. Introduced with a discussion of stereotypes of mixed-race women, the tone is defiant throughout. Includes black-and-white photos.

Christine. "Color-blind." In *Souls Looking Back: Life Stories of Growing up Black*, edited by Andrew Garrod et al. New York: Routledge, 1999.

In this essay the author describes the stages of her identity development as a racially mixed woman of Black and White heritage. Raised in a Northern, mostly White community, she felt insulated from hostility and disapproval about her racial make up, and only began examining what it means to be mixed-race in her senior year of high school. She found herself unprepared for the challenges that Black peers in college brought to her view that race was not important and society should strive to be "color-blind." She relates her experiences as she tries to find a sense of community, explores racial issues in history and contemporary society, begins dating, and faces pressures to identify as Black.

Collins, J. Fuji. "Biracial Japanese American Identity: An Evolving Process." *Cultural Diversity and Ethnic Minority Psychology* 6, no. 2 (May 2000): 115-133.

This study of fifteen biracial Japanese adults shows that the identity development process varies from one individual to the next and is a long-term process. Environmental circumstances and life experiences can influence changes in racial identification. The interviews conducted by Collins indicate that the subjects recognize the positive values of both cultures and have developed an integrated racial identity. Though there were some common trends, the paths that led there varied greatly from one individual to the next. Collins describes common experiences such as self-evaluation, searching for group acceptance, exploration of identity possibilities and situational use of identity. The author encourages researchers to explore each developmental stage instead of one fixed time period and offers a model based on the identified trends.

de Bruin, John H. "Self-Representation and Choice among Korean-Americans and Japanese-Americans: Toward an Interdisciplinary Theory of Biracial Identities." Ph.D. diss., Boston University, 1998.

This study uses data from ten Japanese American and ten Korean American biracial adults to examine the influences on racial identity development. Findings show three ways that subjects' identities develop: Race Coupled (identify as both races side by side); Race Blended (identify with both races blended into a third category); and Race Divested (rejects Asian identity). Using case studies, de Bruin discusses the factors that predict the three developmental paths, and life experiences that can trigger the re-enactment of the developmental process, such as job change, marriage, and aging.

Deters, Kathleen A. "Belonging Nowhere and Everywhere: Multiracial Identity Development." *Bulletin of the Menninger Clinic* 61, no. 3 (1997): 368-384.

With a focus on assisting therapists in working with multiracial patients, this article examines the impact of societal notions of race on racial identity development. Deters examines social constructions such as marginality, the "one-drop rule," status, and prejudice. Therapists are advised to adopt a nonoppressive perspective, stay familiar with current theories, and be mindful of biracial identity issues when diagnosing developmental disorders. This study also highlights issues brought up in interviews with six therapists experienced in this area.

Frazier, Sundee. *Check All That Apply: Finding Wholeness as a Multiracial Person*. Downers Grove, Ill.: InterVarsity, 2002.

Written with a strong Christian viewpoint, this work aims to help mixed-race people come to find joy and a sense of wholeness in life. Essays, advice, anecdotes, and poems are centered on three themes: identity, relationships, and purpose. Each chapter ends with questions for reflection and exercises for personal exploration. Frazier deals with some issues not found in other, nonreligious works, such as frank talk about avoiding temptations (of bitterness, opportunism, or shame); handling disappointment with family relations; deciding whom to date; and advice to spouses. Includes a bibliography, glossary of terms, an appendix on "historical examples of multiracial people," and lists of websites, organizations, videos, and print resources.

Funderburg, Lise. *Black, White, Other: Biracial Americans Talk about Race and Identity*. New York: W. Morrow and Co., 1994.

Focusing on Black/White biracial subjects, this collection contains personal narratives based on interviews with forty-six Americans under the age of twenty-five, conducted from 1992 to 1993. Subjects were asked to talk about their lives, concentrating on the development of their ideas about race and their own racial identity. Chapters are divided by theme, such as family, neighborhood, school, friends, romance, religion, work, politics, and prejudice. Each chapter includes selections from the personal narratives, with some longer "self-portraits" between chapters. This format shows the wide range of individual experiences among mixed-race people. Includes many photos of interviewees.

Gaskins, Pearl Fuyo. *What Are You? Voices of Mixed-Race Young People*. New York: Henry Holt, 1999.

Gaskins, an award-winning journalist of Japanese and White ancestry, has collected interviews with eighty mixed-race young people, combined with poems, essays, and "expert" insights. Topics include identity struggles, the "What are you?" phenomenon, racial categories, family issues, dating, and prejudice. Appendices provide lists of advocacy groups, magazines, young adult books, videos, organizations, campus student groups, and college courses. Photographs of contributors add to the experience of hearing the true voices of biracial young people.

Gillem, Angela R., Laura Renee Cohn, and Cambria Throne. "Black Identity in Biracial Black/White People: A Comparison of Jacqueline Who Refuses to Be Exclusively Black and Adolphus Who Wishes He Were." *Cultural Diversity and Ethnic Minority Psychology* 7, no. 2 (May 2001, special issue): 182-196.

Gillem analyzes in-depth interviews with two biracial college students to trace the experiences on their paths to identity resolution. Though both students claim a Black identity, the differences in their experiences and perspectives serve to complicate notions of race and racial identity and call into question the helpfulness of racial identity development theories.

Johnson, Kevin R. *How Did You Get to Be Mexican? A White/Brown Man's Search for Identity*. Philadelphia, Pa.: Temple University Press, 1999.

This memoir by Johnson, a law professor of White and Mexican descent, describes the fluctuations in his level of comfort with his biracial heritage. He talks candidly about experiences throughout his life, such as moving back and forth between his divorced parents' worlds, trying to assimilate with White culture in adolescence, self-identifying on applications, avoiding race issues at work, and his relationship with other family members. He also discusses affirmative action policies and the issues that have come up with his own interracial children and their ethnic identities.

Kahn, Jack S., and Jacqueline Denmon. "An Examination of Social Science Literature Pertaining to Multiracial Identity: A Historical Perspective." *Journal of Multicultural Social Work* 6, no. 1/2 (1997): 117-138.

By analyzing the history of the multiracial identity construct within social science literature, Kahn shows the following shifts in thinking: from regarding interracial individuals as inferior to striving to understand their experiences; from emphasizing biological differences to focusing on social ones; and from using behavioral observation to relying on self report. He proposes that these shifts reveal the struggle rooted in the ethnocentric beliefs of researchers. Studies of the empirical literature are presented chronologically, with the majority to be found after 1990. Kahn lists databases searched and includes a list of keywords used.

Kennedy, N. Brent. *The Melungeons: The Resurrection of a Proud People*. Macon, Ga.: Mercer University Press, 1994.

Kennedy, who has worked with the Melungeon Research Committee, shares his family background and personal history as he relates the history of Melungeon people in the United States. Informal rather than scholarly in tone, his work includes many photographs as well as genealogical information. He covers various theories of the group's origins, and gives an overview of research on other "mystery" peoples of the American Southeast.

Kerwin, Christine, and Joseph G. Ponterotto. "Biracial Identity Development: Theory and Research." In *Handbook of Multicultural Counseling*, edited by Joseph G. Ponterotto et al. Thousand Oaks, Calif.: Sage Publications, 1995.

The authors provide an overview of the issues surrounding biracial identity development, including demographic trends, stereotypes, and current theories. They include very helpful summaries of the various biracial identity development models proposed up to that point and offer a new model with an integrated framework that emphasizes continuing development over the lifespan of biracial individuals.

Kich, George Kitahara. "Eurasians: Ethnic/Racial Identity Development of Biracial Japanese/White Adults." Ph.D. diss., Wright Institute, Graduate School of Psychology, 1982.

This study explores identity development in biracial Japanese/White adults using data collected from fifteen subjects. Kich identifies three stages: feeling different and separate; moving outside the home among peers and developing a complex identity through contact with extended family, travel, language study, and other experiences; and the resolution of biracial identity with an assertion of self-label. He also examines the historical background of Japanese-White marriages in America.

Kidd, Mae Street. *Passing for Black: The Life and Careers of Mae Street Kidd*. Lexington, Ky.: University Press of Kentucky, 1997.

Oral historian Wade Hall edited this memoir from approximately forty hours of interviews with Kidd, taped in 1993. Born in 1904 to a White father and Black/White/Native American mother, Kidd states that she is technically "more than 80 percent White," yet she identifies as Black, grew up in Black communities, attended Black schools, and became a successful businesswoman with a Black-owned life insurance company. She served in England in the American Red Cross, became a politician in her sixties, and then served seventeen years in the Kentucky General Assembly, overseeing important civil rights legislation. This story provides an inspirational and educational account of this savvy woman who is proud of her heritage.

Kilson, Marion. *Claiming Place: Biracial Young Adults of the Post-Civil Rights Era.* Westport, Conn.: Bergin & Garvey, 2001.

This ethnographic study is based on interviews with fifty-two biracial subjects in their mid-twenties to early thirties. These subjects grew up after the Civil Rights era and are considered an important transitional generation by the author. Participants answered questions about childhood, families, identity choices, perceived advantages and disadvantages of being biracial, dating, and employment. Kilson provides a wealth of quotations that illustrate the wide diversity of viewpoints among mixed-race people.

Korgen, Kathleen Odell. *From Black to Biracial: Transforming Racial Identity Among Americans.* Westport, Conn.: Praeger Publishers, 1998.

Korgen provides a sociological examination of the "changing dialectic between society and the racial identity of biracial individuals" using a symbolic interactionism approach combined with postmodern theory. Interviews with forty adults and data from secondary sources show that the majority of people born before the Civil Rights era identify as Black, while the majority of those born afterward identify as biracial. Discussion topics include the historical context of the multiracial movement; societal factors that have assigned new meaning to biracial identity; the question of marginality; a new theory of identity development; and public policy implications. Case studies of three subjects born before, during, and after the Civil Rights Movement are provided, as well as many quotations from interviewees.

Major, Clarence. *Come by Here: My Mother's Life.* New York: J. Wiley, 2002.

Major, a poet, essayist, and novelist, wrote this memoir of his mother's life from taped conversations with her, supported by historical research. A single mother raising children in poverty, she left the children with her parents and passed as White to gain employment. Full of rich details of her childhood, abusive marriage, and family life, this account illustrates the fluidity of race and the history of color bias in the South. Includes two black-and-white photos.

McCunn, Ruthanne Lum. "Arlee Hen and the Black Chinese." In *Chinese American Portraits: Personal Histories, 1822-1988*. San Francisco: Chronicle Books, 1988.

This article presents a biographical portrait of Arlee Hen, a Black Chinese American woman born in 1893. Raised in rural Mississippi, her father was a Chinese sharecropper who opened a store for African Americans. McCunn also discusses the history of Black/Chinese marriages in Mississippi. Includes black-and-white photos.

Mihesuah, D.A. "American Indian Identities: Issues of Individual Choices and Development." *American Indian Culture and Research Journal* 22, no. 2 (1998): 193-226.

This article examines issues surrounding the identity choices of American Indians. Mihesuah presents a model for the life stages of American Indian identity and lists the variety of backgrounds that may influence the identity development of mixed blood individuals. The discussion explores various identity choices using Rockquemore's model (1999) of four types of identity development resolutions and examines life experiences that may prompt re-evaluation of ethnic identity.

Morrison, Johnetta Wade. "Developing Identity Formation and Self-Concept in Preschool-Aged Biracial Children." *Early Child Development and Care: Focus on Caregivers* 111 (July 1995, special issue): 141-152.

Interviews with eleven mothers of biracial preschool-aged children reveal the methods that mothers use to promote racial identity development. Discussion includes racial labeling and development of a positive self-concept. Most mothers felt it was important to make efforts to expose children to information about African American heritage.

"No Passing Zone: The Artistic and Discursive Voices of Asian-Descent Multiracials." *Amerasia Journal* 23, no. 1 (1997).

This issue of *Amerasia*, devoted to mixed-race issues, provides a variety of viewpoints that challenge notions of race and ethnicity. Contributors come from a variety of backgrounds and provide works that include sociological and historical examinations as well as poetry and prose. Articles include "Multiracial Asians: Models of Ethnic Identity" by Maria P.P. Root, "What Must I Be? Asian Americans and the Question of Multiethnic Identity" by Paul Spickard, and "Race-ing and Being Raced: The Critical Interrogation of 'Passing'" by Teresa Kay Williams.

O'Hearn, Claudine C., ed. *Half and Half: Writers On Growing Up Biracial and Bicultural*. New York: Pantheon Books, 1998.

This anthology includes short personal essays by eighteen authors with a wide variety of backgrounds, covering many topics. Contributors include literary authors such as Julia Alvarez, Bharati Mukherjee, Gish Jen, and others. All are children or parents of biracial or bicultural families.

Penn, William S., ed. *As We Are Now: Mixblood Essays On Race and Identity*. Berkeley, Calif.: University of California Press, 1997.

This collection includes thirteen first-person narratives on mixed-blood identity that focus on the urban experience and reveal the complexities of modern Native American identity. The essays are rooted in the oral tradition using experimental styles, and several first-time authors are included. Issues explored include the connections between Native American and Chicano identities, questions surrounding "authenticity" of Native Americans, and the role of tradition in contemporary society.

Pinderhughes, Elaine. "Biracial Identity: Asset or Handicap?" In *Racial and Ethnic Identity: Psychological Development and Creative Expression*. Florence, Ky.: Taylor & Francis/Routledge, 1995.

This study provides brief case studies of troubled mixed-race patients taken from Pinderhughes' work as a clinician. She presents research findings and expert opinions to examine healthy biracial identity development and proposes that healthy development includes transcending two barriers: societal prejudice against minorities, and the lack of a mixed-race group to provide a sense of belonging. Factors that influence development in a positive way are a diverse community, parental understanding, support networks, and acceptance of both sides of one's racial heritage.

Poston, W.S.C. "The Biracial Identity Development Model: A Needed Addition." *Journal of Counseling and Development* 69, no. 2 (1990): 152-155.

This article reviews models of racial identity development and discusses their shortcomings in regard to biracial identity. Poston presents a new five-stage model of development that has a life-span focus and incorporates the factors that affect that the identity development process. He includes a brief discussion of the implications for counseling and further research.

Quintana, Elena Diana. *Racial and Ethnic Identity Development in Biracial People*. Ph.D. diss., DePaul University, 1998.

A survey conducted at a small college revealed that 17 percent of respondents had at least one relative in the last four generations who was described as a different race than others in the family.

Only one-third claimed a biracial identity, while the rest identified monoracially with their non-White reference group. Quintana uses interviews with this group to explore the reasoning behind identity choices and identify coping mechanisms used in identity formation.

Rockquemore, Kerry Ann, and David L. Brunsma. *Beyond Black: Biracial Identity in America.* Thousand Oaks, Calif.: Sage Publications, 2002.

This study by two sociology professors was written in response to the 2000 census debate. The authors feel that little empirical research of good quality was available to decision makers during that time, only personal testimony and many disconnected studies of small sample size. This work provides an in-depth analysis of data that strives to overcome the limitations of earlier studies. It includes an overview of the census debate and examines the positive and negative implications of adding a new census category. The authors offer four categories of biracial identity choices based on Rockquemore's model presented in her 1999 dissertation, which is cited in many other studies. The discussion analyzes the social factors that shape those choices and how the same set of factors works differently in each category. Includes methodological instruments.

———. "Socially Embedded Identities: Theories, Typologies, and Processes of Racial Identity Among Biracials." *Sociological Quarterly* 43, no. 3 (2002): 335-356.

Using Rockquemore's model (1999) of four ways biracial individuals may understand their racial identity, the authors address issues of identity development, including the social factors that influence choices, and generate hypotheses based on the model. Questionnaires were given to 177 subjects with one Black and one White parent, and results supported the hypothesis that more identity options than Black or biracial would be chosen by respondents. At least six categories were apparent, with only thirteen percent of respondents self-identifying as singularly Black. Results also showed that social networks, appearance, and experiences with members of racial groups influence identity choices.

Root, Maria P.P. "Resolving 'Other' Status: Identity Development of Biracial Individuals." *Women and Therapy* 9, no. 1/2/3 (1990): 185-205.

Root describes the need for a new model of identity development that allows for the multiple strategies by which biracial individuals arrive at and maintain a positive sense of identity in the face of societal pressures. She discusses social influences, including the "hierarchy of color in the U.S.," and how they contribute to the conflict surrounding biracial people. Four general resolutions are presented which individuals may move between: accept the identity society assigns, identify with both races, identify with race of person's choosing, or identify as a new racial group. She identifies the following as being important to healthy development: accepting both sides of one's heritage; understanding the right to choose one's identity; developing strategies for coping with social resistance without internalizing; and refusing to base self-worth on acceptance by any racial group.

————. "Rethinking Racial Identity Development." In *We Are a People: Narrative and Multiplicity in Constructing Ethnic Identity.* Philadelphia: Temple University Press, 2000.

In this article, Root outlines the effects of choosing a multiracial identity over a monoracial one, including group empowerment; inspiring and informing current thinking about race and racial identity; and revealing inadequacies in the current racial system. She also reacts to questions brought up by opponents of the multiracial movement. For example, when asked if multiracial identity creates a new class structure, Root says that the movement fights negative classification and instead attempts to deconstruct such notions and open the door to change. She responds to suggestions that choosing a multiracial identity is really racial hatred in disguise by insisting that such an attitude is a misunderstanding directly attributable to society's monoracial framework. She also discusses the biracial models that have been proposed and offers new research questions to be considered in the future.

————, ed. *The Multiracial Experience: Racial Borders as the New Frontier.* Thousand Oaks, Calif.: Sage, 1996.

This collection of scholarly essays covers a wide variety of issues, including identity development, education, adoption, classification, the multiracial movement, and appearance. The first contribution is Root's "A Bill of Rights for Racially Mixed People." Essays are divided into six sections: human rights; identity; blending and flexibility; gender and sexual identity; multicultural education; and the new millennium. Includes black-and-white photos of contributors and a glossary.

————, ed. *Racially Mixed People in America.* Newbury Park, Calif.: Sage, 1992.

This collection of essays is often credited with starting the discussion among social scientists on mixed-race issues and the need to rethink racial categories. It features contributions by many authors who went on to perform important research in the field. Topics covered include identity development, blood quantum, appearance, history, and racial categorization. Includes black-and-white photos of contributors.

Standen, Brian Chol Soo. "Without a Template: The Biracial Korean/ White Experience." In *The Multiracial Experience: Racial Borders as the New Frontier*, edited by Maria P.P. Root. Thousand Oaks, Calif.: Sage, 1996.

This study gathers life histories and demographic information from eight college students who have first-generation Korean immigrant mothers and White fathers. Standen examines the data to better understand influences on identity resolution within a specific ethnographic sample. Participants in the study discuss how they identify in different situations, showing the fluidity of racial identity. A review of the literature dealing with Asian mixed-race issues is also provided.

Storrs, Debbie. "Whiteness as Stigma: Essentialist Identity Work by Mixed-Race Women." *Symbolic Interaction* 22, no. 3 (1999): 187-212.

Using data from a larger study, this article discusses how some mixed-race women, who choose to identify as non-White rather than mixed-race, challenge the meaning of race by assigning stigma to Whiteness. Storrs examines the history of various identity options and the reasons these women reject those choices. She explores the meanings assigned to Whiteness and how they affect self-identification. Storrs warns readers not to interpret this study using a psychological model of identity development, which might suggest that the subjects have yet to reach the final stage of identifying as biracial. Instead, she suggests using a symbolic interactionist perspective and predicts that individuals would not move to a biracial identity without changes that assign new meaning to that category.

Sturm, Circe. *Blood Politics: Race, Culture, and Identity in the Cherokee Nation*. Berkeley: University of California Press, 2002.

In this examination of the politics of identity in the Cherokee Nation, Sturm combines historical and sociological research with her own experiences as a mixed-blood dealing with identity development in college and while conducting fieldwork among the Cherokee in Oklahoma. Using many archival sources, she examines how Cherokee identity is socially and politically shaped and defined. Sturm examines blood quantum, lineal descent, phenotype, politics of marriage choices, and the status of the offspring of Cherokee slave owners and their slaves in local communities. Discussion also includes local (rather than federal) interpretations of Cherokee identity (including appearance, social behavior, language, and religion). Includes black-and-white photos and a map of Cherokee communities in Oklahoma.

Talalay, Kathryn M. *Composition in Black and White: The Life of Philippa Schuyler.* New York: Oxford University Press, 1995.

Based on firsthand interviews, unpublished letters and diaries, and research, this biography of a world-renowned pianist, journalist, and author provides a thorough examination of the life of an interracial woman in the public eye. Schuyler was known as a child prodigy whose career covered the globe. Her father was a noted Black journalist of the Harlem Renaissance, and her mother was from a wealthy White Texan family. Her parents viewed having a mixed child as a genetic experiment and sought to "create" a musical genius. This account of the ups and downs of her unique experience often focuses on Schuyler's racial identity and her interactions with various racial groups. Includes black-and-white photos.

Tashiro, Cathy J. "Standing on Both Feet: History and the Construction of Identity for Older Mixed-Race Americans." Ph.D. diss., University of California, San Francisco, 1998.

Observing that most studies of biracial identity development focus on children or young people, Tashiro presents case studies of twenty racially mixed middle-aged and elderly adults. The participants, who were either of Black/White or Asian/White backgrounds, show through their life histories how racial identity development is influenced by such factors as aging, gender, class, and historical circumstances. Five dimensions are discussed: cultural identity, ascribed identity, public identity, self-identification, and situation-based identity. Also shown are the ways that social and historical influences shape mixed-race identity.

Tatum, Beverly Daniel. "Identity Development in Multiracial Families: 'But Don't the Children Suffer?'" In *Why Are All the Black Kids Sitting Together in the Cafeteria?* New York: BasicBooks, 1997.

Tatum uses an engaging and accessible style to give a clear explanation of how racial identity develops. Each chapter of her book sheds light on the difficult issues involved, and the chapter on multiracial identity is no exception. Tatum begins by asking a number of questions that reveal the multidimensional nature of multiracial identity development. She highlights points from the literature on multiracial identity while addressing topics such as racial categorization, stereotypes, racial awareness over life stages, and identity in adoptive families. Reading this chapter as part of the larger work helps the reader gain insight into the broader issues of race and racial identity as well as those specific to racially mixed individuals.

Walker, Rebecca. *Black, White and Jewish: Autobiography of a Shifting Self.* New York: Riverhead Books, 2001.
Walker is the daughter of acclaimed African American author Alice Walker and Jewish civil rights lawyer Mel Leventhal. In this memoir she relates her experiences growing up as a mixed-race child shuttling back and forth between her divorced parents living in various cities; her involvement with drugs, sex, and dangerous people; and her thoughts on race, sexuality, memory, and identity.

Wallace, Kendra R. *Relative/Outsider: The Art and Politics of Identity among Mixed Heritage Students.* Westport, Conn.: Ablex Publishers, 2001.
This study provides portraits of fifteen biracial high school and college students from a variety of backgrounds. Wallace presents findings from interviews without trying to advance a common identity development model for all biracial individuals. In-depth discussions cover issues such as family relations, community, religion, language, views on ethnicity and race, and the meanings associated with being biracial. Wallace also examines the students' choices among four visual representations of ways to relate to different communities of heritage (discussed in Root, 1996). The appendices include the interview questions, survey, and recruitment flyer.

Wijeyesinghe, Charmaine L. "Racial Identity in Multiracial People: An Alternative Paradigm." In *New Perspectives on Racial Identity Development: A Theoretical and Practical Anthology*, edited by Charmaine L. Wijeyesinghe and Bailey W. Jackson. New York: New York University Press, 2001.
Based on the assumption that there is no single appropriate outcome for multiracial identity development processes, Wijeyesinghe proposes the Factor Model of Multiracial Identity (FMMI), structured around the factors that influence racial identity rather than stages of development. The factors identified include racial ancestry, physical appearance, cultural attachment, early experience and socialization, political awareness and orientation, social and historical context, and spirituality. She also reviews monoracial and multiracial identity development models and analyzes their limitations.

Williams, Gregory Howard. *Life on the Color Line: The True Story of a White Boy Who Discovered He Was Black.* New York: Dutton, 1995.
This account of a man who identifies as a Black person in a White body is an example of a common theme in mixed-race literature. Williams, a law professor, grew up believing he was White. After

being abandoned by his mother at age ten, his alcoholic father revealed that his own mother was Black, and he had been passing for
White most of his life. Williams relates how he spent the rest of his
life gradually coming to terms with being Black, dealing with challenges to his identity from both races, and confronting prejudice
and limitations imposed by his race. Williams does not identify as
mixed-race and does not explore this issue in his memoir, but he
provides important insights into race in American society.

Williams, Teresa Kay. "Re-Conceptualizing Race: The Identity Formation of Biracial Japanese-European Americans." Ph.D. diss., University of California, Los Angeles, 1997.

This study of the racial identity development of biracial Japa-
nese/White Americans stresses the importance of social influences
and the fluidity of identity choices. Using data from interviews
with fifty-three adults, Williams examines how racial and ethnic
identities are socially constructed. Discussion includes stereotypes
of Asian/White marriages and issues surrounding assimilation.
Williams suggests that positive identity resolution comes from the
ability to "operate within, between and across social borderlands."

Williams-Leon, Teresa, and Cynthia L. Nakashima, eds. *The Sum of
Our Parts: Mixed-Heritage Asian Americans*. Philadelphia, Pa.:
Temple University Press, 2001.

This collection of sociological studies focuses on Asian American
mixed-race identity, including combinations besides Asian and
White. It explores the social construction of identity and how it is
shaped by concepts of ethnicity, gender, sexuality, and nationality.
Discussion includes how multiracial issues are viewed in various
national settings. The introduction provides a helpful discussion of
relevant terminology.

Wilson, Timothy L. "The Multiracial Majority: Biracial Student Identity Development and the College Experience." Ph.D. diss, University of Vermont, 1997.

The focus of this dissertation is on how college student affairs professionals can support biracial students. After providing background information on the biracial experience in America and reviewing the literature on biracial identity development, Wilson
outlines the many ways that biracial students' identities are af-
fected by the college experience. His discussion includes strategies
for dealing with the issues that arise with admissions, curriculum,
dating, student organizations, and counseling.

Winters, Loretta I., and Herman L. DeBose, eds. *New Faces in a Changing America: Multiracial Identity in the 21st Century.* Thousand Oaks, Calif.: Sage, 2003.

This collection brings together top names in the literature on multiracial issues and covers a variety of topics, including identity development, the multiracial movement, census issues, global perspectives, and media images.

Wrathall, Mark William. *What about the Children? The Psychosocial Well-Being of Multiracial Individuals.* Ph.D. diss., Azusa Pacific University, 2002.

This literature review on the topic of multiracial identity development includes an examination of identity development models proposed by Jacobs (1992), Kich (1992), Poston (1990), Collins (2000), and Root (1990). It includes research studies with clinical and nonclinical populations that examine social and psychological adjustment of multiracial individuals as well as relevant literature with therapeutic implications. Wrathall discusses factors influencing identity development, the nature of the development process, and the limitations of these studies.

Zack, Naomi, ed. *American Mixed Race: The Culture of Microdiversity.* Lanham, Md.: Rowman & Littlefield Publishers, Inc., 1995.

This collection of essays features noted authors who explore multiracial issues from a variety of perspectives. Contributions are divided into areas of autobiography, art, social science, public policy, and identity theory.

11   The Intersection of Race and Queer Sexuality

Joseph Diaz

This bibliography is a gathering of works about gay, lesbian, bisexual, and transgendered individuals in multiracial relationships and other works that deal with the intersection of sexual and racial identity among gays, lesbians, bisexuals, people of color, and "Whites."

The bulk of literature found here falls into the following distinct categories: (1) biography/autobiography/testimony, (2) literature by therapists and for therapists, and (3) theory and literary analysis, often referred to as cultural studies.

Only a handful of works of literature or film deal directly with interracial gay relationships. The most noteworthy works (which I mention now rather than in the body of the bibliography simply because there are so few examples) are *Vanishing Rooms*, a fine novel by the deceased novelist Melvin Dixon, and the movie *My Beautiful Laundrette*, whose main character is a young gay Pakistani/British male with a White lover whose gang affiliations leave one wondering why these two are together. Both of these works are readily available and treat the subject of gay interracial relationships quite well, given the complexities involved in such relationships.

Most of the resources compiled here are from academic journals and scholarly anthologies. As the compiler of this information, I am the first to acknowledge my lack of sophistication in thoroughly understanding some of these works, but particularly those that fall within the realm of cultural studies. I can only hope that the reader will find these annotations useful as a starting point, and not rely on them as a substitute for reading the original works. I could never claim to fully capture the essence of some of these complex writings with a brief description.

It is clear that the study of gay interracial relationships has a long way to go, be it from the sociological, psychological, historical, or literary perspective. Much of the psychological literature, for example, stresses the importance of this as an area of study and identifies issues without providing any academic study or analysis. While these works present many creative ideas and arguments and reading this material is indeed worthwhile, all the same there is very little written at the pragmatic level. It was interesting to find, for example, that almost none of these works consist of formal studies that include sampling of populations, analysis of data, or conclusive findings that one could then test and refute or confirm. There is clearly room for further investigation and certainly a need for a deeper understanding.

Allman, Karen Maeda. "Unnatural Boundaries: Mixed Race, Gender, and Sexuality." In *The Multiracial Experience: Racial Borders as the New Frontier,* edited by Maria P.P. Root. Thousand Oaks, Calif.: Sage, 1996.
This essay explores multiracial, queer identity through the lenses of gender, sex, and race. Arguing that each is a social construct that helps one define the world, the author notes that the "sex/gender system is profoundly and interdependently racialized and racializing; that race is also thoroughly engendered and engendering; and that compulsory heterosexuality depends upon rigidity in gender roles and is reinforced by the promotion of racial purity." Any intersection of race, gender, or sexuality that traverses traditional boundaries has the potential to create a sense of marginalization for the individual who is crossing those boundaries.

Almaguer, Tomas, Rudiger Busto, Ken Dixon, and Ming-Yeung Lu. "Sleeping with the Enemy? Talking about Men, Race and Relationships." *Out/look*, no. 15 (Winter 1992): 30.
A frank conversation held between four gay men of color—two Latinos, one Asian American, and one African American—all college-educated members of the *Out/look* editorial board, about interracial gay relationships. Among the topics discussed are the unique individual experiences of each person vis-à-vis coming out within the contexts of both their own culture and the dominant culture, and the tension between one's individual sexual desires and the growing pressure to maintain primary relationships within one's own ethnic group. Each participant provides a unique perspective from which to explore how race, ethnicity, and sexual orientation intersect with desire.

Aura, Jan. "Gender Orientation/Case Illustration of Toni: A 19-Year-Old Biracial Man." In *Child and Adolescent Therapy: A Multicultural-Relational Approach*, edited by Faith H. McClure and Edward P. Teyber, 219-250. Orlando, Fla.: Harcourt, Brace College Publishers, 1996.

In this book, intended for mental health practitioners, a model of child/adolescent therapy called the multicultural-relational approach is outlined. This approach recognizes that a plurality of cultural factors and experiences contributes to each individual's subjective worldview. Chapter 8 of this volume tells the story of a client named Toni, a biracial nineteen-year-old, and of his coming to terms with his sexuality and biracial ethnic identity. According to the chapter's author, "The resolution of positive identity formation depends on the ability of a person to feel belonging as an integrated member of various groups (broad social community, ethnic community, lesbian or gay community, friendship network, family, and possibly romantic partnership), while simultaneously maintaining autonomy and a unique sense of self." The author provides detailed account of sessions held with this client, and how the author helped the client come to understand and accept his sexual and ethnic identity.

Chu, Wei-cheng Raymond. "Some Ethnic Gays Are Coming Home; or The Trouble with Interraciality." *Textual Practice* 11, no. 2 (1997): 219-235.

This essay provides a clear overview of the issues and controversies surrounding interracial romance among gay men, as manifested in various works of literature and film by American and British authors. This is one of several essays falling within the realm of critical theory/cultural studies that addresses the following question: "Is desire by men of color for White men a result of internalized racism and self-hatred?" The author analyzes literary works and feature films illustrating the various angles of the debate, and argues that the issues at play are too complex to be reduced to simplistic explanations and that further study and analysis are needed to fully understand the underlying dynamics of interracial relationships among gay men.

Collins, J. Fuji. "Biracial-Bisexual Individuals: Identity Coming of Age." *International Journal of Sexuality and Gender Studies* 5, no. 3 (2000): 221-253.

Collins presents a study of the identity development of biracial, bisexual Japanese Americans. Based in grounded theory, the focus of the study is on how Japanese Americans perceive themselves in relation to other individuals, groups, and/or their environment. The findings show that the degree of support or negative experience within one's social networks plays a primary role in influencing an individual to identify or not identify as biracial. The author also argues that there are parallels between identity development in biracials and bisexuals. The author concludes by pointing out the need to further study the intersection of race, sexual identity, and gender, especially as they relate to individuals who do not fit the "White, middle class" mold.

Connolly, Medira L., and Debra A. Noumair. "The White Girl in Me, the Colored Girl in You, and the Lesbian, in Us: Crossing Boundaries." In *Off White: Readings on Race, Power and Society*, edited by Michelle Fine et al. New York: Routledge, 1997.

Two psychologists, one Black, the other White, both lesbian, engage in a "deeply personal" dialogue on race, gender, and sexuality. They follow a "group relations perspective," which has theoretical roots in pyschoanalytic and social systems theories and allows for an understanding of both the irrational and unconscious forces as well as the group processes involved in creating a denigrated other. The authors conclude that projecting and stereotyping are insidious processes and that what must happen to combat them is to accept all aspects of one's identity and to keep one's internal identities in dialogue with each other. Addressing these ultimately helps to combat the "isms": racism, sexism, and heterosexism.

Cutrone, Christopher. "The Child with the Lion: The Utopia of Interracial Intimacy." *GLQ* 6, no. 2 (2000): 249-285.

Full of quotations by writers like Adorno, Foucault, Hegel, and Fanon, this lengthy essay, written by a White gay male artist and writer, is a combination of philosophical and literary treatise on the notions of race and sexuality as they concern gay Black-White interracial intimacy. The author, having himself been attacked for including Black-White erotic content in his work, defends the rights of individuals who wish to cross racial lines and engage in interracial relationships, and calls to task those who argue that the use of Black imagery in essentially White artistic media is used in a racist manner. He argues that his essay "The Child with the Lion" "recognizes how intimate refuge can be found between those who would otherwise be estranged by race."

de Romanet, Jerome. "A Conversation with Melvin Dixon." *Callaloo* 23, no.1 (2000): 84-109.

Published posthumously (both de Romanet and Dixon passed away in the early 1990s), this is a fascinating conversation between professor of English and African American studies Jerome de Romanet and Melvin Dixon, also a professor of English and author of several critically acclaimed literary works that deal with being gay and African American. A wide variety of issues are touched upon, including the issue of interracial intimacy between Black and White men in Dixon's novel *Vanishing Rooms*; Dixon's thoughts on the international impact of African American writers, particularly James Baldwin; and Dixon's thoughts on the state of the contemporary African American literary scene. This is a fascinating look at Dixon's views and experiences. While it is a lengthy piece, it is engaging to the end.

Foulke, Mary L., and Renee L. Hill. "We Are Not Your Hope for the Future: Being an Interracial Lesbian Family Living in the Present." In *Our Families, Our Values: Snapshots of Queer Kinship*, edited by Adam E. Goss and Amy Adams Squire Strongheart. New York: Haworth Press, 1997.

This is the story of an interracial lesbian couple who describe the many challenges that confront them as they strive to live happy lives. Included in the discussion are descriptions of relations with each woman's family and reactions to the couple's desire to have children. Differences between the two women are acknowledged and celebrated, not the other way around. Accordingly, they argue that "we are all different from the idealized norms, and we all benefit from questioning and dismantling those norms."

Freedman, Estelle B. "The Prison Lesbian: Race, Class and the Construction of the Aggressive Female Homosexual, 1915-1965." In *Sex, Love, Race: Crossing Boundaries in North American History*, edited by Martha Hodes, 423-443. New York: New York University Press, 1999.

This article offers a historical review of the criminological literature on lesbianism in women's prisons and describes how views of it have evolved over the course of the twentieth century. Central to this discussion is the mythology around the Black lesbian in prison. During the first half of the twentieth century, for example, these women were usually described as playing the aggressive, male role and preying on White women, who were not viewed necessarily as lesbians themselves but as potential victims of this pathological behavior. Race thus substituted for gender in women's prisons, according to the authors. They note, however, a shift in emphasis after World War II, and argue that all lesbians became demonized and were portrayed in the criminological literature as menacing social types. By the 1960s, the focus on lesbians in prison had completely shifted from a focus on Black women to all working-class lesbians. An interesting historical look at how notions of race and class have contributed to shifting views of lesbianism in prison settings.

Greene, Beverly. "Lesbian Women of Color: Triple Jeopardy." In *Women of Color: Integrating Ethnic and Gender Identities in Psychotherapy*, edited by Lillian Comas-Diaz and Beverly Greene. New York: Guilford Press, 1994.

Greene notes that very little mental health research has been done on lesbian women of color and that there is clearly a need for the exploration of the complex interaction between sexual orientation and ethnic and gender identity development. This article provides practitioners with a framework from which to begin looking at lesbians and women of color from a more diverse perspective and at lesbians of color with greater cultural sensitivity. In reviewing some general cultural characteristics of various subgroupings of lesbian women, such as Native American lesbians and Latina lesbians (although it is emphasized that there is much diversity in these communities), Greene discusses the dilemmas associated with interracial relations between women of color and White women. The author concludes by stating that mental health professionals must make themselves aware of the distinct combinations of stressors and psychological demands made on lesbians of color, particularly the potential for isolation, anger, and frustration.

Greene, Beverly, and Nancy Boyd-Franklin. "African American Lesbians: Issues in Couples Therapy." In *Lesbians and Gays in Couples and Families: A Handbook for Therapists*, edited by Joan Laird and Robert Jay Green. San Francisco: Jossey-Bass, 1996.

The authors bemoan the lack of research on Black lesbian issues, noting that research on lesbians has typically focused on White, middle-class women. Triple jeopardy, a term applied to these women, refers to being vulnerable to the social discrimination and internalization of all the negative stereotypes traditionally aimed at African Americans, women, and lesbians. In their discussion of the issues related to this group, the authors note that lesbians of color are more likely to be involved in interracial relationships than White women and that lesbian interracial couples face additional challenges such as increased public visibility and family pressure.

Grinker, Roy Richard. *In the Arms of Africa: The Life of Colin M. Turnbull*. New York: St. Martin's Press, 2000.

This is a biography of the late English anthropologist, Colin Turnbull. Known for his innovative studies of African tribal societies, he upset his colleagues by ignoring established boundaries set in his field. It was not unusual for him to become highly involved in the lives of the people he studied or to wake up in the arms of one of his male hosts. He was an Oxford graduate and a homosexual with a Black gay lover named Joe Towles. While his attraction to Towles puzzled his contemporaries, as they didn't see the two as a good match, the author of this biography argues that Towles was an indispensable part of Turnbull's life and that Turnbull loved him dearly. A worthwhile, interesting story.

Hall, Lisa Kahaleole Chan. "Eating Salt." In *Names We Call Home: Autobiography on Racial Identity*, edited by Becky Thompson and Sangeeta Tyagi. New York: Routledge, 1996.

In this revealing autobiographical essay, Lisa Kahaleole Chan Hall takes the reader on an excursion through her multicultural, multiracial life, where we learn about her Hawaiian, American, African, and Chinese roots and her conflicts with the issue of identity. Compounding her conundrum is the fact that her physical features change over time, prompting her friends and acquaintances to question who she is, and she is left to wonder the same. Of particular note is her struggle with labels and her determination to find community. A well-told story of a lesbian woman coming to terms with the various aspects of her multicultural, multiracial self.

Kanuha, Valli. "Compounding the Triple Jeopardy: Battering in Lesbian of Color Relationships." In *Diversity and Complexity in Feminist Therapy*, edited by Laura S. Brown and Maria P.P. Root. New York: Haworth Press, 1990.

The author explores how racism in feminist and lesbian communities plus sexism and internalized oppression in communities of color contribute to the silencing of lesbians of color, especially those in abusive relationships. Acknowledging that the issues facing lesbians of color in violent relationships are complex, confusing, and painful, the author argues that therapists working with lesbians of color must understand these myriad issues, but more importantly they must understand the interface between violence, homophobia, and racism. Of particular interest is a discussion of the role of power dynamics and the use of violence in interracial lesbian relationships.

Kich, George Kitahara. "In the Margins of Sex and Race: Difference, Marginality and Flexibility." In *The Multiracial Experience: Racial Borders as the New Frontier*, edited by Maria P.P. Root. Thousand Oaks, Calif.: Sage, 1996.

This article describes the experience of identifying as both bisexual and biracial. It also addresses the issue of marginality in relationship to the monoculture and the issue of flexibility, or being comfortable with ambiguity and paradox as a way of life, as well as the similarities of experiences one encounters as a biracial and bisex-

ual individual. The article provides a review of theories related to
identity formation. According to the author, "The task is to see past
the distorted and cloudy mirror of the majorities, through the cru-
cibles of the struggles, experiences and relatedness of the chorus of
the marginalized."

Leslie, Dorian, and Lauren MacNeill. "Double Positive: Lesbians and
Race." In *Racism in the Lives of Women: Testimony, Theory, and
Guides to Anti-Racist Practice*, edited by Jeanne Adleman and
Gloria M. Enguidanos. New York: Haworth Press, 1995.
This article concerns the multiple oppressions confronting lesbians
of color and how racism within the lesbian community and homophobia in communities of color impacts these women. It also focuses on identity development and the challenges of facing one's
own internalized racism and homophobia. The article concludes
with a discussion of interracial relationships and offers to interracial couples strategies for dealing with racism and homophobia.

Moraga, Cherrie. "The Breakdown of the Bicultural Mind." In *Names
We Call Home: Autobiography on Racial Identity*, edited by Becky
Thompson and Sangeeta Tyagi. New York: Routledge, 1996.
Cherrie Moraga writes about being "mixed-blood" and lesbian,
about her Mexican / Indian / Mestiza heritage and her French / Canadian / White heritage. Through a series of vignettes that take the
reader from New York to Mexico to Navajo country, she weaves
stories about intimate relationships with other women of color and
about the different sides of her family. Boldly stating her position,
she writes: "I am that raging breed of mixed-blood person who
writes to defend a culture that I know is being killed. I am of that
endangered culture and of that murderous race, but I am loyal to
only one. My mother culture, my mother land, my mother tongue,
further back than even she can remember."

Otalvaro-Hormillosa, Gigi. "Racial and Erotic Anxieties: Ambivalent
Fetishization from Fanon to Mercer." In *Postcolonial and Queer
Theories: Intersections and Essays*, edited by John C. Hawley.
Westport, Conn.: Greenwood Press, 2001.
Falling within the realm of cultural studies, this dense article relies
heavily on postmodern social theory. In this case, the author uses
the work of Frantz Fanon, author of *Black Skin, White Masks*, to
argue that the notion of hybridity "creates possibilities for identifi-
cations that can lead to cross-race-class-gender-sexuality coalitions
in the perpetual struggle against an imperial system that maintains
multiple structures of repression in place." The author analyzes a
variety of works, including the films of Isaac Julien, whose work
deals with gay interracial themes. This article is written primarily

for those academics involved in critical theory, cultural studies, or queer studies.

Pearlman, Sarah F. "Loving across Race and Class Divides: Relational Challenges and the Interracial Lesbian Couple." *Women and Therapy: Couples Therapy: Feminist Perspectives* 19, no. 3 (1996, special issue): 25-36.

More lesbians are finding themselves in interracial relationships and as a result, are often confronted with unique challenges. These include issues of homophobia, racism, and limited social support systems. This article provides narratives of the story of two interracial lesbian couples to illustrate the challenges of dealing with race and class. The author recommends psychotherapeutic care that is sensitive to race, class, and culture. This approach allows for the articulation of perspectives, which reframes and depersonalizes power struggles.

Poon, Maurice Kwong-Lai. "Inter-Racial Same-Sex Abuse: The Vulnerability of Gay Men of Asian Descent in Relationships with Caucasian Men." *Journal of Gay and Lesbian Social Services* 11, no. 4 (2000): 39-67.

Drawing from his experience working for several years with gay Asian men, Poon describes the need for greater understanding of abusive relationships in Asian-White interracial couples. The author notes that as victims of abuse, gay Asian men frequently do not seek help or do anything to end the violence, due to their internalization of cultural shame. The purpose of the article is to examine the issue of abuse and to raise public concern about the matter. The author discusses the risk factors that leave Asian men prone to violence in intimate relationships with White partners.

Scott, Darieck. "Jungle Fever? Black Gay Identity Politics, White Dick and the Utopian Bedroom." *GLQ* 1, no. 3 (1994): 299-321.

This article is set within the framework of cultural studies. Easier to read and more informative than others within this framework, the author confronts the issue of Black gay identity development and the issue of interracial attraction among Black and White men. Through a review of the literary writings and other works, he argues, as have others, that the complexities of human sexuality result in multiple realities and motivations.

Trujillo, Carla. "Confessions of a Chicana Ph.D." *Out/look*, 5, no. 3 (Winter 1992): 23-27.

In this first person narrative, Carla Trujillo discusses the development of her awareness of her own ethnic background as a Chicana, her attraction to women of various racial and ethnic backgrounds, and of the different challenges that come into play when one is involved intimately with someone from one's own race versus someone from another race. She also discusses the issues that arise from class differences. While she argues that there may very well exist a certain degree of self hatred among people of color who are only attracted to Whites, she also challenges the rhetoric of nationalism and contends that to be attracted to people from different races or classes does not necessarily mean one is full of self-hatred for doing so or has "issues" to resolve.

Weiner-Mahfuz, Lisa. "Organizing 101: A Mixed-Race Feminist in Movements for Social Justice." In *Colonize This! Young Women of Color on Today's Feminism*, edited by Daisy Hernandez and Bushra Rehman. New York: Seal Press, 2002.

This is an essay by a lesbian woman of mixed-race heritage—Jewish and Arab—who shares with the reader stories about her family and the tensions experienced as a result of having parents whose cultures and politics are in conflict. She also discusses the many challenges she faces as an individual with roots in two cultures. While on the surface, she can pass as a White woman, she insists on acknowledging her full self. Accordingly, her "struggle and that of other mixed-race people is to not internalize these dualisms—Jewish/Arab Black/White Privilege/Oppression—and become paralyzed by a society that rejects our complexity in the name of keeping things simple and easy to categorize." An insightful look at identity politics.

Williams-Leon, Teresa. "The Convergence of Passing Zones: Multiracial Gays, Lesbians, and Bisexuals of Asian Descent." In *The Sum of Our Parts: Mixed-Heritage Asian Americans*, edited by Teresa Williams-Leon and Cynthia L. Nakashima. Philadelphia: Temple University Press, 2001.

This article deals with how Asian-descent gay, lesbian, and bisexual multiracial individuals deal with what the author refers to as their "converging passing zones" of race and sexuality. It also illustrates how these individuals "perform their social identities and develop strategies of negotiation and navigation within and across social boundaries, transforming their 'passing zones' into 'no passing zones' which are defined as critical spaces of resistance and empowerment." The author's ultimate aim is to argue for the need for alliances among marginalized peoples in the quest for inclusive politics and shared emancipation.

Wu, Judy Tzu-Chun. "Mom Chung of the Fair-Haired Bastards: A Thematic Biography of Doctor Margaret Chung, 1889-1959." Ph.D. diss., Stanford University, 1998.

This essay provides interesting details of the life of Margaret Chung (1889-1959), whose life unfolds during the transition from the Victorian era to the modern twentieth century in San Francisco's Chinatown. Mom Chung, a doctor, never married and had affairs with White women and engaged in gender bending, but never solidly identified herself as a lesbian. The article examines the historical significance of her life, and explores how this fascinating woman negotiated sex, race, and gender during the early part of the twentieth century.

12 Representations of Interracial Relationships and Multiracial Identity on the American Screen

Helen Look and Martin Knott

The representations of interracial relationships and multiracial persons in American cinema have steadily evolved over time, moving from taboo status to common occurrence. The root of this forbidden status was the fear of sexual relations across races and ethnicities and a belief in White/European racial purity and superiority. Just as there were laws in parts of the United States for much of the seventeenth through twentieth centuries that prohibited interracial marriage (Alabama was the last state to have such a law, finally repealing it in 2000), there was an understanding amongst American filmmakers, especially prior to the civil rights movement, that interracial romance and sex were topics to be avoided or to at least not endorse. Historically, the few films that dealt with interracial relationships often ended tragically for the couples, though that has changed in recent years. Seen even less frequently on film, but with similar consequences, are multiracial characters who typically lead lives dominated by suffering and anger as a result of society's rejection of them. They have been portrayed as denying their mixed heritage and "passing" as White people. In place of these more controversial representations, filmmakers have often used platonic interracial relationships to promote racial harmony. These are especially common in buddy action films. Fortunately, the slow process of changing these representations progressed through the latter half of the twentieth century and continues into the twenty-first.

An increasing prevalence of interracial relationships in American society can be traced in American film. As the civil rights movement gained momentum beginning in the post-World War II period, American filmmakers generated controversy and discussion by addressing this and other race related topics. *Sayonara* (1957) offered the story of two relationships between American servicemen and Japanese women during the Korean War. Both cultures, the American military and Japanese society, discouraged and even punished such love relationships, leaving the two couples with difficult choices. The couple at the center of the story, portrayed by Marlon Brando and Miko Taka, sacrifice their social standing to be together, while the second couple, Red Buttons and Miyoshi Umeki in Supporting Actor Oscar-winning performances, commit suicide together to avoid being separated.

Shadows, directed by John Cassavetes in 1959, addresses the issue of "passing" for White and the sense of isolation and bigotry in the face of love that multiracial people typically have to confront. In the film, three siblings of varied skin tones, two brothers and a sister, struggle to make their way in the Manhattan jazz world. The sister, Lelia, is light-skinned enough to pass for White and falls in love with Tony, a White musician. The relationship ends when Tony meets Lelia's brothers and realizes she is part Black. The younger brother, Ben, also light-skinned, has difficulty fitting in with either White or Black social groups and becomes increasing isolated and disillusioned. Hugh, the oldest and darkest of the siblings, struggles to get singing gigs at the better jazz clubs. At the time of their premieres, *Shadows* and *Sayonara* were groundbreaking in their frank portrayal of the social obstacles faced by interracial couples and multiracial individuals. However, *Sayonara* is often criticized for its stereotypical portrayal of Japanese women as subservient.

A number of classic films on interracial relationships were produced during the height of the civil rights movement in the 1960s. *A Patch of Blue* (1965) sought to answer the question of whether romantic love could truly be color-blind by depicting a romance between a blind White woman and a sighted Black man, portrayed by newcomer Elizabeth Hartman and Sidney Poitier. The relationship is opposed by the man's brother and the woman's mother, portrayed by Shelley Winters in a Best Supporting Actor Oscar-winning performance. Poitier's own Best Actor Oscar for *Lilies of the Field* two years earlier and resulting box office clout may have been major factors in the filmmakers having the courage to present such a relationship in a studio picture. However, Poitier was still frustrated that his character's romantic relationships continued to be nonexistent or, at best, limited to taboo status. *A Patch of Blue* was a critical and financial success, even in Southern states where the civil rights movement met significant resistance. In fact, an eight-second kiss between the central characters was cut from film prints shown in the region.[1]

Possibly the first film people think of when reflecting on interracial relationships in movies is the landmark *Guess Who's Coming to Dinner* (1967), which also starred Sidney Poitier alongside screen legends Spencer Tracy and Katharine Hepburn. In the film, a long-time liberal White couple is forced to confront their principles head-on when their daughter brings home for the first time her fiancé, a Black doctor, and his parents. Both sets of parents disapprove of the pending union, citing the harsh social judgments such a pairing would face rather than their own biases. In the end, the parents are forced to face their prejudices and accept their children's relationship. Many consider the film groundbreaking because it was the first major Hollywood studio picture on interracial relationships to end happily for the couple. *Guess Who's Coming to Dinner* received ten Oscar nominations, with the lead actors Tracy and Hepburn both winning Best Actor Oscars for their roles. The film went on to become the Columbia Pictures' highest-grossing picture at that point in its history.[2]

The box office success of *Guess Who's Coming to Dinner* suggested to television and film producers that American moviegoers and television viewers might be ready to confront interracial relationships, leading to more films and television episodes on the topic. Television, being the medium with most direct access to audiences, has probably been the greatest media influence in evolving people's attitudes toward different ethnic groups. The process began early in network television's history. Although it is rarely discussed in terms of race and ethnicity, the television sitcom classic *I Love Lucy* (1951-1957), with Cuban Ricky Ricardo and his White wife, Lucy, was the earliest multiethnic marriage regularly presented on television. However, this pioneering aspect of their relationship was never the subject of an episode. Though not within the context of an interracial romance, the most widely accepted example of the first interracial kiss on television was from the 1968 *Star Trek* episode "Plato's Stepchildren" in which White Captain Kirk (William Shatner) kisses Black Lieutenant Uhura (Nichelle Nichols). The storyline had the two characters under the control of powerful aliens when the kiss occurred but this did not reduce the controversy of the event. Despite the unwilling nature of the kiss, broadcasters in some Southern states refused to air the episode.

In the late 1960s, daytime soap opera programs began to add African American characters that were not merely domestic servants as had previously been the case. In 1968, *One Life to Live* was the first soap opera to have a major storyline focus on a Black character. Actress Ellen Holly portrayed Carla Gray, the light-skinned daughter of a Black hospital custodian, who secretly passed for White for years. Although she was engaged to a White doctor, Carla found herself attracted to a Black intern. Shamed by her mother into accepting her true heritage, Carla chose to end her engagement to the doctor and pursue a relationship with the intern. It was not until 1988, twenty years later, that *General Hospital* featured the first interracial marriage on a daytime drama. Since then, portrayals of interracial couples have become more commonplace, with some soap operas, such as *All My Children*, featuring the relationships as major storylines.

In primetime television, the first show to include an interracial couple and their children as show regulars was *The Jeffersons*, which debuted in 1975 as a spin-off from the successful and controversial *All in the Family*. Neighbors Tom and Helen Willis, portrayed by Franklin Cover and Roxie Roker, were often the targets of verbal attacks from bigoted, Black entrepreneur George Jefferson, who was written as a Black version of *All in the Family*'s Archie Bunker. Perhaps George's sharpest barbs were saved for their adult multiracial children Jenny and Allan who he often referred to as "zebras." The popular long-running sitcom *M*A*S*H* (1972-1983) added the interracial marriage between White Sergeant Max Klinger and Korean Soon-Lee, portrayed by Jamie Farr and Rosalind Chao, in its final season. This relationship was carried over to the short-lived follow-up series *After MASH* (1983-1984). Interestingly, both actors were portraying ethnicities different than their own: Farr is Lebanese and Chao is Chinese. It was not until *True Colors* premiered on Fox in 1990 that a major network series had an interracial family as the central characters. Starring Frankie Faison and Stephanie Faracy, the show borrowed the Brady Bunch concept of a merged family but added the feature of a Black husband with two sons and a White wife with a daughter. Racial and cultural differences were often central to the story but the episodes focused more on the children's adjustment to the new family rather than the issues the parents faced.

By the 1990s, it became common to see interracial couples in films and television without it being central to the storyline of the film. In what may be well-meaning attempts by producers and directors to improve race relations, interracial relationships are now often treated as unexceptional and commonplace. Movies such as *The Bodyguard* (1992) and *There's Something About Mary* (1998) contain interracial couples but characters make little more than passing comments about this aspect of the relationships. However, many movies and television shows still address the intolerance and family disapproval many of these relationships continue to face and ask whether American society has made as much progress as believed.

While most films on the topic continue to focus on White/non-White relationships, a few movies have dealt with romance between two ethnic minorities. *Mississippi Masala* (1991), for example, looked at the developing love between an African American man (Denzel Washington) and a Ugandan East Indian woman (Sarita Choudhury). Like conventional White/non-White interracial relationship representations in film, the lovers must overcome bigotry from both groups of family and friends. Director Spike Lee was inspired to make *Jungle Fever* (1991) by the beating death of Yusef Hawkins in the Benson-hurst section of New York City. The Black youth was targeted by a mob of White youths, predominantly of Italian American descent, be-cause it was believed he was dating a White girl in the neighborhood. In the controversial film *Jungle Fever*, director Spike Lee tells the story of an African American architect (Wesley Snipes) who has an extra-marital affair with his Italian American secretary (Annabella Sciorra). Lee depicted the interracial affair as driven by taboo sexual desire rather than romantic love.

A number of films have taken inspiration from Shakespearean classics to explore modern interracial relationships, the most frequently adapted source being *Romeo and Juliet* with its tragic star-crossed lov-ers. The conflict between the Capulets and the Montagues serves as an ideal model for representing the gulf in relations between racial groups. As in the original work, the outcome is often tragic for the central char-acters. Rather than taking their own lives, it is often the circumstances created by an intolerant society that lead to the death of one or both of the lovers. Examples of these Romeo and Juliet inspired films are Oscar-winning *West Side Story* (1961) and *China Girl* (1987). *Romeo Must Die* (2000) is a martial arts-action retelling of the story without the central romance between the interracial characters.

Shakespeare's *Othello*, which has an interracial relationship at the center of the story, has also been adapted a number of times. Although revenge and envy are the central themes of the play, Othello's North African Moorish ethnicity elicits prejudice from other characters throughout the play. The pervasive prejudice and Othello's own sense of being unworthy of Desdemona's love due to his ethnicity make him susceptible to the villain Iago's manipulations. Again, the end is tragic for the lovers as Othello takes Desdemona's life and then his own. The most recent film adaptations of the play are *Othello* (1995) and *O* (2001). The 1995 adaptation is set in the play's original time period and stars Laurence Fishburne and Kenneth Branagh in the roles of Othello and Iago. Set in a modern, well-to-do high school, *O* casts the central character as the school's star basketball player and the only Black stu-dent, Odin James as portrayed by Mekhi Phifer.

The most common interracial relationship portrayed on the big and small screens has been the close male friendship, especially in action films. An early classic of this style of film is *The Defiant Ones* (1958) starring Sidney Poitier and Tony Curtis as escaped convicts chained together and on the run. They are forced to overcome their racist atti-tudes toward each other and cooperate to flee the posse pursuing them. The television classic *I Spy* (1965-1968) centered on the interracial partnership of spies played by Bill Cosby and Robert Culp who exchanged witty banter but without the racial tension that preoccupied much of American society at that time.

In the 1970s and 1980s, it became more common to see Black and White cops as both partners and best friends on police televisions shows like *The Rookies* (1972-1976) and *Miami Vice* (1984-1989). The box office success of *48 Hours* (1982) revived the unwilling partners model on the big screen, leading to such films as the *Die Hard* (1988-1995) and the *Lethal Weapon* (1987-1998) series of films. The most recent trend in films of this style of action buddy movies has been to join African American and Asian actors in what appears to be an attempt to capitalize on urban hip-hop culture's affection for Hong Kong martial arts films. Examples of these films are the previously mentioned *Romeo Must Die* (2000), *Cradle 2 the Grave* (2003), and the *Rush Hour* (1998-2001) series. It might be said that there are more interracial buddy action films than interracial romantic films because the action films have been more successful financially. However, this financial success may actually indicate that while American society is ready to accept the concepts of interracial friendship and cooperation, it is not ready for interracial love and romance.

While the number of interracial couples in American films and television shows has been limited, even fewer multiracial characters have been represented. A handful of films have attempted to tell the stories of interracial people, sometimes resorting to the "tragic mulatto" narrative. One might get the impression that American filmmakers are preoccupied with the concept of "passing" for White. Films such as *Imitation of Life* (1934 and 1959), *Pinky* (1949), and *Mixing Nia* (1998) attempt to explore multiracial self-identification, usually by having the character initially deny their ethnic heritage until they are forced to look inward and embrace it. *Devil in a Blue Dress* (1995) and *The Human Stain* (2003), both adapted from best-selling novels, focus on characters struggling to maintain the secret of their racial heritage to continue "passing" as Whites. Within the preoccupation with "passing," one may detect a strain of superiority because there seems to be an assumption that any non-White person given the opportunity to be perceived as White would jump at the chance.

On occasion, television shows have featured interracial characters and had storylines that dealt with their multiracial backgrounds. In 1988, the soap opera *As the World Turns* added the character of Lien Hughes, the daughter of a White American Vietnam War soldier and a Vietnamese nurse, who was initially portrayed by Ming-Na. The character had a difficult time fitting into her new American community and, most importantly, with her new White stepmother. The police drama,

Homicide: Life on the Street (1993-1999) included the character Lieutenant Al "Gee" Giardello, the product of a Sicilian American father and African American mother. Gee often made reference to and expressed pride in both aspects of his heritage. The sitcom *Girlfriends* (2000-), which centers on the friendship of four Black women, includes a biracial woman raised by an adoptive White family. The character has dealt with many aspects of her multiracial background, including confronting her adoptive White sister who acts "more Black" than herself, and meeting her free-spirited, White birth mother for the first time. A recent dramatization of race relations from the perspective of multiracial individuals is the miniseries adaptation of author Anne Rice's *Feast of All Saints* (2001). Set in pre-Civil War New Orleans, the story depicts the struggles faced by a society of free people of color, the offspring of White plantation owners and light-skinned octoroon mistresses. Although these children enjoyed privileges of White society, they were still not considered equals and faced racial oppression. The complex story questioned whether people could escape their predetermined fate in a racially divided society.

It has also become more common to see actors who have multiracial backgrounds on television and the silver screen. Keanu Reeves, Halle Berry, Catherine Bell, Frankie Muniz, Rob Schneider, Lou Diamond Philips, and Carol Channing are just a few examples of well-known actors who have diverse racial heritages and successful careers. However, their roles often do not acknowledge that the actors are multiracial. In the case of Channing, her African American heritage was not known until the publication her autobiography in 2002. Vin Diesel is perhaps the ultimate multiracial actor. Though he has not given any details, Diesel self-identifies as "multiracial" and has portrayed characters of various ethnicities in his film roles. He has portrayed an Italian American World War II soldier in *Saving Private Ryan*, an African American convict in the futuristic *Pitch Black*, and a Jewish gangster in *Knockaround Guys*. Though multiracial actors are not new in Hollywood, Diesel and these other actors represent what is likely to be an increasing presence in film and television of actors of ambiguous ethnicity as the population of multiracial people in America continues to grow.

Since the civil rights movement, representations of interracial couples have become more common on the small and large American screen but the underlying messages of these representations have changed little. The themes of the tragic lovers and the "passing, tortured mulatto" are still frequently used in these films. The makers of these films seem self-righteous in their attempts to illustrate the anguish that can be caused by racism and intolerance. Other writers, directors, and producers, wishing to promote interracial brotherhood without treading into controversial subject matter, have chosen to represent interracial couples and multiracial people as ordinary, everyday people rather than focus on the experiences unique to them. Unfortunately, the most common interracial relationship seen on screens continues to be the platonic interracial buddy action film, though even these films are moving in new directions. The intent here is not to minimize the stories told in all of these films and television shows. The messages they share about acceptance, cooperation, and tolerance must be continuously voiced if the dream of a color-blind society is to be achieved. However, there are more profound stories about interracial relationships and multiracial identity that have yet been told. Hopefully, as the numbers of multiethnic actors, writers, and directors increase, new perspectives and themes will arise that give America a deeper understanding of the challenges and rewards of interracial lives.

Search Strategies

When searching for films with interracial themes, you may encounter some difficulties. Although a film may be cited as having an interracial/multiracial cast (actors of different racial groups), it may not have a storyline that deals with interracial relationships. When a film has an interracial theme, the film description might not have the term "interracial" but may simply state the two ethnic groups, such as "African American and White." Here are some keywords and strategies to use when searching for interracial films.

When searching general resources, remember to limit your searches to visual materials. This can be done by including keywords for the format such as: "video," "videocassette," "movie," "motion picture," "film," "cinema," "media," "television," "TV," "documentary," "screen," or "visual materials." If you are searching a film catalog, it would not be necessary to include a keyword for the format.

When searching for the racial aspect, use keywords such as: "race," "mixed race," "miscegenation," "interracial," "inter-racial," "multiracial," "multi-racial," "multiethnic," "multi-ethnic," "biracial," "bi-racial." Use keywords for specific racial or ethnic groups such as: "mulatto," "quadroon," "octoroon," "amerasian," "mestizo," "hapa," and so forth. It is important to realize that there are many different words and phrases to describe interracial and multiracial. (See Appendices I and II for more comprehensive lists of these terms.) Some of the words may be offensive but were commonly used during the time period when the film or show was made.

When searching for the relationship aspect, use keywords such as: "relationship," "love," "romance," "marriage," "dating," "attraction," and "relations."

General searches on the Internet often retrieve pornographic web sites. Use the advanced search mode of the search engines to utilize term exclusion features to try to eliminate the pornographic interracial materials from search results. There are web sites about interracial films that are maintained by individuals or by organizations. Typically, these web resources will focus on a particular ethnic group such as African Americans or Asian Americans. To find additional information about any film, reliable information can be found at the Internet Movie Database, http://www.imdb.com.

The best search results are achieved by searching film catalogs and/or library catalogs that use controlled vocabulary. Look for common subject headings or keywords used in the database to describe the topic. This will help limit search results to visual materials related to interracial relationships or multiracial individuals.

Some film catalogs are available at the Public Moving Image Archives and Research Centers web site at http://lcweb.loc.gov/film/arch.html. This web site has links to numerous film catalogs. Local libraries may be able to provide access to subscription resources such as OCLC's WorldCat and A/V Online Database. OCLC's WorldCat has over 49 million bibliographic records from libraries worldwide. A/V Online Database is a comprehensive database of audiovisual materials for educators. Searching of either of these two resources will exclude references to pornographic materials.

Finally, a general literature search can often retrieve articles, book chapters, or books that deal with the subject of representation of race in American cinema. Reading these sources and checking their bibliographies can sometimes help identify lesser-known films with interracial themes. The literature will often focus on particular ethnic groups, time periods, or subject matter.

Selection Criteria

The following list of films focuses on how interracial relationships are portrayed in American cinema, but a few foreign films and documentaries were included. There is an emphasis on films that were considered landmarks in film and social history and are commonly mentioned in literature about media representations of interracial relationships. This is by no means meant to be a comprehensive list. A number of films were excluded from the list if the storyline did not explicitly address the interracial relationship and/or the film has not received recognition for the interracial relationship. Films with White actors portraying non-White characters are also excluded from this list. Some foreign films and documentaries/videos were included because they are commonly mentioned as media resources dealing with interracial relationships. All of these films are influential (either negatively or positively) on perceptions of interracial relationships.

Selected Filmography

Documentaries and Videos

American Love Story, directed Jennifer Fox, New Video Group, 500 min. 1999. Videocassette.

The documentary *American Love Story* focuses on the thirty-year marriage of Bill Sims, an African American blues musician, and Karen Wilson, his Caucasian wife. Through a series of ten episodes, director Jennifer Fox documents the relationship of this interracial couple and their two daughters, Cicily and Chaney. The documentary provides an in-depth look at the issue of race from one family's perspective.

Banana Split, produced and directed Kip Fulbeck, National Asian American Telecommunication, 37 min., 1990. Videocassette.

This experimental film explores issues of biracial identity. Director Kip Fulbeck examines his own life as a Hapa with a White father and an Asian mother. The film combines narratives, stories, and media clips to explore issues of self-identity and interracial dating.

Coffee Colored Children, produced and directed Ngozi A. Onwurah, Women Make Movies, 17 min., 1988. Videocassette.

This semi-autobiographical story explores the director's difficult childhood growing up with White and Nigerian parents in England. It examines how incidents of prejudice can lead to internalized racism and confusion of self-identity. The director recounts painful memories of wearing White makeup and scouring her skin with chemical abrasives to make herself more White.

Days of Waiting, produced and directed Steven Okazaki, National Asian American Telecommunication Association, 30 min., 1990. Motion Picture.

The documentary *Days of Waiting* tells the story of the artist Estelle Ishigo, one of the few Caucasians who lived in an internment camp during World War II. Over one hundred thousand Japanese Americans were forced to relocate to internment camps.

Estelle refused to abandon her Japanese American husband. They were both forced to move to Heart Mountain, Wyoming. The experience of life in an internment camp is shared through her sketches and memories. *Days of Waiting* was honored with an Academy Award for Best Documentary, Short Subjects.

Domino: Interracial People and the Search for Identity, Films for the Humanities & Sciences, 45 min., 1994. Videocassette.

Domino portrays the stories of six multiracial individuals and their search for their own identities. Children of interracial relationships are often pressured to choose between two cultures. This film explores how self-identity is influenced by the parents' history; family politics; a search for community; and hierarchies of race, gender, and class.

Doubles: Japan and America's Intercultural Children, directed Reggie Life, Global Film Network, 58 min. [English version], 83 min. [Japanese version], 1995. Videocassette.

During World War II, the fraternization of American soldiers and Japanese women resulted in a number of children born in and out of wedlock. Some of the children were taken to America, while many stayed in Japan and were abandoned by both their mother and father. The film *Doubles* takes an in-depth look at the lives of the children who stayed in Japan and those who left. Over fifty years since World War II, there is a new generation of interracial/intercultural children of Japanese and American descent. How is the next generation being treated? Have things changed? Have they remained the same?

En Ryo Identity, produced and directed Paul Mayeda Berges, National Asian American Telecommunications Association, 23 min., 1991. Videocassette.

The experimental film *En Ryo Identity* explores the complexity of claiming a "biracial identity." The director Mayeda Berges interweaves the subject of the media's construction of Asian American identity, the representations of Asians in movies, and interviews with his Japanese American grandmother about her internment camp experiences.

Interracial Marriage: Blending the Races in America, produced and directed Howard Mass, Films for the Humanities & Science, 52 min., 1992. Videocassette.

This film explores how difference in color, religion, and ethnicity can influence interracial marriages. Some topics include: how and why interracial couples are drawn to each other, how their differences affect their marriage, and how to handle these differences with friends and parents.

Just Black? Multi-Racial Identity, produced Francine Winddance Twine, directed Jonathan F. Warren, Francisco Ferrandiz, and Francine Winddance Twine, Filmakers Library Inc., 57 min., 1992. Videocassette.

In this documentary, anthropologist Francine Winddance Twine interviews young people of multiracial heritage where one parent is African American and the other parent is Asian, Hispanic, or White. Some of the subjects explored include dating, family relationships, friendships, and growing up multiracial in America.

Mixed Blood, produced and directed Valerie Soe, National Asian American Telecommunications Association, 21 min., 1992. Videocassette.

Using interviews and clips from television and film, Soe explores the personal, social, and political implications of interracial relationships between Asian Americans and non-Asian Americans.

Politics of Love in Black and White, directed Ed Burley and Chris Weck, California Newsreel, 33 min., 1993. Videocassette.

In this documentary on interracial relationships on college campuses, interracial couples discuss the pressures they face from friends and family. Black and White students comment on the personal and political implications of interracial relationships.

Roots in the Sand, produced and directed Jayasri Majumdar Hart. 57 min., 1998. Videocassette.

This film is a portrait of Punjabi Mexican families who settled in Southern California's Imperial Valley, just north of the Mexico border, during the early twentieth century. The film uses archival and family photographs, personal and public documents, and film footage to document the history of men from Punjab who because of immigration laws were not allowed to import brides from India. These men, many farmers, married Mexican women and raised families. This documentary portrays the obstacles these interracial families faced from anti-immigration and anti-miscegenation laws, as well as social and institutional discrimination.

Films

The Bodyguard, produced Kevin Costner, directed Lawrence Kasdan and Jim Wilson, Mick Jackson. Roadshow Films International, 130 min., 1992. Motion Picture.

Bodyguard Frank Farmer (Kevin Costner) is hired to protect pop singer Rachel Marron (Whitney Houston), who has been receiving death threats. As things begin to escalate, the two characters fall in love. *The Bodyguard* was a box office success. This film may be considered a landmark because of its color-blind treatment of love. Although the main characters are in an interracial relationship, there is no mention of race in the movie. *The Bodyguard* was originally proposed as a concept back in the 1970s with Diana Ross and Steve McQueen. It was considered too controversial at the time because of the interracial relationship.

Catfish in Black Bean Sauce, produced and directed Chi Moui Lo. Iron Hill Productions, 119 min., 1999.

Siblings Dwayne and Mai, Vietnamese refugees adopted by Harold and Dolores Williams, are reunited with their birth mother, Thahn, as adults. This situational comedy highlights the romantic involvement of Dwayne to an African American woman and Thahn's objection to his interracial love interest. Movie stars veteran actors Paul Winfield as Harold and Mary Alice as Dolores.

China Girl, produced Mitchell Cannold, Mary Kane, Michael Nozik, and Steven Reuther, directed Nicholas St. John. Great American Films Limited Partnership, Street Lite, Vestron Pictures, 89 min., 1987. Motion Picture.

Like *West Side Story*, this film is a modern day *Romeo and Juliet* set in the lower east side of New York City. Chinese and Italian gangs have been fighting over control of the neighborhoods. The Italian pizza delivery boy Tony (Richard Panebianco) falls in love with Tyan (Sari Chang), the sister of one of the Chinese gang members. Neither faction can accept the interracial relationship. Like the original Shakespeare work, the star-crossed lovers' story ends in tragedy.

Come See the Paradise, produced Robert F. Colesberry and Nellie Nugiel, directed Alan Parker. 20th Century Fox, 138 min., 1990. Motion Picture.

Come See the Paradise tells the love story of second generation Japanese American Lily Kawamura (Tamlyn Tomita) and Irish American Jack McGurn (Dennis Quaid). The couple first faces opposition from Lily's family and then from society. The story takes place during World War II when Japanese Americans were forced into internment camps.

Corrina, Corrina, produced Joseph Fineman, Bernie Goldmann, Paula Mazur, Eric McLeod, Jessie Nelson, Steve Tisch, and Ruth Vitale, directed Jessie Nelson. New Line Cinema, 115 min., 1994. Motion Picture.

After the death of his wife, Manny Singer (Ray Liotta) hires Corrina Washington, an African American housekeeper (Whoopi Goldberg), to help raise his daughter Molly (Tina Majorino). Set in the 1950s, the growing relationship between Corrina and the

Singer family raises concern among family members and the community.

Devil in a Blue Dress, produced Jesse Beaton, Jonathan Demme, Donna Gigliotti, Gary Goetzman, Thomas A. Imperato, Walter Mosley, and Edward Saxon, directed Carl Franklin, Clinica Estetico. Mundy Lane Entertainment, TriStar Pictures, 102 min., 1995. Motion Picture.

In the film, Ezekiel "Easy" Rawlins (Denzel Washington) is hired to find the missing Daphne Monet (Jennifer Beals), the mistress of a powerful mayoral candidate. Issues of race and interracial relationships are explored in this film noir set in 1948 Los Angeles.

Double Happiness, produced Stephen Hegyes and Rose Lam Waddell, directed Mina Shum. Fine Line Features, 87 min., 1994. Motion Picture.

Double Happiness is the story of Jade Li (Sandra Oh), a young Chinese Canadian woman, who is trying to find the balance between her desires and the wishes of her traditional parents. Jade finds it difficult to maintain this balance after she falls in love with Mark (Callum Rennie), a White university student.

Dragon: The Bruce Lee Story, produced John Badham, Kelly Breidenbach, Raffaella De Laurentiis, Hester Hargett, Rick Nathanson, Charles Wang, and Dan York, directed Rob Cohen. Universal Pictures, 107 min., 1993. Motion Picture.

Based on biographies of the international martial arts superstar, the film *Dragon* portrays the challenges encountered by Bruce Lee (Jason Scott Lee) when he immigrates to the United States and builds an acting career. Bruce falls in love and marries Linda Emery (Lauren Holly), a White college student, despite the disapproval of her family and friends. The film has several scenes depicting the discrimination that Bruce Lee experienced personally and professionally. One of the scenes is the loss of the lead role in *Kung Fu*, a television show he helped develop, to Caucasian actor David Carradine.

Far from Heaven, produced Declan Baldwin, George Clooney, Jean-Charles Levy, Jody Patton, Eric Robison, Bradford Simpson, John Sloss, Steven Soderbergh, Christine Vachon, and John Wells, directed Todd Haynes. Focus Features, 107 min., 2002. Motion Picture.

In *Far from Heaven*, the Whitakers seem to have the ideal life. Set in the 1950s, the director Todd Haynes looks below the surface to see the emotionally repressed lives of housewife Cathy Whitaker (Julianne Moore) and her husband Frank (Dennis Quaid). When Cathy discovers that her husband is having an affair with a man, she finds her world out of control. She finds comfort in her friendship with Raymond (Dennis Haysbert), their African American gardener, but their relationship spurs gossip in their community.

Feast of All Saints, produced Peter R. McIntosh, Anne Rice, Bart Wenrich, Forest Whitaker, and John Wilder, directed Peter Medak. Showtime Network, 100 min., 2001. Television Miniseries.

Based on a novel by Anne Rice, this miniseries set in nineteenth-century New Orleans describes the world of the *gens de couleur libre*, or the Free People of Color. These were the children of wealthy White men and their light-skinned Black mistresses. Although granted special privileges normally afforded to Whites, these children were still never considered equal to their White siblings. The daughters were encouraged to continue this lifestyle by becoming mistresses for wealthy White men. The stories of the Free People of Color are told through parallel stories within several generations of one family trying to break from their predetermined destiny. It is a complex look at interracial relationships and biracial identity in the history of New Orleans.

Flirting, produced Barbara Gibbs, Terry Hayes, George Miller, and Doug Mitchell, directed John Duigan. Samuel Goldwyn Company, 99 min., 1991. Motion Picture.

Set in 1965, the film *Flirting* is the story of first love. Danny Embling (Noah Taylor) is attending an Australian all-boys prep school when he meets Thandiwe Adjewa (Thandie Newton), a biracial African girl at a nearby all-girls school. The two characters are outcasts at their schools—Danny is an outcast because of his "rebellious spirit" and Thandiwe is an outcast because of her race. Despite the rules of society and their schools, the two loners continue to secretly meet, flirt during school functions, and eventually fall in love. An upperclassman Nicola Radcliffe (Nicole Kidman) helps the couple keep their secret.

Fools Rush In, produced Anna Maria Davis, Doug Draizin, Michael McDonnell, and Steven P. Saeta, directed Andy Tennant. Columbia TriStar, Sony Pictures Entertainment, 109 min., 1997. Motion Picture.

Businessman Alex Whitman (Matthew Perry) meets Isabel Fuentes (Selma Hayek), a Mexican American photographer. After one night of passion, the couple does not meet again until months later when Isabel discovers she is pregnant. The sparks are rekindled and the couple decides to get married. When the couple meets their respective families, there is the typical comedy of cross-cultural assumptions.

Guess Who's Coming to Dinner, produced George Glass and Stanley Kramer, directed Stanley Kramer. Columbia Tristar Home Entertainment, 108 min., 1967. Motion Picture.

This classic film is considered a landmark with regard to interracial relationships. The story focuses on a daughter (Katharine Houghton) who brings her fiancé (Sidney Poitier) home to meet her liberal parents (Spencer Tracy and Katharine Hepburn). It is a surprise to her wealthy White parents when they learn their future son-in-law is Black. The film explores the issues related to interracial marriages and the acceptance of these relationships by family members. Controversial at the time of its release, the film is named one of the top 100 films by the American Film Institute.

Imitation of Life, produced Carl Laemmle Jr., John M. Stahl, and Henry Henigson, directed John M. Stahl. Universal Pictures, 111 min., 1934. Motion Picture.

Imitation of Life is one of Hollywood's earliest attempts to seriously address the question of race. Stahl's 1934 film adaptation featured African American actors in major roles. After her husband's death, Bea Pullman (Claudette Colbert) and her daughter Jessie (Rochelle Hudson) struggle to make ends meet. Their lives change for the better when African American Delilah Johnson (Louise Beavers) and her daughter Peola (Fredi Washington) move in. Delilah works as the housekeeper in exchange for room and board. The film explores the biracial friendship between these women. One subplot focuses on how light-skinned Peola decides to pass for White. Growing up in an integrated household, Peola enjoys the privileges of Whiteness and rejects her race to continue that lifestyle. The film was later remade in 1959.

Jefferson in Paris, produced Humbert Balsan, Paul Bradley, Ismail Merchant, and Donald Rosenfeld, directed James Ivory. Beuna Vista Pictures, 136 min., 1995. Motion Picture.

Jefferson in Paris depicts President Thomas Jefferson's five years of diplomatic service with France, following the death of his wife. The film primarily focuses on the women in his life. One of the women is his African American slave Sally Hemings (Thandie Newton), who is accompanying his daughter (Gwyneth Paltrow). The film depicts the alleged interracial relationship between Jefferson and Hemings. It was released prior to the controversial DNA study of real-life descendents of Jefferson.

Joy Luck Club, produced Ronald Bass, Patrick Markey, Jessinta Liu Fung Ping, Oliver Stone, Amy Tan, and Janet Yang, directed Wayne Wang. Beuna Vista Pictures, 139 min., 1993. Motion Picture.

Based on the best-selling novel by Amy Tan, this film follows the story of four Chinese women and their relationships with their American daughters, two of whom are in interracial relationships. Although her mother does not approve nor understand, Waverly Jong (Tamlyn Tomita) is in a happy relationship with her White boyfriend. On the opposite end of the spectrum, Rose Hsu Jordan (Rosalind Chao) has a White husband who does not give her the respect her mother thinks she deserves. The author Amy Tan has been criticized for her portrayal of interracial relationships as an integral part of becoming "Americanized." Tan has also been criticized for negative portrayal of Chinese/Chinese American men as being emasculated and/or chauvinists with traditional expectations.

Jungle Fever, produced Jon Kilik, Spike Lee, and Monty Ross, directed Spike Lee. MCA Home Video, 132 min., 1991. Motion Picture.

Flipper (Wesley Snipes) is a successful, married African American man who has an affair with Angie (Annabella Sciorra), an Italian American woman at work. Although Flipper loves his wife and Angie is engaged to marry another man, the couple acts upon their sexual attraction for one another. The film explores the repercussions of an interracial affair, and is often cited as one of the landmark films on interracial relationships. This film is often criticized as being negative about interracial relationships for its failure to distinguish between interracial romance and interracial relationships built on curiosity or "primal lust."

Lone Star, produced Jan Foster, R. Paul Miller, Maggie Renzi, and John Sloss, directed John Sayles. Sony Pictures Classic, 135 min., 1996. Motion Picture.

Director John Sayles tells the story of Sheriff Sam Deeds (Chris Cooper) who is investigating a murder committed 40 years ago. Through the course of his investigation, Sam reveals the uneasy tension of racial groups along the border of Texas and Mexico. One of the story's subplots is the interracial relationship between Anglo Sam and Chicana Pilar Cruz (Elizabeth Peña). Long ago, the couple were high school sweethearts until their parents forced them to break up. They always believed that their parents objected to their relationship because of society's ethnic boundaries. Now as adults, the couple's paths cross and they are tempted to resume their taboo relationship. By the end of the film, we grow to understand why the parents strongly objected to their relationship.

Love Field, produced George Goodman, Kate Guinzburg, Sulla Hamer, Sarah Pillsbury, Don Roos, and Midge Sanford, directed Jonathan Kaplan. Orion Pictures Corporation, 102 min., 1992. Motion Picture.

Set in 1963, *Love Field* is the story of Dallas housewife Lurene Hallett (Michelle Pfeiffer) whose world is shattered after witnessing JFK's assassination. Against her husband's wishes, Lurene embarks on a bus trip to attend the funeral in Washington, D.C. Along the way, she meets African American Paul Cater (Dennis Haysbert) and his young daughter Jonell (Stephanie McFadden). Paul is the complete opposite of her redneck husband. A romance begins to blossom between Lurene and Paul. Through a serious of mix-ups, the threesome is soon trying to evade the law.

The Lover, produced Claude Berri and Jacques Tronel, directed Jean-Jacques Annaud. Metro-Goldwyn-Mayer (MGM), 115 min. [unrated] or 103 min. [R-rated], 1991. Motion Picture.

The art house film *The Lover* (also known as *L'Amant*) is based on the semi-autobiographical novel by Marguerite Duras. Set in 1920s Saigon, a poor French teenager (Jane March) and a wealthy Chinese businessman (Tony Leung Ka Fai) begin a torrid love affair. The couple continues their taboo relationship even though they know their respective families and society would not approve. The characters' names are simply listed as "The Young Girl" and "The Chinaman" in the film's credits.

Mississippi Masala, produced Lydia Dean-Pilcher, Mitch Epstein, Mira Nair, Michael Nozik, and Cherie Rodgers, directed Mira Nair. Samuel Goldwyn Company, 118 min., 1991. Motion Picture.

The film starts with the story of an Asian Indian family expelled from Uganda. The family immigrates to America—specifically Mississippi. The daughter Mina (Sarita Choudhury) falls in love with African American Demetrius (Denzel Washington). The respective families come to terms with their interracial relationship. This is one of the few films where both individuals comprising the interracial couple are ethnic minorities.

Mixing Nia, produced Paul F. Bernard, Sylvia Caminer, Mathew Dunne, James Scura, Gabriella Stollenwerck, and Jedd Wider, directed Alison Swan. Xenon Entertainment Group, 92 min., 1998. Motion Picture.

After being forced to market beer to African American inner city youth, Nia (Karyn Parsons) quits her job at an ad agency. Disillusioned about her job and her lifestyle, Nia decides to write a book and searches for an understanding of her biracial identity. Through her relationships with a Black activist and a White co-worker, Nia soon discovers her roots and finds her true self.

Monster's Ball, produced Milo Addica, Michael Burns, Lee Daniels, Eric Kopeloff, Michael Paseornek, Will Rokos, and Mark Urman, directed Marc Forster. Lee Daniels Entertainment, 111 min., 2001. Motion Picture.

Monster's Ball tells the story of the relationship between White prison guard Hank Grotowski (Billy Bob Thornton) and Leticia Musgrove (Halle Berry), the African American wife of a prisoner he has just executed. Despite the deep-rooted racial prejudice of Hank and his family, the two main characters are drawn together after they suffer unexpected personal tragedies. Halle Berry received an Academy Award for Best Actress for her performance in this film. She was also the first African American to receive the Best Actress Award.

Mr. and Mrs. Loving, produced Eric Buchanan, Timothy Hutton, Dan Paulson, Susan Rose, and Chi-en Telemaque, directed Richard Friedenberg. Hallmark Home Entertainment, 105 min., 1996. Television Movie.

Based on a true story, the film *Mr. and Mrs. Loving* takes place in the 1960s, when sixteen states still enforced laws that prohibited interracial marriages. When White Richard Loving (Dennis Quaid) decides to marry his pregnant African American girlfriend Mildred Jeter (Lela Rochon), the couple does not believe the Virginia law would be enforced. The newlyweds are arrested on their wedding night. They are given the option of spending three years in prison or leaving the state for twenty-five years. The couple decides to move from Virginia. The Lovings eventually take their case to the Supreme Court, which strikes down the state laws forbidding interracial marriage.

My Beautiful Laundrette, produced Sarah Radclyffe, directed Stephen Frears. Orion Classics, 97 min., 1986. Motion Picture.

Omar (Gordon Warnecke) is a young Pakistani man trying to live up to the expectations of his wealthy extended family. He runs a laundry in a poor London neighborhood with an old classmate, the white, unemployed, and formerly fascist Johnny (Daniel Day-Lewis). Set during the Thatcher era when rampant unemployment and the fear of immigrants "taking jobs" led to racial tensions, a secret romance develops between the two young men despite their ethnic and class differences. Omar and Johnny's relationship is contrasted by Omar's uncle's long-term affair with a white mistress and complicated by Omar's attraction to his uncle's daughter.

Both Omar and Johnny are forced to confront this tension with their family and friends.

O, produced Betsy Danbury, Zack Estrin, Daniel Fried, Eric Gitter, Lisa Gitter, Fred Goodman, Brad Kaaya, Stephen A. Kepniss, Michael I. Levy, Anthony Rhulen, William Shively, and Tom Tucker, directed Tim Blake Nelson. Lions Gate Film Inc., 95 min., 2001. Motion Picture.

O is a modern teenage version of Shakespeare's *Othello*. *O* is Odin (Mekhi Phfifer), the school's star basketball player and the only African American student in a White boarding school. Odin has everything he wants—a chance for a good education, a winning basketball season, and his loving girlfriend Desi (Julia Stiles). His teammate Hugo (Josh Hartnett) grows jealous of all the attention given to Odin—especially the attention given by their coach, who is Hugo's father. Hugo devises an elaborate plan to bring the eventual down fall of Odin. Although Odin and Desi are in an interracial relationship, the racial differences are only subtly explored.

One Night Stand, produced Michael De Luca, Robert Engelman, Mike Figgis, Ben Myron, Richard Saperstein, and Annie Stewart, directed Mike Figgis. New Line Cinema, 102 min., 1997. Motion Picture.

One Night Stand is a morality tale of casual sex during the age of AIDS epidemic. African American Max Carlyle (Wesley Snipes) comes to New York City to visit his old friend Charlie (Robert Downey Jr.). Max winds up having a passionate one night stand with White Karen (Nastassja Kinski). The affair leads Max to question his L.A. life and his relationship with demanding Asian American wife Mimi (Ming-Na Wen). A year later when Max returns to visit Charlie who is now dying of AIDS, he meets Karen again, who is married to Charlie's brother. In interviews, actor Wesley Snipes commented that he wanted to have the role of his wife played by an Asian American or Spanish actress. He did not want the audience to mistake the interracial aspects of the affair to be the main storyline like it was in one of his previous movies, *Jungle Fever*.

Othello, produced David Barron, Jonathan Olsberg, and Luc Roeg, directed Oliver Parker. Sony Pictures Entertainment, 123 min., 1995. Motion Picture.

This is one of the many film adaptations of Shakespeare's play *Othello*. Iago (Kenneth Branagh) manipulates Othello (Lawrence Fishburne) to believe that his wife Desdemona (Irene Jacob) has been unfaithful. Since Othello was a Moor (North African), the character is often portrayed as being dark-skinned. Although he loves his wife, Othello's jealousy leads to a tragic ending to the interracial marriage.

A Patch of Blue, directed Guy Green. Metro-Goldwyn-Meyer, 105 min., 1965. Motion Picture.

A Patch of Blue tells the story of a blind White girl, Selina D'Arcy (Elizabeth Hartman), who lives a sheltered life with an abusive family. One day in the park, Selina meets Gordon Ralfe (Sidney Poitier). He is the first person to show her kindness and friendship. Her feelings for Gordon deepen over time. Things change when Selina's mother discovers that Gordon is African American. *A Patch of Blue* is considered one of Hollywood's earliest attempts at portraying an interracial relationship. By having the main character Selina be blind, the story explores the issue of whether true love is color-blind.

Queen, produced Bernard Sofronski, directed John Erman. CBS Television, 281 min., 1993. Television Miniseries.

Queen is the television adaptation of the last novel written by Alex Haley (known for *Roots*). The title character Queen (Halle Berry) is the daughter of an African American slave woman and a White plantation owner. Queen experiences prejudice because of her light-skinned complexion. Her story spans the time period from just prior to the Civil War through the early twentieth century.

Sally Hemings: An American Scandal, produced Craig Anderson, Tina Andrews, Wendy Kram, Ric Rondell, Marty Eli Schwartz, and Gerrit van der Meer, directed Charles Haid. CBS Television, 87 min., 2000. Television Movie.

This television miniseries provides a fictionalized account of the illicit affair between the third president of the United States, Thomas Jefferson (Sam Neill), and his slave Sally Hemings (Carmen Ejogo). During their thirty-eight-year relationship, the interracial couple allegedly had six children. This miniseries explores the couple's relationship more in-depth than *Jefferson in Paris*.

Save the Last Dance, produced Marie Cantin, Robert W. Cort, Scarlett Lacey, David Madden, and Douglas Curtis, directed Thomas Carter. Paramount Pictures, 112 min., 2001. Motion Picture.

Until her mother's accidental death, teenager Sara Johnson (Julia Stiles) dreamed of becoming a professional ballet dancer. She is uprooted from her quiet small town life and must adjust to her predominantly Black high school on the south side of Chicago. She soon meets Derek Reynolds (Sean Patrick Thomas) a popular African American student. The characters' mutual love of hip hop dancing further blossoms into a growing love for each other. The main characters must overcome their racial differences and face opposition to their interracial relationship.

Sayonara, produced William Goetz, directed Joshua Logan. MGM/UA
Home Entertainment Inc., Warner Bros., 147 min., 1957. Motion
Picture.

Based on James Michener's best-selling novel, *Sayonara* tells the
story of the difficulties of interracial relationships in Japan during
the Korean War. An American serviceman Gruver (Marlon
Brando) realizes that his long-distance relationship is no longer
working. Although the military and Japanese society strongly dis-
courage interracial relationships, Gruver falls in love with a Japanese performer (Miko Taka). The couple face prejudice because of
their relationship. After Gruver sees the tragedy that has befallen
his friend Joe (Red Buttons) and his Japanese wife (Miyoshi
Umeki), he begins to question whether love can withstand the
hardships of interracial relationships. Both Buttons and Umeki
won Oscars for their supporting roles in the film.

Secrets & Lies, produced Simon Channing-Williams, directed Mike
Leigh. October Films, 142 min., 1996. Motion Picture.

Set in London, *Secrets & Lies* tells the story of a Black professional woman Hortense Cumberbatch (Marianne Jean-Baptiste)
who is searching for her biological mother. She discovers that her
mother is Cynthia Purley (Brenda Blethyn) a White working-class
woman who has another daughter. There is awkwardness when
Cynthia's family realizes that she had given up her Black daughter
for adoption. The mother and daughter eventually come to terms
with the reason why Cynthia gave Hortense up for adoption. Director Mike Leigh is known for encouraging his actors to improvise
the dialogue, which helps this story seem authentic in the flow of
conversation.

Shadows, directed John Cassavetes. Orion Home Videos, 81 min.,
1959. Motion Picture.

In *Shadows*, director John Cassavetes explores issues of racism in
the 1950s' New York music scene. The light-skinned African
American Lelia (Lelia Goldoni) falls in love with Tony (Anthony
Ray), a White man. Once he meets her musician brothers, Tony realizes that she is Black, which forces him to evaluate his feelings
for her.

Snow Falling on Cedars, produced Ronald Bass, Carol Baum, David
Guterson, Kerry Heysen, Kathleen Kennedy, Frank Marshall,
Lloyd A. Silverman, Harry J. Ufland, and Richard Vane, directed
Scott Hicks. MCA/Universal Pictures, 127 min., 1999. Motion Pic-
ture.

Set in the 1950s, *Snow Falling on Cedars* explores post-war anti-Japanese sentiments in a small fishing community in the Pacific Northwest. Reporter Ishmael Chamber (Ethan Hawke) is investigating the murder of a local fisherman. The accused murderer, Japanese American Kazuo Miyamot (Rick Yune), is the husband of Hatsue (Youki Kudoh), the only woman Ishmael has ever loved. Through flashback sequences, the film shows how Japanese American Hatsue and White Ishmael fall in love, but they are forced to keep their romance a secret. Growing societal pressure and World War II forces the young couple apart until the meet again at the trial.

A Walk in the Clouds, produced James D. Brubaker, Bill Johnson, Stephen Lytle, Gil Netter, David Zucker, and Jerry Zucker, directed Alfonso Arau. 20th Century Fox Film Corporation, 102 min., 1995. Motion Picture.

After returning from World War II, Paul Sutton (Keanu Reeves) accidentally meets the pregnant Victoria Aragon (Aitana Sánchez-Gijón) who is on her way home to her family's vineyards. She is afraid to tell her family that she is pregnant and unmarried. Although he is already married, Paul offers to pretend to be her husband to help her face her domineering father (Giancarlo Giannini). Mr. Aragon immediately forms a dislike for Paul who is unaware of the old Mexican traditions. Over time, the couple's love for each other blossoms. Although this is an interracial relationship, most of the opposition from the father is based on cultural differences.

The Wedding Banquet, produced Dolly Hall, Ted Hope, Li-Kong Hsu, Feng-Chyt Jiang, Ang Lee, and James Schamus, directed Ang Lee. Samuel Goldwyn Company, 106 min., 1993. Motion Picture.

The Wedding Banquet is a comedy about Wai-Tung (Winston Chao), a gay Taiwanese American man, who is afraid to tell his parents about his happy long-term relationship with his Caucasian lover Simon (Mitchell Lichtenstein). To stop his parents from pressuring him to marry, Wai-Tung decides to marry his tenant Wei-wei (May Chin), an immigrant in desperate need of a green card. Wai-Tung's parents come to America to throw him a wedding and a banquet. The threesome tries to maintain the secret, which leads to humorous cross-cultural situations.

West Side Story, produced Saul Chaplin, Robert Wise, and Walter Mirisch, directed Jerome Robbins and Robert Wise. United Artists, 151 min., 1961. Motion Picture.

West Side Story is a musical adaptation of *Romeo and Juliet* set in New York City. The rival street gangs, the Jets and the Sharks, battle for control of the neighborhood. The interracial love of Puerto

Rican Maria (Natalie Wood) and White Tony (Richard Beymer) cannot survive in a world of prejudice and violence.

Zebrahead, produced Matthew Coppola, Jeff Dowd, Charles Mitchell, Peter Newman, Oliver Stone, William F. Willett, Stan Wlodkowski, and Janet Yang, directed Anthony Drazan. Ixtlan Corporation, 100 min., 1992. Motion Picture.

In the film *Zebrahead*, the Jewish Zack (Michael Rapaport) and African American Dee (DeShonn Castle) are best friends. Everything starts to change once Zack begins to date Dee's cousin, Nikki (N'Bushe Wright), who has just moved into town. The friendship between the teenaged Zack and Dee is put to the test. The couple encounters prejudice from friends and family, and Nikki begins to mistrust Zack. Set in Detroit, this film combines issues of interracial dating and urban violence.

Notes

1. Fristoe, Roger. *A Patch of Blue*. http://www.turnerclassicmovies.com/thisMonth/Article/0,,12485,00.html

2. McGillicuddy, Genevieve. *Guess Who's Coming to Dinner*. http://www.turnerclassicmovies.com/ThisMonth/Article/0,,403,00.html

Appendix I: Subject Heading/Descriptor Vocabulary to Assist in Searching

Karen Downing

Vocabulary to Assist in Your Search

Searching techniques will change based on whether you are using paper or electronic catalogs and indexes, and between each separate index. Generally, it is much easier to use online resources because you can use keyword searching to combine terms such as "children AND interracial." One common technique is to start with a keyword search, like the one above, then browse through the retrieved records to look at the subject headings used. Catalogers and indexers assign these descriptors to each resource to describe the subject content. When you do a subject search, you must use the particular language of that catalog or index. Once you find a subject heading that is descriptive of your topic, re-do your search as a subject search.

Library Catalogs

Library of Congress Subject Headings
The following list reflects the Library of Congress Subject Headings (LCSH) that relate to interracial subject matter. Knowing these headings will help in the search for interracial materials. Be aware that headings change regularly, so always check the current LCSH list to ensure you are using the most recent headings for your subject searches.

> *Indians of North America—Mixed descent*
> *Interethnic marriage*
> *Intermarriage* (NOTE: may be subdivided in any number of ways.
>   For example: *Intermarriage—Psychological aspects)*
> *Interracial adoption* (NOTE: may be subdivided)
> *Interracial dating* (NOTE: may be subdivided)
> *Interracial marriage* (NOTE: may be subdivided)
> *Interracial marriage in art*
> *Interracial marriage in literature*
> *Miscegenation* (NOTE: may be subdivided)

Miscegenation in literature
Miscegenation in motion pictures
Mulattoes (NOTE: may be subdivided)
Mulattoes in literature
Passing (Identity) (NOTE: may be subdivided)
Passing (Identity) in literature
Passing (Identity) in motion pictures
Racially mixed children (NOTE: may be subdivided)
Racially mixed people (NOTE: may be subdivided by geographic
  area. For instance, *Racially mixed people—United States)*
Racially mixed people in art
Racially mixed people in literature

Sometimes interracial materials are not specifically assigned interracial subject headings. *Crossings: A White Man's Journey into Black America* and Judy Scales-Trent's *Notes of a White Black Woman* are two examples of important interracial books that have no interracial subject headings assigned to them at all. Therefore, it may be necessary to widen your search to include a variety of broader subject headings. The following headings are often used to describe materials that have interracial components to them, such as an anthology on race related topics.

African Americans—Relations with Indians
Black Race—Color
Ethnicity
Human skin color
Race
Race Identity
United States—Race Relations

Indexes

Indexes are important tools for any researcher looking for periodical literature on interracial issues. There are indexes for newspapers, scholarly journals, and popular magazine articles. The following selection of social science indexes highlights how different the subject terms assigned to interracial articles can be from one index to another.

Alternative Press Index
Alternative Press Index (API) is a major index to the North American "alternative press." *API* indexes 380 alternative, radical, and left publications, which report and analyze the practices and theories of cultural,

economic, political, and social change. Ninety percent of these publications are not indexed elsewhere. Some terms used in *API* are:

Ethnic identity
Identity, politics of
Interracial families
Interracial heritage
Interracial identity
Interracial relationships

America: History and Life

This resource indexes social science and humanities literature on all aspects of U.S. and Canadian history, culture, and current affairs. It is a primary resource for finding articles on U.S. history, yet many articles that are relevant to interracial topics have no interracial headings at all. Beware of ambiguous headings such as "race relations"—they are often the only way to get at the interracial literature in this index.

Creoles
Marriage (Mixed)
Miscegenation
Mulatto
Mulattoes
Race Relations

Biblioline

Biblioline provides electronic access to eight databases from the National Information Services Corporation (NISC), including *African Studies*, *Alternative Press Index*, *Black Studies Database*, *Gay & Lesbian Abstracts*, and other less relevant indexes. It is useful for locating "nonmainstream" publications which more commercial indexes overlook. As important as these resources are, there is very little in the way of interracial subject headings. Users of this product must choose very general terms such as "adoption" rather than "interracial adoption."

Interracial Marriage

Chicano Index

Chicano Index indexes articles on a wide range of subjects relating to Mexican Americans, and since 1992, the broader Latino experience, including Puerto Ricans, Cuban Americans, and Central American immigrants. While *Chicano Index* is an important resource for finding articles written within the Hispanic community, there are virtually no interracial headings. You must search broadly under "marriage" for interracial marriage, or under "adoption" for interracial adoption.

Dissertation Abstracts

Doctoral students in their dissertations are publishing some of the most exciting and important interracial research today. Therefore, *Dissertation Abstracts* is an important source to use. Unfortunately, *Dissertation Abstracts* does not use subject headings, rather they have an ever-changing list of keywords that are extracted from the titles of the dissertations. Keep in mind these change from month to month depending on the titles of the dissertations. Recent keywords include: *Interracial Couples, Interracial Relationships, Racial Identity, Miscegenation.*

ERIC

ERIC indexes journal articles, government publications, and unpublished materials such as conference papers, reports, and theses, on the broad topics of education and developmental/cognitive psychology. ERIC is one of the better indexes for subject headings specifically describing interracial topics. Check the *Thesaurus of ERIC Descriptors* for changes in subject headings.

> *Biracial Committees*
> *Cultural Interrelationships*
> *Cultural Pluralism*
> *Intermarriage*
> *Multiracial Persons*
> *Racial Identification*
> *Transracial Adoption*

Ethnic Newswatch

One of the most comprehensive sources for interracial articles written from within the interracial community, *Ethnic Newswatch* is not without problems. If you were to do a subject search on the term "interracial," you would not find articles on interracial topics. This is due to the fact that their subject term is "inter-racial." They do however, maintain indexes by race, and using the term "multi-ethnic" will allow entrée into the interracial literature as well. It is also possible to access a plethora of interracial articles via keyword searching, however, the results are imprecise.

> *Culture/Ethnicity (Bi-Racial)*
> *Culture/Ethnicity (Bi-Racial, Heritage)*

Culture/Ethnicity (Multi-ethnic)
Human/Interpersonal Relations (Family, Inter-Racial Marriage)
Human/Interpersonal Relations (Inter-Racial Marriage)
Inter-racial

InfoTrac

InfoTrac is a general topic database that indexes articles from newspapers, reference books, and periodicals, many with full text and images. It is especially helpful for current events and popular culture coverage of interracial topics.

Council on Interracial Books for Children
Interracial Adoption
Interracial Dating
Interracial Marriage
Miscegenation
Mulatto
Racially Mixed People

International Index to Black Periodicals

Provides indexing for over 150 scholarly and popular periodicals in Black Studies, with links to full text for forty of them. Most articles on interracial topics are assigned one of two broad subject headings, with a plethora of general headings for each article.

Interracial Relationships
Racially Mixed People

ISI Web of Science (Social Science Citation Index and Science Citation Index)

A unique tool that allows users to trace citations used in a given article, and to see who is citing any given author. A user can search *ISI* to find articles on an interracial topic, then view that article's bibliography to find related articles. Unfortunately, many articles on interracial topics do not carry specific interracial subject headings; making it necessary to do inaccurate keyword searching on terms such as "interracial."

Intermarriage

JSTOR (Journal STORage)

JSTOR, a full text database of the sciences and social sciences, contains unique features that make it both important and frustrating to use. It is important to use because it allows entrée into literature that many libraries do not have in paper format. It has many pre-1990 issues of scholarly journals that other databases do not contain. Here is where you will find many articles on interracial topics from the 1970s when sociologists first started writing about interracial issues. It is frustrating to use because unlike other databases, it only searches full text, authors, titles, and abstracts—no subject headings. Therefore, you must use keywords such as "interracial," "biracial," "interracial marriage," etc. These searches will result in many articles that are off topic. Still, the database is very helpful in finding resources you won't find elsewhere.

ProQuest Research Library

ProQuest is an important resource because it indexes more than two thousand periodicals, many of which have full text articles available. It is a general topic index, yet the subject access to interracial topics is not great. One must use the general terms such as "Multiculturalism & pluralism" or a general heading such as "Race relations" to find a full array of articles. Keyword searching on "Interracial" gives an overwhelming array of resources that includes many irrelevant items.

> *Interracial relationships*
> *Multiculturalism & pluralism*
> *Race relations*

Psychological Abstracts

Psychological Abstracts (or its online counterparts, *PsycINFO* or *PsycARTICLES*) indexes periodical literature, some book chapters, and dissertations in the field of psychology and other closely related fields (social work, sociology). This is a very important database because so much has been written about interracial identity development, interracial family dynamics, and causation for interracial relationships. Though many relevant subject headings are used, there are still many articles that have not been assigned any of these specific headings.

> *Ethnic Identity*
> *Interracial Adoption*
> *Interracial Family*
> *Interracial Marriage*
> *Interracial Offspring*

Public Affairs Information Service (PAIS)

Contains references to over 450,000 journal articles, books, government documents, statistical directories, research and conference reports, publications of international agencies, microfiche, Internet material, and so on, concerning public affairs worldwide.

Mixed marriage
Plural societies
Race relations

Wilson Indexes to Journal Articles

A combination of indexes from H.W. Wilson (including *Social Sciences Index*) covering a wide variety of subjects, representing mainstream scholarly journals, popular magazines, and some books. *Wilson Indexes* provides citations to articles, essays in collections, and book and film reviews. Library of Congress Subject Headings are assigned to resources fairly consistently and accurately. We found no interracial articles without specific interracial subject headings attached.

Interracial adoption
Interracial adoption—United States
Interracial dating
Interracial marriage
Interracial marriage—Law and legislation—United States
Interracial marriage—United States
Miscegenation—Law and legislation—United States
Racially mixed people

Appendix II: Definitions of Terms Used in Interracial Literature

Karen Downing

This is a list of terms and phrases that have been used in information resources to describe various individuals or groups of racial and interracial people. Many of the terms are also used by indexers and catalogers to classify interracial articles, books, and other resources. Today, some of these terms may be viewed as being hurtful, hateful, and derogatory in nature. It is, however, essential to know about these terms and their uses in literature in order to find resources on many interracial topics, particularly those that are historical in nature. Some of these terms have been used for centuries; some are very new. Some have dictionary meanings that are separate from their vernacular use. Where appropriate, their idiomatic and classification uses are noted.

Terms and Definitions

African American: Also known as Black, Negro, and Afro-American, depending on the time period of the literature. "Individuals of African ancestry, born in or resident in the United States."[1]

Afro-Asian: An individual who is both Black and Asian.

Afro-Cuban: A person, group, or cultural expression that has elements of Black and/or African culture with those of Cuban culture.

Amerasian: Of mixed American and Asian parentage, especially used when fathered by an American serviceman stationed in Asia.

American Indian: Also known as Native American, Indigenous Americans, Indians of North America (in Library of Congress terminology), Amerinds, Amerindians, and Indians. "A member of the aboriginal people of America."[2]

Anglos: Refers to European Americans or Whites, even if they are not Anglo-Saxon. Used particularly in the Southwest United States. A person of English (or non-Latin European) origin, especially a resident in the United States, distinguished from a Mexican-American.

anti-miscegenation laws: Laws passed by states in the North and the South to prohibit people of color from marrying White European

Americans. The first such law was passed in 1622 in Virginia (Russell, 1992, p. 13). These laws were declared unconstitutional in 1967 after the famous *Loving v. Virginia* Supreme Court case.

Asian: Belonging to, situated in, or characteristic of the countries or regions lying to the east of the Mediterranean. A person native to Asia. The term Oriental was previously used, but is now considered derogatory by many.

Asian-American: One who is a citizen or resident of the United States, and of Asian birth or descent.

biracial: People who are born of parents of two different "races." Sometimes referred to as bi-racial, interracial, inter-racial, multiracial, multi-racial, mixed, mixed-race, or more specific mixes such as Amerasian.

Black Indian: Individuals who are of both African and Native American descent. This mixing has been very common since colonial times when the mistreatment of Native Americans and the enslavement of African Americans brought many people from these two groups together.

blended people/families: The process of mixing intimately; the blending of two races.

blood quantum: Traditionally this phrase has been used to measure the degree of Native American heritage in fractions such as one-half, one-quarter, one-eighth, etc.

blue-vein societies: Social groups of multiracial elites found mainly in urban settings before the civil rights period. The name arose from the members' light skin color that allowed their veins to be seen.

Brass Ankles: Triracial isolate group located on the coastal plain area of South Carolina.

Cajuns: A triracial isolate group found in Mississippi and Alabama.

Cape Verdians: A group of Portuguese Africans who in the 1993 federal hearings on Directive 15 expressed a desire to have their own census category.

Caublinasian: The term Tiger Woods coined to describe his ancestry combining Caucasian, Black, Indian, and Asian.

Caucasian: Refers to White people; specifically, "a name given to the 'white' race of mankind, which derived from the region of the Caucasus."[3]

cephalometry: The science of measuring human racial traits such as head shape and size. The science of measuring the head, especially for determining the characteristics of a particular race, sex, or somatotype.

Chicanos: Americans of Mexican descent.

Creole: During slavery, Creoles were mostly "free people of color" located in Louisiana. They are mixtures of French, Native American, and Black who were afforded higher status than Blacks, but were not on par with Whites.[4] They remain a distinct culture today. The *Encyclopaedia Britannica Online* acknowledges that the term is used with various and often conflicting meanings. They share an intertwined African and Romance languages grammatical base.

Criollos: A person born in Latin America, but of European descent.

Croatans: A triracial isolate group found in North and South Carolina and Virginia.

culture: The accumulation of customs, symbols, ideas, values, norms, beliefs, and products associated with a group of people (a family up to an entire society or nation).

Directive 15: The federal government Directive issued in 1977 that regulated racial categories for all federal paperwork and reporting. The directive did not allow for a multiracial category, or allow multiracial individuals to choose more than one race.

endogamy: Marriage within a specific tribe or similar social group.

ethnicity: A broader term than culture (many cultures can be found within one ethnicity). Ethnicity includes elements of shared culture and way of life, reflected in language, religion, dress, and food. Ethnicity, unlike culture, does not encompass any one social system, which implies regular interaction, but instead refers to a category of peoples.

Eugenics: The study of or belief in the possibility of improving the qualities of the human species or a human population, especially by such means as discouraging reproduction by persons having genetically undesirable traits. Unfortunately, many older interracial resources are cataloged under this terminology.

Eurasian: An individual who is half White European, half Asian.

European American: Used to refer generally to White people, and specifically to those Whites who themselves or whose ancestors immigrated to the United States from any of the European countries.

exogamy: "Marriage outside a specific tribe or similar social unit."[5] Older interracial information was classified under this terminology in reference resources and indexes.

Griquas: "A person of mixed ethnic or racial heritage."[6] Non-White people of mixed "Bushman-Hamite, Bantu and European descent inhabiting chiefly South Africa."[7]

Guineas: A triracial isolate community in West Virginia and Maryland.

Haafu: An individual who is half Japanese and half anything else. Can be an Afro-Asian, Amerasian, or Eurasian.

half-breed: A disparaging term referring to the offspring of parents of different racial origins, especially Native American and European American parents.

Hapa: (or Hapa Haole) A Hawaiian term meaning "half." Refers to a person of part White ancestry or origin, especially a mixture of White and Hawaiian ancestry.

Hispanic: Common usage refers to Americans of Latin American descent. Synonymous with Latino (male) or Latina (female). Hispanic is the ethnic descriptor used by the U.S. government as designated by Directive 15.

Hispanic American: An American citizen or resident, having Spanish or Latin American ancestors or origin.

hybrid: A term used mostly in the field of botany to refer to nonhuman animals, it came into use to describe interracial offspring as early as the 1600s. Refers to the offspring of cross-fertilization between distantly related parents of different races or species.

hypodescent: The eugenic idea that when two races mix, the offspring take on the characteristics and designation of the least desirable race.

hypo-descent rule: "Racially mixed persons are assigned the status of the subordinate group." Also known as the "one-drop rule" or the "traceable amount rule."[8]

integrated family: Refers to an interracial family. The term is sometimes used by indexers rather than "interracial family."

intercountry marriage: Term used to describe marriages between persons from two different countries of origin, but also often includes interracial marriages.

intercultural: Of more than one culture. Often used by indexers and in the vernacular instead of, or related to, interracial.

interethnic: Term sometimes used to define individuals who belong to more than one ethnic group. Often used by indexers and in the vernacular instead of, or related to, interracial.

intermarriage: Term used by many indexers to describe interracial marriages and interfaith marriages. The term is used differently by many different sources.

interracial: Often refers to individuals who belong to more than one race. Used synonymously with multiracial, but is often used more broadly by social scientists to refer to any interaction between members of different races.

invisible Blackness: A phrase used to describe individuals who have some African ancestry but who phenotypically appear White or European American.

issues: A triracial isolate group from Virginia. The "name is derived from the term applied to free Negroes prior to the Civil War."[9]

Jackson Whites: A triracial isolate community from New Jersey and New York. The "name is said to be derived from 'Jackson and White' which are common surnames. . . . Still another idea is that Jackson was a man who imported some of the ancestors of these people during the Revolutionary War."[10]

Latinos/Latinas: A Latin American inhabitant of the United States. Colloquially used as a synonym for Hispanic.

Maroon: Mixed Indian and African fugitive slaves who developed communities in remote areas of South America, the Caribbean, and the Eastern areas of North America.

mélange: A French word for mixture; is sometimes used by interracial people to indicate their mixed racial heritage.

Melungeons: A triracial isolate community located first in Tennessee, then Kentucky. Melungeons are thought to be the product of the mixing of runaway slaves, Native Americans, and European Americans.

Mestizaje: In the Americas, "the mix of Spanish and Portuguese colonizers first, then of English and French, with American Indians, to which the African slaves were added."[11]

Mestizo/a: (also spelled Mestises) Refers to the offspring of White and Native American parents.

Metis: A person of mixed American Indian and European ancestry, or other persons of mixed descent. The term is mainly used in Canada.

miscegenation: The mixing of races; specifically refers to the sexual union of people of different races, with particular negative attention drawn to Black/White mixing, but more broadly used to describe marriage between races. Miscegenation was outlawed in many states until the 1967 *Loving v. Virginia* Supreme Court decision that determined anti-miscegenation laws were unconstitutional. Many indexes and catalogs still use this term to describe interracial marriage.

mixed bloods: Persons derived from more than one race. Used interchangeably with "mixed heritage."

mixed marriage: Synonym for "interracial marriage," but it can also refer to a marriage between persons of different religions.

mongrels: Any animal or plant resulting from the crossing of different breeds or varieties, especially if inharmonious or indiscriminate.

monoracial: Refers to people who identify themselves by a single race.

Montuvios: Coastal Equadorians of mixed descent. "Coastal farmers, called Montuvios, are usually mixed-race Black and Indian, or negros de monte, 'Blacks of the mountain.'"[12]

Moor: A triracial isolate community from Delaware and New Jersey. The "name 'Moor' traditionally derived from ship-wrecked Moorish sailors."[13]

Mulatto/a: (also spelled mollatto, mulata/o, mulatow, mallatto, melotto, molata/o, muletto, mulattoe) One who is half Black and half White. Also used loosely for anyone of mixed race.

Mulattress: A female mulatto.

multiethnic: A term used in the vernacular interchangeably in the vernacular with "multiracial" or "interracial."

multiracial: Often refers to an individual or family belonging to more than one race. Used synonymously with interracial, but also has a broader meaning whereby an individual or group is composed of, involves, or represents various races.

Nanticokes: A triracial isolate community located in Delaware and New Jersey.

Native American: An individual who has indigenous American Indian heritage.

Negro(es): A term used for people of African descent until the 1960s when Black or Afro-American was adopted. Today, the term African American is most commonly used.

New People: A term referring to mixed-race individuals who wish to identify themselves fully as being interracial. The term is thought to originate in 1900 novel by Charles W. Chesnutt called *The House Behind the Cedars*.[14]

Octoroons: A term used during slavery through the civil rights era, meaning a person of one-eighth Black ancestry.

one-drop rule: Related to hypodescent, an idea, and later a series of laws originating in the South beginning in early slavery, that states if a person has even one drop of African blood (ancestry), they are considered Black. This naturally benefited slaveholders who could then enslave mixed-race offspring.[15]

Oriental: "Belonging to, found in, or characteristic of, the countries or regions lying to the east of the Mediterranean or of the ancient Roman empire, or Asiatic countries generally."[16] An outdated, term that is often viewed as offensive today. Most often people use the term Asian today.

outbreeding: Like the terms exogamy or hybrid, a scientific term originally meant to describe nonhuman animals or plant crossings that was adapted to indicate displeasure with interracial unions.

passing: Refers to any light-skinned person of color, who, by pheno-typical stereotype, appears to be White. Someone who chooses a white racial identity to the exclusion of any other, no matter what their actual racial heritage may be. It most commonly refers to a deliberate act of crossing the color line, but can also be inadvertent when others misidentify one's race.

Quadroon: (also spelled Quarteron or Quatron) refers to a person who has one-quarter Black ancestry. Synonymous with the term Ter-ceroon.

Quintroon: An individual who is one-fifth Black.

race: A term that is defined differently in each and every source one uses. Commonly refers to a human social construct involving groups of people including a family, profession, tribe, nation, be-longing to the same "stock." Also, defined as a class or kind of people unified by community of interests, habits, or characteristics. Also, a division of mankind possessing traits that are transmissible by descent and sufficient to characterize it as a distinct human type.

race crossing: Refers both to interracial individuals and relationships that cross racial lines.

racially mixed: A phrase used to mean a person who is descended from more than one race.

Red Bones: a triracial isolate community from Louisiana. The "name 'Red Bone' is derived from the French *Os Rouge*, for persons partly of Indian blood."[17]

Terceroon: (also spelled Terceron) The offspring of a White person and a Mulatto; a person who is one-quarter Black. Synonymous with the term Quadroon.

transracial: Refers to crossing racial boundaries. Used most often when referring to interracial or cross-racial adoptions.

triracial isolates: Small communities of racially mixed families that traditionally lived apart from mono-cultural communities. The in-dividuals within these communities are usually mixtures of White or European American, African American, and Native American peoples. There have been over two hundred triracial isolate com-munities identified.[18]

Wesorts: Triracial isolate group in Maryland.

White: Refers to people of European or Middle Eastern descent. A fluid group of people over time, used to exclude Jews and Italians, and sometimes excludes people of Middle Eastern descent.

Notes

1. *Oxford English Dictionary Online*, Second Edition (Oxford: Oxford University Press, 1996).

2. *Random House Unabridged Dictionary*, Second Edition (New York: Random House, Inc., 1993).

3. See note 1.

4. Root, Maria P.P., *Racially Mixed People in America* (Newberry Park, Calif.: Sage Publications, 1992), 104.

5. See note 2.

6. Ibid.

7. See note 1.

8. Davis, James F., *Who is Black? One Nation's Definition* (University Park, Pa.: Pennsylvania State University Press, c1991), 5.

9. Gilbert, William Harlen, Jr., "Memorandum Concerning the Characteristics of the Larger Mixed-Blood Racial Islands of the Eastern United States," *Social Forces* 24, no. 4 (May 1946), 442.

10. See note 9, p. 443.

11. Smelser, Neil J., and Paul B. Baites, eds. *Encyclopedia of the Social and Behavioral Sciences* (Amsterdam: Elsevier, 2001), 7095.

12. *The Experts Equador* http://www.ecuadorial.com/coast.htm.

13. See note 9, p. 445.

14. Williamson, Joel, *New People: Miscegenation and Mulattoes in the United States* (Baton Rouge: Louisiana State University Press, 1995), xi.

15. Russell, Kathy Y., Midge Wilson, Ronald E. Hall, *The Color Complex* (New York: Harcourt Brace Jovanovich, Publishers, 1992), 14.

16. See note 1.

17. See note 9, p. 445.

18. See note 4, p. 98, Daniel, G. Reginald, *More Than Black? Multiracial Identity and the New Racial Order* (Philadelphia: Temple University Press, 2002), 68; see note 9.

Appendix III: Sociology 412—Ethnic Identity and Intergroup Relations Syllabus

David Schoem

This course looks at multiracial, multiethnic, and multifaith identities and relationships as a focal point for the exploration of a wide range of questions on racial, ethnic, and religious identity and intergroup relations. It considers frameworks for community building, taking into account issues of conflict and power and competing social interests.

Students are encouraged to bring personal experience and perspective to enrich the discussion of theoretical readings. Active participation, a research paper, and two other shorter papers are required.

Required Texts

Root, Maria P.P. *Racially Mixed People in America.* Thousand Oaks, Calif.: Sage, 1992.

———. *The Multiracial Experience.* Thousand Oaks, Calif: Sage, 1996.

Tatum, Beverly. *Why Are All the Black Kids Sitting Together in the Cafeteria?* New York: BasicBooks, 1997.

Zack, Naomi. *American Mixed Race.* Lanham, Md.: Rowman & Littlefield, 1995.

Coursepack

Alba, Richard. *Ethnic Identity: The Transformation of White America*, Chapter 1. New Haven, Conn.: Yale University Press, 1990.

Bayme, Steven. "Intermarriage and Communal Policy: Prevention, Conversion, and Outreach." 285-293 in *The Jewish Family and Jewish Continuity*, edited by Steven Bayme and Gladys Rosen. Hoboken, N.J.: KTAV, 1994.

Brown, Yasmin A., and Anne Montague. "Choosing Sides" *New Statesman and Society* (February 7, 1992).

Calderon, Jose. "Latinos and Ethnic Conflict in Suburbia: The Case of Monterey Park." *Latino Studies Journal* 1, no. 2 (1990): 23-32.

Chesler, Mark. "Racetalk: Thinking and Talking about Racism." *Diversity Factor* 3, no. 3 (Spring 1995): 37-45.

Cohen, Steven. 10-18 in *American Assimilation or Jewish Revival.* Bloomington: Indiana University Press, 1988.

———. "The One in 2000 Controversy." *Moment,* March 1987.

Cose, Ellis. "One Drop of Bloody History: Americans Have Always Defined Themselves on the Basis of Race." *Newsweek,* February 13, 1995.

Espiritu, Yen Le. Chapter 7 in *Asian American Panethnicity: Bridging Institutions and Identities.* Philadelphia, Pa.: Temple University. Press, 1992.

Fisher, Roger, and William Ury. 17-39 in *Getting to Yes.* New York: Viking, 1991.

Gilbreath, Edward. "How Our Children Surprised Us." *Christianity Today,* March 7, 1994.

Gordon, Milton."Toward a General Theory of Racial and Ethnic Group Relations." 84-110 in *Ethnicity: Theory and Experience,* edited by Nathan Glazer and Daniel P. Moynihan. Cambridge, Mass.: Harvard University Press, 1975.

Hacker, Andrew. "Race and Racism: Inferiority vs. Equlaity." 17-30 in *Two Nations: Black and White, Separate, Hostile, Unequal.* New York: Charles Scribner, 1992.

Hoffman, Paul. "The Science of Race." *Discover,* November 1994.

Hughes, Langston. "Let America Be America Again" in *ReReading America: Cultural Contexts for Critical Thinking and Writing,* edited by Gary Columbo et al. Boston: St. Martin's Press, 1992.

Leo, John. "Community and Personal Duty." 29-32 in *The Graywolf Annual Ten: Changing Community,* edited by Scott Walker. St. Paul: Graywolf Press, 1993.

Lorde, Audre. "Age, Race, Class and Women Redefining Difference." 503-509 in *Race, Class, and Gender,* edited by Margaret Andersen and Patricia Hill Collins. Belmont, Calif.: Wadsworth, 1992.

Njeri, Itabari. "The Last Taboo: Does Wave of Interracial Movies Signal a Real Change?" *Ebony,* September 1991.

Omi, Michael, and Howard Winant. 57-68 in *Racial Formation in the United States.* New York: Routledge, 1986.

Parker, Pat. "For the White Person Who Wants to Know How to Be My Friend." 180 in *Reconstructing Gender,* edited by Estelle Disch. Mountain View, Calif.: Mayfield, 1997.

Pinderhughes, Elaine. "Biracial Identity: Asset or Handicap?" 73-93 in *Racial and Ethnic Identity: Psychological Development and Creative Expression,* edited by H.W. Harris, H.C. Blue, and Ezra E.H. Griffith. New York: Routledge, 1993.

Poston, W.S. Carlos. "The Biracial Identity Development Model: A Needed Addition." *Journal of Counseling and Development* 69, no. 2 (1990): 152-155.

Reagon Johnson, Bernice. "Coalition Politics: Turning the Century." In *Race, Class, and Gender*, edited by Margaret Andersen and Patricia Hill Collins. Belmont, Calif.: Wadsworth, 1992.

Rodriguez, Clara E. "Race, Culture, and Latino Otherness in the 1980 Census." *Social Science Quarterly* 73, no. 4 (December 1992): 930-937.

Russell, Karen. "Growing Up with Privilege and Prejudice." 82-87 in *Race, Class, and Gender*, edited by Margaret Andersen and Patricia Hill Collins. Belmont, Calif.: Wadsworth, 1992.

Sandor, Gabrielle. "The 'Other' Americans." *American Demographics*, (June 16, 1994): 36-42.

Schumer, Fran. "Star-Crossed: More Gentiles and Jews Are Intermarrying—and It's Not All Chicken Soup." *New York*, April 2, 1990.

Waxman, Chaim. "Is the Cup Half-Full or Half-Empty?" 31-43 in *American Pluralism and the Jewish Community*, edited by Seymour Martin Lipset. New Brunswick, N.J.: Transaction Books, 1990.

Wertheimer, Jack, Charles Liebman, and Steven Cohen. "How to Save American Jews." *Commentary* 101 (January 1996): 47-51.

Wilson, William Julius. "The Cost of Racial and Class Exclusion in the Inner City." *Annals of the American Academy of Political and Social Science* 501 (January 1989): 8-25.

Week-to-Week Outline

c = *coursepack*
t = *textbook*

Week One: Introduction; Communication
  Film: *None of the Above.*
  Hughes, "Let America Be America Again."
Week Two: Group Identities and Personal Identities
  Film: *Skin Deep.*
  c - Chesler, "Racetalk."
  c - Parker, "For the White Person Who Wants to Know How to Be My Friend."
  c - Pinderhughes, "Biracial Identity: Asset or Handicap?"
  t – Tatum, parts 1 and 2.

Week Three: Race, Racism, and Racial Identity
Films: *True Colors; LA is Burning; America in Black and White.*
c - Cose, "One Drop of Bloody History: Americans Have Always Defined Themselves on the Basis of Race."
c - Hacker, *Two Nations*, chapter 2.
c - Hoffman, "The Science of Race."
c - Omi and Winant, *Racial Formation in the United States*, chapter 4.
t - Spickard, "The Illogic of American Racial Categories." 12-23 in *Racially Mixed People in America.*
t - Tatum, chapters 6 and 8.
Week Four: Assimilation, Cultural Pluralism, Multiculturalism
Film: *Crossing Delancey.*
c - Alba, *Ethnic Identity.*
c - Cohen, *American Assimilation or Jewish Revival.*
c - Espiritu, *Asian American Panethnicity: Bridging Institutions and Identities*, chapter 7.
c - Waxman, "Is the Cup Half-Full or Half-Empty?"
Week Five: Assimilation, Cultural Pluralism, Multiculturalism
t - Shrage, "Ethnic Transgressions: Confessions of an Assimilated Jew" in *American Mixed Race.*
t - Daniel, "Passers and Pluralists: Subverting the Racial Divide" in *Racially Mixed People in America.*
t - Fernandez, "La Raza and the Melting Pot: A Comparative Look at Multiethnicity" in *Racially Mixed People in America.*
Week Six: Multiracial Identity
Films: *Politics of Love in Black and White; Just Black.*
Guest Speaker
c - Brown and Montague, "Choosing Sides."
t - Streeter, "Ambiguous Bodies: Locating Black/White Women in Cultural Representations." 305-320 in *The Multiracial Experience.*
t - Tatum, chapter 9.
t - King and Da Costa, "Remaking of Race in the Japanese American and African American Communities." 227-244 in *The Multiracial Experience.*
t - Weisman, "An 'Other' Way of Life." 152-164 in *The Multiracial Experience.*
Week Seven: Multiracial Identity
Guest Speakers
c - Njeri, "The Last Taboo: Does Wave of Interracial Movies Signal a Real Change?"
c - Poston, "The Biracial Identity Development Model: A Needed Addition."

t - Kich, "Development Process of Asserting Biracial Bicultural Identity." 304-317 in *Racially Mixed People in America.*

t - Nakashima, "Voices from the Movement: Approaches to Multiraciality." 79-97 in *The Multiracial Experience.*

t - Ramirez, "Multiracial Identity in a Color-Conscious World." 49-62 in *The Multiracial Experience.*

t - Williams, "Race as a Process: Reassessing the 'What Are You?' Encounters of Biracial Individuals." 191-210 in *The Multiracial Experience.*

Week Eight: Interracial Relationships

Film: TBA.

t - Johnson, "Offspring of Cross-Race and Cross-Ethnic Marriages." 239-249 in *Racially Mixed People in America.*

Week Nine: Multifaith Identity

Films: *School Ties; Gefilte Fish.*

c - Bayme, "Intermarriage and Communal Policy: Prevention, Conversion, and Outreach." 285-293 in *The Jewish Family and Jewish Continuity.*

c - Cohen, "The One in 2000 Controversy."

c - Greenberg, "The One in 2000 Controversy"

c - Wertheimer, Liebman, and Cohen, "How to Save American Jews."

Week Ten: Interfaith Relationships

Observation and Analysis Paper or Group Identity Paper Due

c - Gilbreath, "How Our Children Surprised Us."

c - Schumer, "Star-Crossed: More Gentiles and Jews Are Intermarrying—and It's Not All Chicken Soup."

Guest Speakers

Week Eleven: Classification and Census-Taking

Students Present Research Papers

Guest Speaker

c - Gabrielle, "The 'Other' Americans."

c - Rodriguez, "Race, Culture, and Latino Otherness in the 1980 Census."

t - Fernandez, "Testimony of the Association of Multiethnic Americans Before the Subcommittee on Census, Statistics, and Postal Personnel of the U.S. House of Representatives." 191-210 in *American Mixed-Race.*

t - Fernandez, "Government Classification of Multiracial / Multiethnic People." 15-36 in *The Multiracial Experience.*

t - Graham, "The Real World." 37-48 in *The Multiracial Experience.*

t - Wilson, "Blood Quantum: Native American Mixed Bloods."
108-125 in *Racially Mixed People in America.*

Week Twelve: Integrating Race, Class, and Gender

Students Present Research Papers

t - Allman, "(Un)Natural Boundaries: Mixed Race, Gender, and
Sexuality." 277-320 in *The Multiracial Experience.*

t - Kich, "In the Margins of Sex and Race." 277-290 in *The Multiracial Experience.*

c - Lorde, "Age, Race, Class and Women Redefining Difference."
503-509 in *Race, Class, and Gender.*

c - Russell, "Growing Up with Privilege and Prejudice." 82-87 in
Race, Class, and Gender.

c - Wilson, "The Cost of Racial and Class Exclusion in the Inner
City."

Week Thirteen: Building Community

Essay/Literature Review Due

Students Present Research Papers

c - Calderon, "Latinos and Ethnic Conflict in Suburbia: The Case
of Monterey Park."

c - Fisher and Ury, 17-39 in *Getting to Yes.*

c - Leo, "Community and Personal Duty." 29-32 in *The Graywolf
Annual Ten: Changing Community.*

c - Reagon Johnson, "Coalition Politics: Turning the Century" in
Race, Class, and Gender.

Week Fourteen: Concluding Discussion and Analysis

Students Present Research Papers

Research Papers Due

Assignments and Grades

Students are expected to maintain the highest level of academic
integrity. Students are expected to submit their own work on
assignments. On assignments in which collaboration is encouraged,
students will be asked to indicate the amount of work submitted that is
their own. Cheating and plagiarism on papers and exams will not be
tolerated and will negatively affect grades.

Active Participation (20 points)

Active student participation is essential to the success of this course. At
a minimum, participation includes regular attendance and attending
class on time. Active participation involves completing readings on

time, exercising good listening skills and paying careful attention to class discussion, contributing analytical comments to discussion, asking probing and clarifying questions, and making good use of office hours. Students will be expected to make presentations to the class on readings and on their research papers. Students who are not active participants as described above will receive a lower grade; students who miss more than three classes will receive a failing grade for the course.

Research Paper (40 points—due April 15)

Research papers will be 10-15 pages and will ordinarily represent an individual effort, although students may request to do collaborative papers. Paper topics must be approved by the instructor.

Observation and Analysis Paper or Group Identity Paper (20 points—due March 18)

This paper (7-10 pages) will ordinarily be completed as collaborative effort with one to three other students. A single grade will be assigned to each paper, credited to each student's name on the paper.

The observation and analysis paper will provide an opportunity to critically observe and record issues of intergroup relations, race and ethnic identity, and multiracial and multifaith identity and relationships. Students should begin their observations at the start of the semester to compile enough data to write a comprehensive essay by the due date. Observations should be linked to reading assignments.

The group identity paper provides an opportunity for a personal exploration of one's group identity(ies). These papers should also be started at the very beginning of the semester in order to allow sufficient time for paper development and revision.

Essay/Literature Review (20 points—due April 8)

Each student will submit a short, critical essay (5-7 pages) reviewing required readings for the course. This assignment provides an opportunity to reflect in an analytic, structured way on course readings and discussions. Rather than asking for a response to specific test questions, it allows each student to think about the whole of the course and focus the substance of the essay as each sees fit.

Students should first review the main themes of the course. Next, students should identify which themes they wish to discuss in this paper and then organize their discussion with reference to the readings.

These essays are intended to be thoughtful and analytical, not merely summaries of readings.

Extended Reading List
(compiled by Diana Alvarado)

Week 3: Race and Racial Identity

"Children as Young as Three Have 'Complex Understanding of Race.'" *The University Record (University of Michigan)*, March 29, 1993.

King, Rebecca Chiyoko, and Kimberly McClain Da Costa. "Remaking of Race in the Japanese American and African American Communities." 227-244 in *The Multiracial Experience: Racial Borders at the New Frontier*, edited by Maria P.P. Root. Thousand Oaks, Calif.: Sage, 1996.

Streeter, Caroline A. "Ambiguous Bodies: Locating Black/White Women in Cultural Representations." 305-320 in *The Multiracial Experience: Racial Borders at the New Frontier*, edited by Maria P.P. Root. Thousand Oaks, Calif.: Sage, 1996.

Thorton, Michael C. "Hidden Agendas, Individual Theories, and Multiracial People. 101-120 in *The Multiracial Experience: Racial Borders at the New Frontier*, edited by Maria P.P. Root. Thousand Oaks, Calif.: Sage, 1996.

Tilove, Jonathan. "Racial Shadings: Mixed Heritages Confound the Question of Color." *Detroit Free Press*, April 29, 1992.

Week 4: Multiracial Identity

Bowles, Dorcas D. "Bi-Racial Identity: Children Born to African-American and White Couples." *Clinical Social Work Journal* 21, no. 4 (1993): 417-428.

Brand-William, Oralandar. "I Just Don't Understand You: In Black and White." *Detroit News*, June 14, 1992.

Forna, Aminatta. "A Racial Caste-Away?" *British Cosmopolitan*, December 1988: 71.

Grove, Kwai Julienne. "Identity Development in Interracial, Asian / White Late Adolescents: Must It Be So Problematic?" *Journal of Youth and Adolescence* 20, no. 6 (1991): 617-628.

Kich, George Kitahara. "Development Process of Asserting Biracial Bicultural Identity." 304-317 in *Racially Mixed People in America*, edited by Maria P. P. Root. Newbury Park, Calif.: Sage, 1992.

Mahdesian, Linda. "It's Not Easy Being Green." *U.S. News & World Report*, November 23, 1987.

Nakashima, Cynthia L. "Voices from the Movement: Approaches to Multiraciality." 79-97 in *The Multiracial Experience: Racial Borders at the New Frontier*, edited by Maria P.P. Root. Thousand Oaks, Calif.: Sage, 1996.

Santiago, Roberto. "Black and Latino." *Essence*, November 1989.

Stevens, Robin. "Growing Up Beige." *Scholastic Update* (1989, teacher's edition): 9.

Weisman, Jan R. "An 'Other' Way of Life: The Empowerment of Alterity in the Interracial Individual." 152-164 in *The Multiracial Experience: Racial Borders at the New Frontier*, edited by Maria P.P. Root. Thousand Oaks, Calif.: Sage, 1996.

Williams, Teresa Kay. "Race as a Process: Reassessing the 'What Are You?' Encounters of Biracial Individuals." 191-210 in *The Multiracial Experience: Racial Borders at the New Frontier*, edited by Maria P.P. Root. Thousand Oaks, Calif.: Sage, 1996.

Week 5: Interracial Relationships

Balzar, John. "Biracial Families See a Road to Equality Paved with Diversity." *Los Angeles Times*, October 7, 1992.

Duke, Lynne. "25 Years after Landmark Decision, Still the Rarest of Wedding Bonds." *Washington Post*, June 12, 1992.

Goldblatt, Henry, and Bethany Robertson. "Interracial Dating: Holding Hands Across Cultures." *Michigan Daily*, February 14, 1992.

"Interracial Dating: Yes or No?" *The Black Collegian* 23, no. 4 (March-April 1993): 31-34.

Kantrowitz, Barbara. "Ultimate Assimilation." *Newsweek*, November 24, 1986.

"The Last Taboo? Does Wave of Interracial Movies Signal a Real Change?" *Ebony*, September 1991.

Minerbrook, Scott "The Pain of a Divided Family." *U.S. News & World Report*, December 24, 1990.

Nicholas, Emilia. "Dating for the Wrong Reasons." *Consider*, University of Michigan, November 26, 1990.

Peterson, Karen S. "Interracial Dating Common Among Teens." *USA Today*, October 3, 1997.

Slaughter, Lynn. "Interracial Couples Express No Regrets." *Ann Arbor News*, June 16, 1991.

Suh, Theresa. "Interracial Dating: Why Not?" *Consider*, University of Michigan, November 26, 1990.

Todd, J., J.L. Mckinney, R. Harris, R. Chadderton, and L. Small. "Attitudes toward Interracial Dating: Effects of Age, Sex and Race." *Journal of Multicultural Counseling and Development* 20 (1992): 202-208.

Tucker, M.B., and C. Mitchell-Kernan. "New Trends in Black American Interracial Marriage: The Social Structural Context." *Journal of Marriage and the Family* 52, no. 1 (1990): 209-218.

Turner, Renee D. "Interracial Couples in the South." *Ebony*, June 1990.

Walsh, Joan "Asian Women, Caucasian Men: The New Demographics of Love." *Image*, December 2, 1990.

Walton, Scott "Crossing the Date Line: Some Teens Make Romance a Matter of Black and White." *Detroit Free Press*, October 9, 1992.

Wilson, Barbara Foley. "Marriage's Melting Pot." *American Demographics* 6, no. 7 (1984): 34-37, 45.

Week 8: Power and Identity

Buckley, Thomas E. "Unfixing Race: Class, Power, and Identity in an Interracial Family." *Virginia Magazine of History and Biography* 102, no. 3 (July 1994): 349-380.

Daniel, G. Reginald. "Beyond Black and White: The New Multiracial Consciousness." 333-341 in *Racially Mixed People in America*, edited by Maria P.P. Root. Newbury Park, Calif.: Sage, 1992.

Weather, Diane. "White Boys." *Essence*, April 1990.

Wiernick, Julie. "Whites Like Limited Integration." *Ann Arbor News*, August 16, 1992.

Week 9: Classification and Census

Fernandez, Carlos A. "Testimony of the Association of Multiethnic Americans Before the Subcommittee on Census, Statistics, and Postal Personnel of the U.S. House of Representatives." 199-210 in *American Mixed Race: The Culture of Microdiversity*, edited by Naomi Zack. Lanham, Md.: Rowman & Littlefield, 1995.

———. "Government Classification of Multiracial/Multiethnic People." 15-36 in *The Multiracial Experience: Racial Borders at the New Frontier*, edited by Maria P.P. Root. Thousand Oaks, Calif.: Sage, 1996.

Gabriella, Sander. "The 'Other' Americans." *American Demographics* 16 (June 1994): 36-42.

Graham, Susan R. "The Real World." 37-48 in *The Multiracial Experience: Racial Borders at the New Frontier*, edited by Maria P.P. Root. Thousand Oaks, Calif.: Sage, 1996.

Rainwater, Catherine. "'Wait Till 2050' Native Americans Recovering the Future." *College Literature* 20 (June 1993): 214-218.

Schmidt, Peter. "U.S. to Let People Choose Multiple Races on Forms; Big Changes Expected in Data." *Chronicle of Higher Education*, October 31, 1997.

Week 10: Integrating Race, Class, and Gender

Allman, Karen Maeda. "(Un)Natural Boundaries: Mixed Race, Gender, and Sexuality." 227-320 in *The Multiracial Experience: Racial Borders at the New Frontier*, edited by Maria P.P. Root. Thousand Oaks, Calif.: Sage, 1996.

Week 11: Assimilation

Daniel, G. Reginald. "Passers and Pluralists: Subverting the Racial Divide." 91-107 in *Racially Mixed People in America*, edited by Maria P.P. Root. Newbury Park, Calif.: Sage, 1992.

References (Book and Article Citations)

Brodkin, Karen. *How Jews Became White Folks and What That Says about Race in America*. New Brunswick, N.J.: Rutgers University Press, 1998.

Fernandez, Carols A. (1992). "La Raza and the Melting Pot: A Comparative Look at Multiethnicity." 126-143 in *Racially Mixed People in America*, edited by Maria P.P. Root. Newbury Park, Calif.: Sage, 1992.

Ignatiev, Noel. *How the Irish Became White.* Cambridge, Mass.: Harvard University Press, 1995.

Kosmin, Barry, Sidney Goldstein, Joseph Waksberg, Nava Lerner, Ariella Keysar, and Jeffrey Scheckner. *Highlights of the CJF National Population Survey*. New York: Council of Jewish Federations, 1991.

Schoem, David. "Teaching about Ethnic Identity and Intergroup Relations" in *Multicultural Teaching in the University*, edited by David Schoem, Linda Frankel, Ximena Zuniga, and Edith Lewis. Westport, Conn.: Praeger, 1995.

————. "College Students Need Thoughtful, In-Depth Study of Race Relations." *Chronicle of Higher Education*, April 3, 1991.

————. *Inside Separate Worlds: Life Stories of Young Blacks, Jews, and Latinos*. Ann Arbor: University of Michigan Press, 1991.

Schoem, David, and Marshall Stevenson. "Teaching Ethnic Identity and Intergroup Relations: The Case of Blacks and Jews." *Teachers College Record* 91, no. 4 (1990): 579-594.

Shrage, Laurie. "Ethnic Transgressions: Confessions of an Assimilated Jew." 287-307 in *American Mixed Race: The Culture of Micro-diversity*, edited by Naomi Zack. Lanham, Md.: Rowman & Little-field, 1995.

Spickard, Paul R. "The Illogic of American Racial Categories." 12-23 in *Racially Mixed People in America*, edited by Maria P.P. Root. Newbury Park, Calif.: Sage Publications, 1992.

Appendix IV: OMB Directive 15

The Office of Management and Budget's Policy for Race and Ethnic Definitions[1]

Directive No. 15
Race and Ethnic Standards for Federal Statistics and Administrative Reporting

This directive provides standard classifications for recordkeeping, collection and presentation of data on race and ethnicity in Federal programs administrative reporting and statistical activities. These classifications should not be interpreted as being scientific or anthropological in nature, nor should they be viewed as determinants of eligibility for participation in any Federal program. They have been developed in response to needs expressed by both the executive branch and the Congress to provide for the collection and use of compatible, nonduplicated, exchangeable racial and ethnic data by Federal agencies.

1. Definitions
The basic racial and ethnic categories for Federal statistics and program administrative reporting are defined as follows:

a. American Indian or Alaskan Native. A person having origins in any of the original peoples of North America, and who maintains cultural identification through tribal affiliation or community recognition.

b. Asian or Pacific Islander. A person having origins in any of the original peoples of the Far East, Southeast Asia, the Indian subcontinent, or the Pacific Islands. This area includes for example, China, India, Japan, Korea, the Philippine Islands, and Samoa.

c. Black. A person having origins in any of the Black racial groups of Africa.

d. Hispanic. A person of Mexican, Puerto Rican, Cuban, Central, or South American or other Spanish culture or origin, regardless of race.

e. White. A person having origins in any of the original peoples of Europe, North Africa, or the Middle East.

2. Utilization for Recordkeeping and Reporting

To provide flexibility, it is preferable to collect data on race and ethnicity separately. If separate race and ethnic categories are used, the minimum designations are:

    a. Race:

—American Indian or Alaskan Native

—Asian or Pacific Islander

—Black

—White

    b. Ethnicity:

—Hispanic origin

—Not of Hispanic origin

When race and ethnicity are collected separately, the number of White and Black persons who are Hispanic must be identifiable and capable of being reported for that category.

If a combined format is used to collect racial and ethnic data, the minimum acceptable categories are:

    American Indian or Alaskan Native

    Asian or Pacific Islander

    Black, not of Hispanic origin

    Hispanic

    White, not of Hispanic origin

The category which most closely reflects the individual's recognition in his community should be used for purposes of reporting on persons who are of mixed racial and/or ethnic origins.

In no case should the provisions of this Directive be construed to limit the collection of data to the categories described above. However, any reporting required which uses more detail shall be organized in such a way that the additional categories can be aggregated into these basic racial/ethnic categories.

The minimum standard follows:

    a. Civil rights compliance reporting. The categories specified above will be used by all agencies in either the separate or combined format for civil rights compliance reporting and equal employment reporting for both the public and private sectors and for all levels of government. Any variation requiring less detailed data or which cannot be aggregated into the basic categories will have to be specifically approved by the

Office of Federal Statistical Policy and Standards [OFSPS] for executive agencies. More detailed reporting which can be aggregated to the basic categories may be used at the agencies' discretion.

b. General program administrative and grant reporting. Whenever an agency subject to this Directive issues new or revised administrative reporting or recordkeeping requirements which include racial or ethnic data, the agency will use the race / ethnic categories describe above. A variance can be specifically requested from the Office of Federal Statistical Policy and Standards but such a variance will be granted only if the agency can demonstrate that it is not reasonable for the primary reporter to determine the racial or ethnic background in terms of the specified categories, and that such determination is not critical to the administration of the program in question, or if the specific program is directed to only one or a limited number race/ethnic groups, e.g. Indian tribal activities.

c. Statistical Reporting. The categories described in this Directive will be used as a minimum for federally sponsored statistical data collection where race and/or ethnicity is required, except when: the collection involves a sample of such size that the data on the smaller categories would be unreliable, or when the collection effort focuses on a specific racial or ethnic group. A repetitive survey shall be deemed to have an adequate sample size if the racial and ethnic data can be reliably aggregated on a biennial basis. Any other variation will have to be specifically authorized by OMB through the reports clearance process (see OMB Circular No. A-40). In those cases where the data collection is not subject to the reports clearance process, a direct request for a variance should be made to the OFSPS.

3. Effective Date

The provisions of this Directive are effective immediately for all new and revised recordkeeping or reporting requirements containing racial and/or ethnic information. All existing recordkeeping or reporting requirements shall be made consistent with this Directive at the time they are submitted for extension, or not later than January 1, 1980.

4. Presentation of Race/Ethnic Data

Displays of racial and ethnic compliance and statistical data will use the category designations listed above. The designation "non-White" is not acceptable for use in the presentation of Federal Government data. It is not to be used in any publication of compliance or statistical data or in the text of any compliance or statistical report.

In cases where the above designations are considered inappropriate for presentation of statistical data on particular programs or for particular regional areas, the sponsoring agency may use:

(1) The designation "Black and Other Races" or "All Other Races" as collective descriptions of minority races when the most summary distinction between the majority and minority races is appropriate;

(2) The designations "White," "Black," and "All Other Races" when the distinction among the majority races, the principal minority race, and other races is appropriate; or

(3) The designation of a particular minority race or races, and the inclusion of "Whites" with "All Other Races," if such a collective description is appropriate.

In displaying detailed information which represents a combination of race and ethnicity, the description of the data being displayed must clearly indicate that both bases of classification are being used.

When the primary focus of a statistical report is on two or more specific identifiable groups in the population, one or more of which is racial or ethnic, it is acceptable to display data for each of the particular groups separately and to describe data relating to the remainder of the population by an appropriate collective description . . . .

Note

1. Taken from the "Federal Measures of Race and Ethnicity and the Implications for the 2000 Census," pages 13-14. Originally printed in the GAO/GGD-93-25 *Agencies' Use of Consistent Race and Ethnic Definition*, pages 10-11.

Appendix V: Resources by Race

African American/White: 24-26, 28-31, 38-52, 57, 59-61, 64-65, 67-68, 71, 81-98, 107-114, 116, 121, 123-133, 135-136, 138-147, 150-157, 159, 162-163, 169-172, 175-176, 188, 190-202

Asian/White: 24, 83, 89, 106, 108, 110-111, 120, 127, 130, 132-133, 135, 139-140, 142, 144, 146, 152, 155, 157, 161, 164, 169, 175-177, 188-192, 194-198, 200-201

Asian/African American: 123, 157, 196

Hispanic/White: 26, 69, 82, 112, 123, 126-127, 129, 141-142, 154, 174-175, 193, 195, 201

Hispanic/African American: 26, 93, 143

Native American/White: 32-33, 43, 60-61, 121-122, 131, 143-144, 157-158, 161

Resources that deal with more than two races: 24, 27-28, 42-48, 50, 52-53, 57-69, 71-77, 80-82, 85-88, 90-98, 106, 108-117, 120-122, 126-130, 132-134, 136, 140-141, 143-144, 146-147, 150-151, 153-156, 158-165, 168-169, 172-176, 189-190, 198

Index

48 Hours, 184

ABA National Resource Center on
  Legal and Court Issues, 129
Adams, Romanzo Colfax, 42
Adoff, Arnold, 138, 139
adolescents: and adoption, 134;
  and identity development,
  150; in film, 199, 202;
  interviews with, 153-154,
  156, 163; parenting of, 111,
  113; resources for, 117, 137,
  142-147
adoption, international, 119, 133;
  from Korea, 108, 120, 130;
  from Vietnam, 123-124; from
  China, 127, 132, 135
adoption, transracial, 119-136; and
  resources for parents, 106,
  117, 120, 130, 132; and
  therapists, 112, 116; in film
  and television, 185, 200;
  opposition to, 121, 122-125,
  126-127, 129, 130, 131. *See
  also* Adoption, international;
  Multiethnic Placement Act
Adoption and Race Work Group
  of the Stuart Foundation, 128
Adoption and Safe Families Act,
  127
Africa, 52, 59, 172
African Americans. *See specific
  topics*
After MASH, 182
Aguirre, Benigno E., 83
Ahmed, Sara, 27
Akaka, Daniel K., 72
Alabama, 49, 59, 60, 87, 179. *See
  also Pace v. Alabama*
Aldridge, Delores P., 80
Alexander, Ralph, Jr., 125, 128,
  130, 132, 136

All in the Family, 182
All My Children, 182
Allen, William G., 41
Allman, Karen Maeda, 168
Almaguer, Tomas, 168
Alperson, Myra, 106
Altstein, Howard, 127, 133-134
Alvarez, Julia, 158
American in Black and White, 20
American Indians. *See* Native
  Americans
American Love Story, 188
Amlani, Alzak, 106
Anderson, David C., 120
Andujo, Estela, 123
animals in children's books, 140,
  141
Annella, Sister M., 87
anti-miscegenation laws, 49, 56-
  57, 60, 63, 90, 92; and the
  Bible, 53; for other than
  Black/White unions, 60, 61;
  in early history, 37, 59-60,
  62-63; opposition to, 49-50;
  twentieth-century, 49, 58, 61-
  62, 63-64, 87, 94. *See also
  specific court cases*
appearance, 23-27, 70; and
  identity development, 114,
  151, 163; and marriage, 84;
  and Native Americans, 34, 36,
  161; and "scientific" studies,
  43-44, 45, 46, 47, 48; and
  White features, 19, 20, 39, 41,
  42; hierarchy based on, 50,
  66, 159; in children's books,
  138, 140, 145; in film and
  television, 180, 181, 188, 199,
  200. *See also* Passing
Appelbaum, Harvey M., 57
Appiah, Anthony, 68
Arabs, 20, 75, 176

Arboleda, Teja, 150
Arkansas, 111, 117
As the World Turns, 184
Asbury, Herbert, 50
Asian Americans, 24, 157, 162, 164; ethnicities within, 16, 17, 89; and homosexuality, 168, 175, 176; and parenting, 106, 108, 111; and terminology, 8, 80. *See also names of specific ethnic groups*; Adoption, international
Asian Indians. *See* Indian Americans
assimilation, 42, 83, 95, 108, 154, 195
Association of American Indian Affairs, 131
Association of Multiethnic Americans, 55, 72, 77, 148
Atlanta, 40, 49
Aura, Jan, 169
autobiography, 23, 29, 149, 165, 167; examples of, 26, 28, 40, 41, 42, 110, 163
Autographs for Freedom, 41
Avens, Alfred, 57

Baber, Ray, 80
Baden, Amanda L., 126
Baird-Olson, Karren, 32
Baldwin, James, 171
Baldwin, Louis Fremont, 50
Banana Split, 188
Barnes, Irene, 43
Baron, Dennis, 70
Barron, Milton Leon, 43, 50
Barth, Richard P., 128
Bausch, Robert S., 126-127
Becker, Stanli K., 65
Bell Curve, 68
Bennett, Juda, 29
Berman, Sandy, 6
Bethel, Kathleen, 7
Bibb, Amy, 112
Biever, Joan L., 96
bisexuals. *See* Homosexual relationships

Black, Algernon D., 50
Blau, Peter M., 81
Blau's theory of composition, 82, 85, 86
Bletzer, Siri S., 83
Blockson, Charles L., 57
blood quantum, 23, 32-36, 160, 161, 212
Blue-Vein Societies, 28, 212
Blustain, Sarah, 150
Boas, Franz, 43
Boateng, Osei, 27
Bobele, Monte, 96
The Bodyguard, 182, 190
Boston, 40, 52, 117
Bowman, Jennifer, 127
Boyd, Aaron, 146
Boyd-Franklin, Nancy, 172
Boyd Krebs, Nina, 65
Bradley, Carla, 127
Bradman, Tony, 139
Bradshaw, Carla K., 24
Brand-Williams, Oralandar, 24
Brandt, Joshua, 127
Braus, Nancy, 147
Brazil, 73-74
Breaux-Schropp, Anissa, 106
Brooks, Devon, 128
Brown, John A., 96
Brown, Nancy G., 76-77
Brown, Ursula M., 150-151
Brown, William Wells, 38
Browne, Eileen, 139
Brunsma, David L., 151, 159
Bullough, Vern L., 120
Bureau of Indian Affairs, 32-34, 121-122, 131
Burma, John H., 43
Bussiere, Alice, 128
Busto, Rudiger, 168
Butler, Judith, 27
Buxenbaum, Kim Una, 151
Byrd, Charles, 55

California, 21, 78n6, 120, 123, 126, 127, 143, 190
call numbers, 6-7, 10
Camper, Carol, 151

Canadians, 151, 174, 192
Cannon, Poppy, 50
Caribbean, 66, 90
Castle, W.E., 43-44
Catfish in Black Bean Sauce, 191
census, the United States: race
        categories in, 59, 65, 66, 68,
        108; of 2000, 24, 56, 67, 70-
        76, 159
Cerroni-Long, E. Liza, 81
Chadwick, Allen, 32
Chai, Lynn, 89
Chan, Anna Y., 97
Chao, Christine M., 24
Cheng, Andrea, 139
Chesnutt, Charles W., 39, 61, 216
Chicago, 45, 111, 124, 129
Child Welfare League of America,
        121-122, 124
children's books, 137-148
Chimezie, Amuzie, 123
China, 127, 132, 135, 139, 146
China Girl, 183, 191
Chinese, 42, 70, 157, 173, 177;
        and adoption, 127, 132, 135;
        and intermarriage, 48, 56-57,
        83, 89; in children's books,
        139, 146; in film and
        television, 182, 191, 192, 195,
        196, 201; life stories of, 157,
        173, 177
Chow, Calire S., 106
Chu, Wei-cheng Raymond, 169
Chung, Margaret, 177
Civil War, 26, 57, 59, 60, 63, 88
class, 160, 175; and identity
        development, 162, 189; and
        mate selection, 80-82, 83, 84-
        86, 88, 89; and passing, 27;
        differences in relationships,
        176, 197. *See also* Merton's
        theory of hypogamy
Coffee Colored Children, 188
Cohn, Laura Renee, 154
Colker, Ruth, 58, 71
college admissions, 35, 78n6
Collins, David R., 141, 146
Collins, J. Fuji, 152, 165, 169

colonial period, 26, 37, 47, 60, 64;
        and legislation, 37, 47, 55, 56,
        59, 61
Come See the Paradise, 191
Connecticut, 43, 144
Connerly, Ward, 56, 78
Connolly, Medira L., 170
Cooney, Teresa M., 113
Corrina, Corrina, 191
Cose, Ellis, 69
Cotter, Holland, 28
counseling: of interracial couples,
        82, 96, 98, 172, 175; of
        mixed-race clients, 151, 153,
        158, 169; of multiracial
        families, 110, 112, 113, 115-
        116
counting by race. *See* Census, the
        United States
Coverdale, Christina, 132
Cradle 2 the Grave, 184
Craft, William, 41
Croly, David G., 49
Cross, Suzanne, 131
Crossing Delancey, 20
Crowder, Kyle D., 81
Cubans, 16, 82, 181
Cuffe, Paul, 146
Curtis, Carla M., 125, 128, 130,
        132, 136
Cutrone, Christopher, 170

Dalmage, Heather M., 65, 107
Daly, Jennifer, 94
Daniel, G. Reginald, 28, 66
Danziger, Paula, 142
Darby, Mary Ann, 147
dating, interracial, 79, 86-87, 151,
        164; and appearance, 26;
        personal accounts of, 143,
        152, 154, 156, 188, 190
Davenport, Charles B., 43, 44
Davidson, Jeanette R., 81
Davis, F. James, 58, 71
Davis, Timothy, 58
Davol, Marguerite W., 139
Day, Caroline Bond, 44
Days of Waiting, 188

de Bruin, John H., 152
de Hartog, Jan, 120
de Romanet, Jerome, 170
Deane, Claudia, 92
DeBose, Herman L., 165
The Defiant Ones, 183
Denmon, Jacqueline, 154
Derricotte, Toi, 28
Desjarlait, Robert, 33
Deters, Kathleen A., 153
Detroit, 40, 202
Devil in a Blue Dress, 184, 192
Die Hard, 184
Dixon, Ken, 168
Dixon, Melvin, 167, 170-171
Dollard, John, 44-45
*Domino: Interracial People and
    the Search for Identity*, 189
Dorris, Michael, 142
Doss, Carl, 120-121
Doss, Helen Grigsby, 120-121
Double Happiness, 192
*Doubles: Japan and America's
    Intercultural Children*, 189
Douglas, Nathan, 72
Douglass, Ramona E., 55, 72, 76-
    77
Downing, Karen, 13, 18
Dragon: The Bruce Lee Story, 192
Drake, St. Clair, 45
DuBois, W.E.B., 61, 87
Duling, Gretchen A., 123
Duras, Marguerite, 196

East Indians. *See* Indian
    Americans
Eckard, E.W., 45
education: elementary, 65, 106,
    111, 115, 116; and interracial
    topics, 13-22, 219-230. *See
    also* Race, teaching about;
    Students, interracial
Ellison, Joe, 107
Embree, Edwin R., 45
En Ryo Identity, 189
England, 37, 42, 59, 114, 156, 188,
    197

enumeration. *See* Census, the
    United States
Ernst, Kathleen, 142
Etzioni, Amitai, 71
eugenics, 38, 44, 51, 61, 213

families, 105-117, 176; acceptance
    of interracial relationships by,
    79, 93, 94, 97, 114; and
    identity formation, 25, 150,
    151, 153, 154, 156; in
    children's books, 137, 138-
    147; in film and television,
    182, 188, 190, 191, 192, 193,
    201; studies on, 42, 44, 45,
    46. *See also* Adoption;
    Parenting
Family Diversity Projects, Inc.,
    109
Fang, Carolyn Y., 82
Fanon, Frantz, 170, 174
Fanshel, David, 121
Far from Heaven, 192
Farmer, Robin, 107
Faulkner, William, 29
Fauset, Jessie, 29
Fears, Darryl, 92
Feast of All Saints, 185, 193
Feldman, Jane, 147
Ferguson, George Oscar, 45
Fernandez, Carlos, 55, 72
fiction, 10, 29-31, 38-41, 170-171.
    See also Children's books;
    Historical fiction
Filipinos, 43, 48, 83, 89, 144
film, 179-202; adaptations, 40, 41-
    42; and homosexuality, 167,
    196, 174; as educational
    resource, 20; trends in, 1, 30,
    31. *See also names of specific
    racial and ethnic groups*
Finkelman, Paul, 58
Fisher, Gene, 89
Fitzpatrick, Joseph P., 82
Fitzpatrick, Kevin M., 81
Fletcher-Stephens, Barbara J., 108
Flirting, 193

Florida, 49, 117. *See also*
    McLaughlin v. Florida
Foeman, Anita Kathy, 97
Fools Rush In, 193
Forbes, Jack D., 66
Forde-Mazrui, Kim, 128
Fosdick, Franklin, 51
Foulke, Mary L., 171
France, 59, 194
Frazier, Sundee, 153
Free People of Color, 28, 185, 193
Freedman, Estelle B., 171
Fricke, Harriet, 121
Friedman, Ina R., 139
Fu, Vincent Kang, 82
Fugitive Slave Law, 38, 42
Fujino, Diane C., 83
Fulbeck, Kip, 188
Funderburg, Lise, 24, 153

Gaines, Stanley O., Jr., 93, 97
Gamache, Gail, 135
Garcia, Stella D., 93
Garland, Sarah, 139
Garland, Sherry, 142-143
Garroutte, Eva Marie, 33
Gaskins, Pearl Fuyo, 143, 154
Gates, Henry Lewis, 30
gays. *See* Homosexual
    relationships
Gefilte Fish, 20
Geidel, Molly, 147
gender: and identity formation,
    160, 162, 164, 177, 189; and
    parental relationships, 113;
    differences in attitudes
    toward intermarriage, 94, 95;
    differences in patterns of
    intermarriage, 86, 90, 91;
    roles, 97, 110. *See also*
    Women
genealogy, 57, 58, 62, 155
Georgia, 41, 59, 114. *See also*
    Atlanta
Gillem, Angela R., 154
Gillespie, Nick, 71
Gillespie, Peggy, 109
Ginsberg, Elaine K., 30, 31

Girlfriends, 185
Goddard, Lawford L., 128
Golden, Joseph, 45-46
Gordon, Linda, 129
Graham, Susan, 55, 72
Granrose, Cherlyn S., 97
Grape, Helen, 131
Greenberg, David, 59
Greene, Beverly, 172
Grinker, Roy Richard, 172
Grow, Lucille J., 123-124
Guess Who's Coming to Dinner,
    180-181, 194
Gurak, Douglas T., 82
Gustavsson, Nora S., 131

Hagan, W.T., 33
Haizlip, Shirlee Taylor, 108
Hall, Lisa Kahaleole Chan, 173
Hall, Ronald, 26
Hall, Wade, 155
Hamilton, Virginia, 143
Hanley-Lopez, Ian Haney, 59
Harlem Renaissance, 26, 40, 67,
    162
Harrington, Glenn, 144
Hatanaka, Herbert, 89
Hawaii, 42, 89, 140, 173
Hawkins-Leon, Cynthia G., 127
Hayes, Janice, 24
Heer, David M., 87
Helbig, Alethea, 147
Hemings, Sally, 58, 194, 199
Hening, William Walter, 37
Henriques, Fernando, 59, 78
Henry, Patrick, 61
Herman, Bobby E., 129
Herskovits, Melville J., 46
Hickey, Gorden, 108
Hickman, Christine B., 67
Higginbotham, A. Leon, 59
Hill, Miriam R., 98
Hill, Renee L., 171
Hines, Alice M., 95
Hispanics: and adoption, 20, 123;
    and census-taking, 69, 76;
    and intermarriage, 67, 85, 89,
    90; as ethnic rather than

racial group, 69, 75, 76; in film, 190, 193, 195. *See also* Cubans, Mexicans, Puerto Ricans
historical fiction, 29, 31, 37-38; examples of, 30, 31, 38-41; for children, 142-143, 145
historical resources, 9, 10, 57-58; examples of, 41-53
history, interracial issues in, 14, 26, 28, 37. *See also specific topics*; Civil War; Colonial period; Legislation, historical
history, issue of race in, 15, 37, 55, 112, 152, 179
Ho, Man Keung, 98
Hodes, Martha, 88
Hoffman, Frederick L., 47, 51
Hollinger, Joan H., 129
Hollingsworth, Leslie Doty, 129-130
Holm, John James, 51
Holmes, Steven A., 67, 72
Homicide: Life on the Street, 185
homosexual relationships: compared to intermarriage, 60; interracial, 95, 109, 115, 167-177, 192
Horse, John, 146
House Committee on Government Reform, 72
Houston, Sam, 61
Howard, Alicia, 124
Howard, John, 30
Hughes, Langston, 29
The Human Stain, 184
Hwang, Sean-Shong, 83

I Love Lucy, 181
I Spy, 183
Ickes, William, 93
identity development, 52-53, 111, 122, 149-165, 169; and appearance, 24; models of, 155, 157, 158, 159-160, 163; parental influence on, 27, 105, 108, 111, 116, 158; studies

on, 151, 152-153, 155; theories of, 112
Imitation of Life, 184, 194
immigration, 68; and intermarriage, 90; European, 61, 67, 71
Indian Adoption Project, 121, 122
Indian Americans: and intermarriage, 89, 106, 110-111; in film, 182, 190, 196, 197-198
Indian Child Welfare Act, 122, 125, 131
intelligence, 45, 46, 51, 52, 126
Interethnic Adoption Provisions, 128, 129
interfaith issues, 14, 15, 17, 18, 20, 50, 80
intermarriage, 79-99, 110; and appearance, 26, 39-40; and political implications, 51, 161; causal factors of, 45, 48, 51, 79-87, 112; demographic trends in, 46, 48, 87-88, 90, 91, 105; in fiction, 39, 40, 41; in film and television, 180-181, 182, 188-189, 194, 195, 197, 198, 201; in history, 43, 52, 87-88, 90, 91, 92, 157; in Hawaii, 42-43, 189; negative attitudes toward, 10, 92-93, 94, 95; public opinion on, 48, 51, 80, 92-95. *See also names of specific racial and ethnic groups*; Anti-miscegenation laws
Interracial Marriage: Blending the Races in America, 189
Ishigo, Estelle, 188
Ito, Naomi, 89

Jacobs, J.H., 165
Jacobson, Matthew Frye, 67
Jamaica, 44
Japan, 119, 139, 140, 189, 200
Japanese, 43, 70, 111; and adoption, 119; and identity development; 152, 155, 164,

169; and intermarriage, 83,
85-86, 89; in children's
books, 139, 140, 144; in film,
179-180, 188, 189, 191, 200-
201
Jefferson, Thomas, 38, 57, 147,
194, 199
Jefferson in Paris, 194
The Jeffersons, 182
Jen, Gish, 158
Jenks, Albert Ernest, 49
Jennings, Herbert S., 43, 47
Jews: and adoption, 127, 130, 133;
and interfaith relationships,
14-15, 18; and intermarriage,
85-86, 150; as racial group,
15-16; in children's books,
141, 146; mixed-race, 110,
114, 176
Johnson, Angela, 139
Johnson, James Weldon, 30, 39
Johnson, Kevin R., 58, 154
Johnson, Penny R., 124
Johnson, Walton R., 93
Johnston, James Hugo, 47, 55, 60
Jones, Edmund D., 121
Jones, J. McHenry, 39
Jones, Nicholas, 73
Jones, William H., 47
Jordan, Winthrop D., 51, 60
Joy Luck Club, 195
Judaism. *See* Jews
Julian, Isaac, 174
Jungle Fever, 183, 195, 198
Just Black? Multi-Racial Identity,
20, 190

Kaeser, Gigi, 109
Kahn, Jack S., 154
Kalmijn, Matthijs, 82, 88
Kandel, Bethany, 141
Kanuha, Valli, 173
Karis, Terri A., 90
Kashef, Ziba, 25
Katz, William Loren, 146
Kearns, Maureen, 130
Kelly, Matt, 55
Kennedy, N. Brent, 155

Kennedy, Randall, 60, 62, 88
Kenney, Kelly R., 115
Kenney, Mark E., 115
Kentucky, 156
Kephart, William M., 47
Kerwin, Christine, 155
Kich, George Kitahara, 155, 165,
173
Kidd, Mae Street, 155
Kilbride, Gina, 94
Killian, Kyle D., 98
Kilson, Marion, 156
Kitano, Harry H.L., 83, 89
Klineberg, Otto, 51
Knockaround Guys, 185
Koenig, Karen, 130
Koreans: and adoption, 108, 119,
120, 130; and identity
development, 152, 161; and
intermarriage, 83, 89, 182; in
Hawaii, 42
Korgen, Kathleen Odell, 156
Kouri, Kristyan Marie, 109
Krouse, Susan Applegate, 34
Kung Fu, 192

L.A. is Burning, 20
Ladner, Joyce A., 125
language ability and racial identity,
25, 26, 107, 155, 161, 163
Lanier, Shannon, 147
Larsen, Nella, 27, 29-31, 39-40
Latinos. *See* Hispanics
Lazarre, Jane, 109
Lee, Sharon, 73
legislation: historical, 37, 47, 55,
59-60, 91; race-defining, 14,
32, 33. *See also specific court
cases*; Anti-miscegenation
laws; Fugitive Slave Law;
One-drop rule
lesbians. *See* Homosexual
relationships
Leslie, Dorian, 174
Lethal Weapon, 184
Leventhal, Mel, 163
Lewis, Allison, 131
Lewis, Edmonia, 146

Lewis, Richard, Jr., 83
Liang, Zai, 89
Liera-Schwichtenberg, Romona, 30
Lilies of the Field, 180
Lincoln, Abraham, 49, 59
Linton, Ralph, 48
literature. *See* Fiction
Little, George, 84
Little, Kimberley Griffiths, 143, 144
Little, Mimi Otey, 140
Liu, Eric, 67
Liu, Liming, 135
Lone Star, 195
Longmore, Amy, 94
Los Angeles, 48, 83, 89, 117, 192, 198
Love Field, 196
The Lover, 196
Lovett-Tisdale, Marilyn, 130
Loving v. Virginia, 37, 49-50, 56, 59, 61, 62, 63, 87, 90, 92, 94; and the Constitution, 57; in film, 197
Low, Gail Ching-Liang, 27
Lu, Ming-Yeung, 168
Lutheran Children's Friend Society, 121
Lyslo, Arnold, 122

MacEachron, Ann E., 131
MacNeill, Lauren, 174
Mahboubi, Jayne, 113
Mahdesian, Linda, 25
Majete, Clayton, 109
Major, Clarence, 156
Makalani, Minkah, 68
Manasseh Societies, 52
Mandelbaum, Phil, 137, 140
marriage. *See* Intermarriage
Martin, Antoinette, 25
Martinez, George A., 58
*M*A*S*H*, 182
Massachusetts, 41, 59
mate selection, 80-87
Mavin Foundation, 55
Mayer, Gina, 141

Mayer, Mercer, 141
McBride, James, 110
McCunn, Ruthanne Lum, 157
McFadden, John, 110
McLaughlin v. Florida, 57
McNamara, Robert P., 94
McPherson, Carolyn Flanders, 131
McRoy, Ruth G., 131
McSween, Rebecca, 107
media, interracial images in, 1, 38, 65; and adoption, 130; and skin color, 26. *See also* Children's books; Film; "Tragic mulatto" theme
Melungeon Research Committee, 155
Melungeons, 155, 215
Melwani, Lavina, 110
memoirs. *See* Autobiography
Mencke, John G., 52
Merton, Robert K., 48, 79, 84
Merton's theory of hypogamy, 82, 84, 85, 86, 88, 89
Messner, Steven F., 85
Mexicans, 16, 17; and adoption, 126, 127, 129; and intermarriage, 48; and parenting, 112; and racial identity, 26, 154, 174; in children's books, 140, 141, 143; in film, 193, 195
Mexico, 140, 143, 174, 190, 195
Meyer, Carolyn, 144
Meyer, Melissa, 34
Miami Vice, 184
Michener, James, 200
Midwest, 52, 90, 94, 143
Mihesuah, D.A., 157
Miller, Jim, 131
Miller-Lachmann, Lyn, 147
Mills, Jon K., 94
Minerbrook, Scott, 111
Minneapolis, 117, 121
Minton, Jeremy Mario, 131
Mississippi, 62, 157, 196
Mississippi Masala, 182, 196
Missouri, 117
Mitchell, Marion M., 122

Mitchell-Kernan, Claudia, 91
Mixed Blood, 190
Mixing Nia, 184, 196
Mjoen, J.H., 43
Model, Suzanne, 89
Momaday, N. Scott, 32
Monahan, Thomas P., 90
Monk, Isabell, 140
Monster's Ball, 197
Moraga, Cherrie, 174
Moran, Rachel F., 60, 90
Morganthau, Tom, 68
Morning, Ann, 73
Morrison, Johnetta Wade, 157
Morrison, Toni, 29
Mosley, Albert, 68
movies. *See* Film
Mr. and Mrs. Loving, 197
Mukherjee, Bharati, 158
Multiethnic Placement Act, 125,
    127-130
multiracial movement, 55-56, 76-
    78, 156
Murphy, Rita, 144
Muse, Daphne, 147
My Beautiful Laundrette, 167, 197

NAACP. *See* National Association
    for the Advancement of
    Colored People
Nackerud, Larry, 135
Naim v. Naim, 56
Nakashima, Cynthia L., 164
Nakazawa, Donna Jackson, 111
Nash, Gary B., 60
National Association for the
    Advancement of Colored
    People, 41-42, 50-51
National Association of Black
    Social Workers, 122-123,
    124
Native Americans, 26, 32-36, 43,
    55, 60, 174; and adoption,
    121, 122, 131; and identity
    formation, 157, 158, 161; and
    intermarriage, 48, 62, 82, 90,
    97; in children's books, 142,

143, 144, 146. *See also* Blood
    quantum
Negro in American Life, 51
Nero, Collette Leyva, 110
New York, 28, 40, 52, 59, 82, 89,
    110, 117, 129, 174; in film
    and television, 180, 183, 191,
    198, 200, 201
Niemann, Yolanda Flores, 112
Nobles, Melissa, 73
None of the Above, 20
The North, 29, 40, 60, 152; and
    trends in intermarriage, 87,
    90
North Carolina, 63
Noumair, Debra A., 170

O, 183, 198
Oglesby, Zena, 131
O'Hare, William, 74
O'Hearn, Claudine C., 147, 158
Ohio, 38, 117, 124
Okimoto, Jean, 144
Oklahoma, 20, 161-162
Okun, Barbara F., 112
OMB Directive 15, 4, 71, 72, 75,
    76, 231-234
One Life to Live, 181
One Night Stand, 198
one-drop rule, 14, 55, 58, 66, 67,
    153, 216; and legislation, 29,
    56; and the census, 71, 72, 76;
    compared to blood quantum,
    33
Open Door Society, 121
Orbe, Mark P., 112
Oriti, Bruno, 113
Otalvaro-Hormillosa, Gigi, 174
Othello, 183, 198-199

Pace v. Alabama, 57
Panunzio, Constantine, 48
parenting, 106, 113, 115, 116; and
    antiracism, 112; and
    appearance, 25; and identity
    formation, 106-107, 108, 110,
    111. *See also* Adoption;
    Families; Identity

development, parental influence on

Park, Robert E., 52

Pascoe, Peggy, 61-62

passing, 27-31, 47, 66, 108, 164, 217; estimates of, 43, 45, 50; in fiction, 27, 29-31, 39, 40; in film and television, 179, 180, 181, 184, 185; inadvertent, 24, 27

A Patch of Blue, 180, 199

Patterson, Glendora, 128

Patton, Sandra Lee, 132

Pearlman, Sarah F., 175

Peirce, Neal R., 74

Penguin Club, 52

Penn, Michael L., 132

Penn, William S., 158

Perkins, Agnes, 147

Perlmann, Joel, 70, 74

Perry, Leslie, 51

Persians, 25

Pewewardy, Cornel, 34

Pfeiffer, Kathleen, 31

phenotype. *See* Appearance

Philadelphia, 46, 59, 117

Phipps case, 58

picture books, 137-141

Pieterse, Jan, 69

Pinderhughes, Elaine, 158

Pinky, 40, 184

Piper, Adrian, 28

Pitch Black, 185

Plessy v. Ferguson, 29, 56, 58

Pocahontas, 61

Politics of Love in Black and White, 20, 190

Ponterotto, Joseph G., 155

Poon, Maurice Kwong-Lai, 175

Porterfield, Ernest, 84, 92

Poston, W.S.C., 158, 165

Powell, Richard, 90

Pratto, Felicia, 82

Prentiss, Suzanne M., 113

prisons, 171-172

Project Race, 55

Pryne, Miki, 147

psychotherapy. *See* Counseling

public opinion on interracial issues, 1, 14, 15, 22, 61, 108; and census-taking, 68, 71

publishing trends, 1, 29, 149

Puerto Ricans, 19, 26; and intermarriage, 82; in film, 201-202; in Hawaii, 42-43

Purnell, Bruce Anthony, 130

Qian, Zhenchao, 85

Queen, 199

Quintana, Elena Diana, 158

race: and appearance, 70; as biological construct, 15, 69, 78n1; as Black/White, 37, 68; as social construct, 15, 69, 78n1; teaching about, 13, 14, 15, 16-17, 20, 21

race categories: and implications of multiracial category, 1, 35, 56, 59, 69, 77, 160; changes in, 15-16, 69, 70; government definitions of, 4, 49, 64, 66, 67, 70-76; politics of, 65-66, 69, 136. *See also* Census, the United States

race relations: in the South, 60, 88, 156; intermarriage as indicator of, 63, 86, 88; film's influence on, 182, 183

racial "purity": and appearance, 45; and European ethnic groups, 16; and literature, 29; as defense for legislation, 55, 56, 59. *See also* Eugenics

Radina, M. Elise, 113

religion: and adoption, 119, 129, 131, 132; and intermarriage, 53, 63, 64, 189; and interracial Christians, 153; and interracial families, 42, 106. *See also* Interfaith issues; Jews

Removal of Barriers to Interethnic Adoption Provision, 125, 127, 129 researching interracial issues: resources for, 10, 38, 105, 149, 187, 203-209. *See also* Terminology

Reuter, Edward B., 48, 52

Rice, Anne, 185, 193

Richardson, Brenda Lane, 25

Rios, Diana I., 97

Rivera, Semilla M., 93

Rockquemore, Kerry Ann, 151, 157, 159

Rodriguez, Clara E., 69

Rojewski, Jacy L., 132

Rojewski, Jay W., 132

Rolfe, John, 61

Romeo and Juliet, 183, 191, 201

Romeo Must Die, 183-184

The Rookies, 184

Roorda, Rhonda M., 134

Root, Maria P.P., 17, 20, 55, 79, 94, 114, 157, 159-160, 165

Roots, 57, 199

Roots in the Sand, 190

Rose, Edward, 146

Rosenberg, Maxine, 144

Rosenberg, Shelley Kapnek, 133

Rosenblatt, Paul C., 90, 94

Royse, David D., 124

Rush, Sharon, 133

Rush Hour, 184

Russell, Kathy, 26

Saenz, Rogelio, 83

Sally Hemings: An American Scandal, 199

San Francisco, 117, 146, 177

Sanders, Dori, 144

Sandor, Gabrielle, 74

Santiago, Roberto, 26

Sato, Jane Takahashi, 83

Savage, Jeff, 147

Save the Last Dance, 199

Saving Private Ryan, 185

Sayonara, 179-180, 200

Scales-Trent, Judy, 26, 29

Schmitt, Eric, 75

School Ties, 20

Schuyler, Philippa, 162

Schwartz, Virginia Frances, 145

Scott, Darieck, 175

Secrets & Lies, 200

Segal, Josylyn Cahn, 114

Selena, 31

Sellers, Martha G., 122

Senisi, Ellen B., 140

Serpe, Richard T., 126-127

sex. *See* Gender

sexual relations: between White men and slaves, 45, 52, 80, 84, 88, 170; in film, 179, 195, 198; in literature, 40; laws against, 37

Shadows, 180, 200

Shange, Ntozake, 30

Shannon, Alexander H., 52

Shapiro, Deborah, 123-124

Shireman, Joan F., 124

Shiu, Anthony, 133

Sickels, Robert J., 61

Sidanius, Jim, 82

Simms, Peggy J., 135

Simon, Rita James, 127, 133-134

Skerl, John A., 124

Skerry, Peter, 75

skin color. *See* Appearance

Skin Deep, 20

Skurzynski, Gloria, 145

A Slave's Story: Running a Thousand Miles to Freedom, 42

slavery, 50, 55, 70, 161; and intermarriage, 41-42; and legislation, 37, 62, 64; in fiction, 38, 39; race-mixing as a result of, 57, 59, 60, 145. *See also* Fugitive Slave Law

Small Business Job Protection Act of 1996, 125

Smith, Amy Symens, 73

Smith, Cynthia Leitich, 148

Smith, Greg Leitich, 148

Smith, Janet Farrell, 134

Smith, Lillian Eugenia, 40

Smolowe, Jill, 135

Snipp, C. Matthew, 35

Snow Falling on Cedars, 200-201

Snowden, Lonnie R., 95
social acceptance. *See* Public opinion
social work: and adoption, 120, 122, 123, 124, 127, 135; with mixed-race children, 115. *See also* Counseling
Society for the Amalgamation of the Races, 50
socioeconomic issues. *See* Class
Sollors, Werner, 29, 31, 61-62, 91
The South: and legislation, 29, 64; in fiction, 39, 40; in film, 180, 181; interracial relationships in, 47, 51, 87, 94; race relations in, 60, 88, 156
South, Scott J., 85
South Africa, 52, 56, 68, 77
South America, 21, 82
South Carolina, 59, 63, 94, 144
Spaulding for Children, 131
Spencer, Jon Michael, 56, 76, 77
Spencer, Rainier, 75
Spickard, Paul, 56, 62, 69, 85, 157
St. Jean, Yanick, 95
Standen, Brian Chol Soo, 161
Stanfield, Rochelle L., 76
Star Trek, 181
Steward, Robbie L., 126
Stonequist, Everett V., 52
Storrs, Debbie, 161
students, interracial, 13-14, 19-20, 151, 158-159, 161, 164; in film, 193, 195; personal accounts by, 111, 150, 152, 153, 154, 163
Sturm, Circe, 161
subject headings. *See* Terminology
Sullivan, Neil, 31
Sumner, Cid Ricketts, 40
Suro, Roberto, 91

Talalay, Kathryn M., 162
Taliman, Valerie, 35
Tashiro, Cathy J., 162
Tatum, Beverly Daniel, 162
Taylor, Mildred, 145
Teague, Allison L., 147

teenagers. *See* Adolescents
television, 181-182, 184, 185, 186, 190, 192, 199
Tempenis, Maria, 94
terminology, 44, 66, 164, 203-209, 211-217; for database searching, 4, 8-9, 136, 138, 149-150, 186-187; lack of standardized, 1-2, 3, 8-9; Library of Congress, 6-7, 8, 38, 138; offensive, 4, 6, 7, 9, 10, 80, 186
Terry-Azios, Diana, 26
Tessler, Richard C., 135
Texas, 144, 195, 196
There's Something About Mary, 182
Thomas, Volker, 98
Thompson, Henry O., 53
Throne, Cambria, 154
Tolnay, Stewart E., 81
Towles, Joe, 173
"tragic mulatto" theme, 27, 30, 38, 39, 40, 41, 184
triracial isolates, 28, 66. *See also* Melungeons
True Colors, 20, 182
Trujillo, Carla, 175
Tucker, M. Belinda, 91
Turnbull, Colin M., 172
Twine, France Winddance, 70, 114

United Nations Convention on the Rights of the Child, 132

Vietnamese: and adoption, 119, 120, 123; and intermarriage, 83; in children's books, 142-143; in film and television, 184, 191
Vigil-Piñón, Evangelina, 140
Virgin Islands, 30, 145
Virginia, 37, 59, 60, 62, 63, 107, 110, 197. *See also Loving v. Virginia*
vocabulary. *See* Terminology
Vonk, M. Elizabeth, 135

Wadlington, Walter, 62
Wakeman, George, 49
Wald, Gayle Freda, 31
Walden-Kaufman, Edie Natalie, 26
Wales-North, Mary, 96
A Walk in the Clouds, 201
Walker, Alice, 163
Walker, Pamela, 141
Walker, Rebecca, 163
Wallace, Kendra R., 163
Wallenstein, Peter, 63, 92
Walton, Beth, 94
Wardle, Francis, 115
Warren, Dennis M., 93
Warren, Jonathan W., 70
Washington, D.C., 46, 47, 87, 108, 116, 196
Waters, Mary, 70, 74
Waters, Maxine, 72
Watson, Kenneth W., 124
Weaver, Hilary N., 35
Webb, Frank, 40
Webster, Yehudi, 68
The Wedding Banquet, 201
Wehrly, Bea, 115
Weiner-Mahfuz, Lisa, 176
The West, 21, 61, 87, 90, 105
West Indians, 59, 89, 90, 101
West Side Story, 183, 191, 201-202
Wethington, Elaine, 97
White, Walter Francis, 40, 42, 50
Wijeyesinghe, Charmaine L., 163
Williams, Garth, 141
Williams, Gregory Howard, 29, 163
Williams, Nancy, 136
Williams, Teresa Kay, 157, 164
Williams, Vera, 141
Williams-Leon, Teresa, 164, 176

Willis, Madge Gill, 136
Wilson, Harriet, 41
Wilson, Midge, 26
Wilson, Robin, 29
Wilson, Terry P., 35
Wilson, Timothy L., 164
Wing, Natasha, 141
Winkel, George, 76
Winters, Loretta I., 77, 165
women: Asian, rate of intermarriage of, 83, 89; Black, and domination of, 55, 59, 61; Black, and effects of interracial marriage on, 79, 81; mixed-race, 23, 160, 161; White, in interracial relationships, 51, 52, 98, 114. *See also* Gender
Woods, Frances Jerome, 42
Woods, Tiger, 140-141, 146-147, 212
Woodson, Carter G., 49, 61
Woodson, Jacqueline, 145
Wrathall, Mark William, 165
Wright, Lawrence, 76
Wright, Marguerite A., 116
Wu, Judy Tzu-Chun, 177
Wyeth, Sharon Dennis, 141, 142, 146
Wyoming, 189

Yancey, George A., 63, 83, 86
Yancey, Sherelyn W., 86
Yep, Laurence, 146
Yeung, Wai-Tsang, 89

Zabel, William D., 49, 64
Zack, Naomi, 17, 64, 68, 165
Zackodnik, Teresa, 64
Zebrahead, 202
Zebroski, Sheryline A., 95

About the Contributors

Joseph Diaz
Music and Dance Librarian at the University of Arizona. He has served in a variety of library positions for over seventeen years. A native of Tucson, Diaz has authored numerous articles on multicultural topics and is currently working on a book on building Latin music collections.

Karen Downing
Foundation and Grants Librarian at the University of Michigan. A librarian for fifteen years who grew up in an interracial family, she has held a variety of positions centered on serving diverse populations. Downing has maintained a website with an extensive bibliography on interracial issues and her family history, and presented nationally on topics relating to interracial matters. Publications include "Instruction in a Multicultural Setting" (in *Teaching the New Library to Today's Users*, 2000), *Reaching a Multicultural Student Community* (1993), and "Multicultural Services at the Undergraduate Library" (in *Cultural Diversity in Libraries*, 1995).

Renoir Gaither
Reference and Instruction Librarian and Coordinator of the Peer Information Counseling Program at the Shapiro Undergraduate Library at the University of Michigan. He has taught writing at Eastern Michigan University and secondary language arts. Gaither's interests include diversity, academic integrity, and American literature. His work has been published in a variety of professional and literary journals.

Alysse Jordan
Social Work Librarian at Columbia University. She holds B.A. and M.I.L.S. degrees from the University of Michigan and has been working in academic libraries since 1993. She contributed a chapter in the book *Diversity in Libraries: Academic Residency Programs* (2001). Jordan has been involved with activities surrounding interracial and multicultural issues for some time as she is multiracial and a member of an interracial family.

Martin Knott

Head, Cataloging Support Services at the University of Michigan Graduate Library. He received his Master of Science in Information from the University of Michigan in 2003. Knott is a member of the American Library Association's Spectrum Scholars Class of 2000 and has been involved in diversity efforts on campus for a decade.

Helen Look

Collection Management Coordinator for the University of Michigan's Public Health Library and Informatics Division. Look has been a librarian for six years and has served in a variety of capacities on diversity-related committees and working groups.

Darlene Nichols

Psychology and Social Sciences Librarian and Coordinator of Graduate Library Instruction, University of Michigan. She has been a librarian for nearly twenty years and has published extensively on instruction and other diversity-related library topics including *Reaching a Multicultural Student Community* (1993) and "Peer Information Counseling: An Academic Library Program for Minority Students" (*Journal of Academic Librarianship*, 1989). Interracially married for almost two decades, Nichols is the mother of two biracial children.

Chuck Ransom

Coordinator of Multicultural Initiatives, University of Michigan, since 1991. He has been a librarian for thirty years. Ransom received his B.A. from Wabash College in 1972 and his M.L.S. degree from Indiana University in 1974. He has published and presented on multicultural issues in librarianship, including interracial student issues.

David Schoem

Faculty Director of the Michigan Community of Scholars Program and lecturer in the Sociology Department at the University of Michigan. He has served as Assistant Dean for Undergraduate Education and Assistant Vice President for Academic and Student Affairs. He is a PEW National Learning Communities Fellow and has led faculty institutes on diversity issues at numerous colleges and universities. Schoem has written extensively on topics in higher education, including his article "Transforming Undergraduate Education: Moving beyond Distinct Undergraduate Initiatives" (*Change Magazine*), and recent book *Intergroup Dialogue: Deliberative Democracy in School, College, Community and Workplace*. He is coeditor of a forthcoming book, *Engaging the Whole of Service: Learning, Diversity, and Learning Communities*.

Kelly Webster
Special Formats Cataloger at the University of Michigan. She has been a librarian for seven years and is active in Native American librarianship, including service in the American Indian Library Association. Webster is a mixed-blood Oneida Indian and is the compiler of the online bibliography *Library Services to Indigenous Populations*.